ROOTS OF MARYLAND DEMOCRACY

Recent Titles in
Contributions in American History

Roots of
Maryland Democracy

1753–1776

DAVID CURTIS SKAGGS

Contributions in American History, Number 30

Greenwood Press, Inc.
Westport, Connecticut • London, England

Library of Congress Cataloging in Publication Data

Skaggs, David Curtis.
    Roots of Maryland democracy, 1753-1776.

    (Contributions in American history, no. 30)
    Bibliography: p.
    1. Maryland—Politics and government—Colonial
period. I. Title.
F184.S65   320.9'752'02   72-833
ISBN 0-8371-6402-8

Library of Congress Catalog Card Number: 72-833
ISBN: 0-8371-6402-8
First published in 1973

Greenwood Press, Inc., Publishing Division
51 Riverside Avenue, Westport, Connecticut 06880
Manufactured in the United States of America

To
Margo, Jason, and Philip
with love

All power is getting fast into the Hands of the very lowest of the People. Those who first encouraged the Opposition to Government, and set these on this licentious Behaviour will probably be amongst the first to repent thereof.

Gov. Robert Eden, 1775

CONTENTS

CONTENTS

EPILOGUE

LIST OF TABLES

ACKNOWLEDGMENTS

My appreciation of the place and importance of state and local history began in classes and seminars directed by two masters of the craft—James C. Malin and George L. Anderson of the University of Kansas. I hope I have not become an apostate by transferring the spatial location of such studies from their beloved American grassland to the Chesapeake shores. This transfer has not altered the impact of their belief that the study of the microcosm helps to better understand the macrocosm. Another intellectual legacy is owed my parents who, in the midst of that grassland, created a household which encouraged the love of learning.

For this particular work, the author owes considerable gratitude to individuals who have helped him along the way. Foremost in such acknowledgments stands my wife, Margo, without whose self-sacrifice, hard work, and constant support these labors might never have reached fruition. Special thanks is acknowledged for the kind hospitality given me and my family by Mr. and Mrs. Daniel A. Spintman of Bowie during several visits to the Old Line State.

The personnel at all the libraries I used were especially helpful. In particular I would like to thank staff members at the Maryland Hall of Records, Maryland Land Office, Maryland Historical Society,

ACKNOWLEDGMENTS

Maryland Diocesan Archives, Library of Congress, Duke University Library, William L. Clements Library, Georgetown University Library, and Bowling Green State University Library.

Many private individuals and several academic colleagues throughout the country provided insights into various issues that were most helpful. Lee Adams, formerly a graduate at the University of Maryland, drew the county map for 1730–1776, which Allan Luczyk, a Bowling Green State University undergraduate adapted for the 1748–1772 map. Their skillfully drawn contributions are especially appreciated. A special debt is owed to Professor Virginia B. Platt and Professor Emerita Dorothy Moulton of Bowling Green State University, who provided much-valued criticisms, and to the Faculty Research Committee of the same institution for financial aid. Patiently typing the manuscript was Miss Patricia Bogni of the history department staff. Professor Stanley I. Kutler, former editor of this series, and the staff at Greenwood have been most cooperative in seeing this study through to publication. Gratitude is due to the editors of the *Journal of American History* and the *Maryland Historical Magazine* who have allowed me to utilize in this book material previously published by them.

Lastly, I owe countless debts for constructive criticism to various faculty members at Georgetown University, particularly Richard Walsh, whose comments have added immeasurably to any significance this study might have.

Invaluable as this help has been, I must take full responsibility for any errors, the presentation of evidence, and any conclusions made herein.

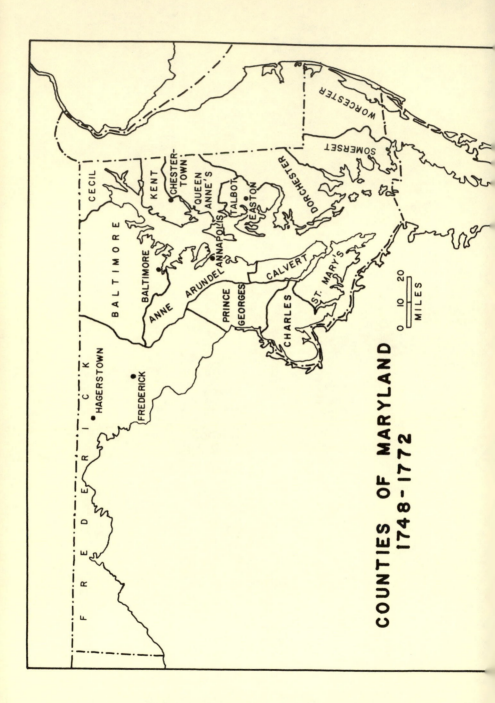

COUNTIES OF MARYLAND
1748-1772

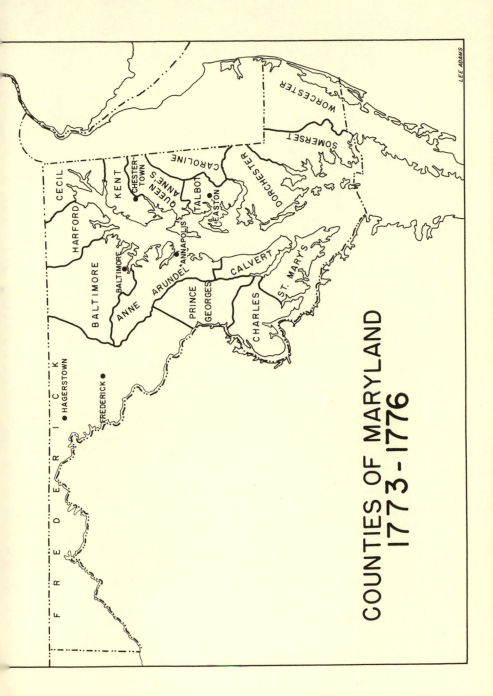

COUNTIES OF MARYLAND
1773-1776

LEE ADAMS

ROOTS OF MARYLAND DEMOCRACY

PROLEGOMENON

A republican spirit appears generally to predominate; and it will undoubtedly require the utmost exertion of legislative wisdom to establish on a permanent basis the future political and commercial connection between Great Britain and America.

William Eddis, April 2, 1770

Chapter

1

THE PROBLEM OF COLONIAL DEMOCRACY

From the day in 1753 when Horatio Sharpe stepped off the vessel which brought him from England to begin service as His Lordship's lieutenant governor until the day in 1777 when Thomas Johnson, Jr., assumed office as the first governor of the State of Maryland, politics on the Chesapeake were in ferment. The course of this turbulent period is the subject of this study.

Much of the social and intellectual background of the period is supplied in the monographs of Charles A. Barker,[1] and it is not the intention of this study to repeat in great detail these excellent studies. Rather, emphasis will be given to religious, ethnic, and economic differences needing more thorough examination, and an analysis of the years 1773–1776, which have not been subject to much recent scholarship. All of this is to be explored in terms of the effect upon political life.

More critical than the narrative of events leading to the Declaration of Independence in one colony is the attempt of this study to define the role of Maryland in the larger context of British North America—to show its similarities to, and differences from, the other colonies during the same period. Such a desire necessitates a brief look at the historiographic problem of the nature of the American Revolution.

Historiography of the revolutionary era has, since World War II, been dominated by the neo-conservative or consensus school. Led by the writings of Robert E. Brown and his wife Katherine, who have done detailed analyses of the colonies of Massachusetts and Virginia, and by the more general approach of Daniel J. Boorstin, scholars of this genre see the Revolution as a movement to preserve an existing colonial democracy, rather than an attempt to overturn the social, political, and economic order. In short, the revolutionary ferment was a quest to secure the blessings of British and colonial liberty for colonists who felt that the drift of imperial developments after the Great War for the Empire (1754–1763) was anti-democratic and un-English. Thus, the American Creoles waged a war for political independence without any design or desire for truly revolutionary consequences. In both Virginia and Massachusetts, the Browns found the Revolution to have been a unique movement "designed primarily to preserve a social order rather than change it." They concluded: "Revolutions usually occur because people are dissatisfied with the status quo, but except for the areas where Britain had prevented normal evolution, Virginians [and Bay Staters] appear to have been satisfied with the social order."[2]

This so-called "Brown Thesis" rests upon two basic assumptions: first, that by the mid-eighteenth century the colonies were "democratic" in their social, economic, and political life, and, second, that the Revolution was fought to preserve that existing democracy. In an extended critique of *Middle-Class Democracy and the Revolution in Massachusetts,* John Cary pointed out that "the validity of his [Brown's] conclusions in the second part of the book depends upon the success with which he establishes his thesis that Massachusetts was democratic."[3]

Direct attack upon the Browns' argument has revolved mostly around the first portion of their thesis. This criticism falls roughly into three categories: (1) an improper use of statistical analysis, (2) a failure to define significant phrases used in the thesis, such as "democracy" and "middle class," and (3) a misunderstanding of the nature of deference shown to the colonial gentry by the general populace and the effect of this upon the general "stake-in-society" concept of government that prevailed in the Hanoverian period.

On the first point, most criticism concerned the sampling techniques used. John Cary made the most significant attack by claiming Professor Brown's "analysis of religious and educational institutions does not prove they were democratic, because he ignores some of the most important materials for determining whether they were. Because of his sampling techniques, his conclusions as to the extent of land ownership and the number of men who were qualified to vote are unreliable." Brown admitted the validity of some of this criticism and tried to solve it in the second book. Nonetheless, Chilton Williamson felt that the use of statistical evidence from only seven of fifty-three countries — none from the Shenandoah Valley — left considerable question as to the validity of the conclusions in *Virginia: Democracy or Aristocracy?*[4]

An indirect attack along the same lines came from a group of young scholars who, like the Browns, began their own detailed analyses of colonial communities. Many such studies resulted in portrayals of communities that were much less democratic in their economic composition than had been implied, if not specifically stated, in the Browns' books. Monographs by scholars such as James T. Lemon, Gary B. Nash, James A. Henretta, and Jackson T. Main found growing indices of social stratification, especially in the more settled areas. In a look at New England society, Kenneth Lockridge concluded: "In terms of land, many 'yeomen' or 'husbandmen' . . . of late eighteenth-century America were not perceptibly better off" than their great-great grandfathers had been in Stuart England. "America," or at least New England, "was no longer the land of opportunity."[5] These challenges brought into question the validity of the Browns' figures, which portrayed a high degree of economic equality.

Initially, the strongest attack leveled against the Browns concerned their alleged failure to define critical words. When Professor Brown tried to correct this deficiency, he clouded the issue by speaking of a "plebeian party" controlling Massachusetts, not a middle-class one. Carl Bridenbaugh found that the Virginia book failed to answer the question of whether the colony was either democratic or aristocratic, the very subjects which the authors sought to investigate. He charged that the defect resulted from vague definitions of "democracy" and "aristocracy."⁶ One of the critical points at issue among historians concerned with the problem of early American politics revolves around defining what is meant by such terms as "democracy."

At least two solutions have been advanced to this problem. Roy Lokken advocated a definition based upon "a study of colonial political institutions and behavior" which would allow historians to arrive at a concept of democracy conforming to that prevalent in colonial America. He felt that any definition based upon observation of the modern scene would become fouled in an argument over semantics in a world filled with "republics" and "peoples' democracies" of all political shades. Similarly, any such definition would immediately be subjected to the charge of subjective relativism, which would invalidate it in the eyes of many of Clio's disciples. Cecelia Kenyon, on the other hand, felt that only a modern description of the term would suffice. First, the semantic argument over definition would end in futility because no two historians could ever agree on what the revolutionaries meant by "democracy." Second, most eighteenth-century men believed in mixed governments, having monarchical, aristocratic, and democratic elements, and accepted Plato's adverse criticism of unfettered democracy noted in the *Republic*. Thus, there was no positive eighteenth-century definition of the term. Kenyon then used "democratic" to denote "a political system in which authority is derived from the majority of adult inhabitants, all of whom enjoy the suffrage and may use it at regular and reasonably frequent intervals and all of whom are legally eligible for office." For her, such a modern definition was a necessary and proper means of investigating historical phenomena.⁷

This author agrees wholeheartedly with Professor Kenyon. The Browns' monographs fail to effectively use the tools of the social sciences in their quest for historical truth and accuracy. Before beginning any inquiry into the subject of colonial democracy, one must solve the problem of definition.

Austin Ranney and Willmoore Kendall satisfied this need in their *Democracy and the American Party System*. They expanded Professor Kenyon's brief definition of the term: democracy, they wrote, consists of four principles—popular sovereignty, political equality, popular consultation, and majority rule. In their model for a democratic nation-state government, "popular sovereignty" means that the "whole power of government resides in the whole people—that is, in *all* the members of the community, and not in any special ruling class or in any single individual." Political equality means "not only 'one man, one vote,' but also an equal chance for each member of the community to participate in the total decision-making process of the community." "In democratic government," they continued, "the people must be 'consulted' about the policy they wish those in power to pursue in a given matter — and the holders of office, having learned the popular desire, should proceed to do whatever the people want them to do." The principle of majority rule is the most controversial, but Ranney and Kendall held that the ideally democratic government must eventually acquiesce in popular demands for governmental action, since this principle must be "consistent with the other three principles of democracy."[8]

Of the problems raised by this definition, one of the most critical involves ascertaining the degree of political equality existing in colonial America: Were all citizens allowed an equal voice in the political process?

Such a question brings us to the third, and probably the most damning, criticism of the Brown Thesis. The Browns are accused of failing to understand the underlying political philosophy of the period, which required *noblesse oblige* on the part of the gentry and a deference to social superiors on the part of the general populace. The structure of ideas required leadership by men of merit, and merit was generally thought to reside among those of wealth and social position. There were representative institutions and some popular participation in government, but these checks on arbitrary rule were "not designed to facilitate the expression of [popular] will but to defend them from oppression." In essence, such critics as J. R. Pole and Richard Buel, Jr., charged that the tally of all the eligible voters and other such quantitative analyses by the Browns failed to meet the real issue: the psychological limitations of prevalent social philosophy upon the existence of political equality.

These critics went even further and argued that the revolutionary experience brought about a change in social attitudes resulting in a more democratic society in 1790 than existed in 1760. Jackson T.

Main's detailed analyses of the social backgrounds of elected officials before and after the Declaration of Independence show that voters tended to select men more plebeian in their class origins after 1776.[9] Such a conclusion compels one to accept the premise that the Revolutionary era promoted a dramatic change in popular attitudes towards community leadership.

There arose among younger scholars in the 1960s a decided disenchantment with the consensus approach to the Revolutionary era personified by the Browns and Boorstin. Staughton Lynd led the assault. His analyses of Revolutionary politics in Duchess County, New York, and the efforts of the New York City working classes to secure a more prominent place in the social and economic order, reveal efforts to modify the pre-Revolutionary milieu.

Most outspoken of these historians has been Jessee Lemisch, who seeks to articulate the inarticulate in a series of articles dealing with artisans, sailors, and prisoners of war. His call to action was to find not the bland generalities upon which the American people agreed, but rather to view the differences which have divided the nation and to delve into the source material to show how the common man has influenced the course of national development. Concerning the Revolution, Lemisch wrote:

"Colonials" meant many people, often people in conflict with one another: there was, from the very beginning, something of a struggle over who should rule at home. The people on the bottom of that conflict were also involved in the struggle for home rule, but their activities have been made to seem an extension of the conduct of the more articulate, who have been seen as their manipulators. The inarticulate could act on their own, and often for very sound reasons. It is time that we examined the American Revolution from their perspective.[10]

Like the Browns, Lemisch and the "New Left" historians tend to insist upon the complete validity of their positions. If the Browns were excessively partisan in maintaining the whole of the Revolutionary experience to have been a reaffirmation of the colonial tradition, so also has the New Left been giving to the "inarticulate" an excessive amount of influence, insight, and lasting contribution to the American heritage. At the same time, one cannot discount their presence.

The purpose of this particular monograph is to explore the degree of democracy in one particular colony. It will use, on the one hand, the concept of dualism embodied in the Brown theme (the existence of an egalitarian social order in colonial America and the lack of any effort to change this situation) and, on the other, a deep awareness of the pitfalls of the Browns' approach, in an attempt to incorporate criticisms of them into a reasoned analysis of the Maryland scene. Of particular importance will be the use of the Ranney-Kendall definition as the basis for judging the degree of democratic social and political order in the colony. Such an assessment is made in the concluding chapter, but the definition should be kept in mind when reading of developments throughout the monograph. The study will also concentrate on political activities in the years 1773–1776, which have been generally neglected in recent scholarship. It is not intended to be a comprehensive history of Maryland's road to revolution (although such is certainly needed), nor is it a comparison of the democratic trends in one colony with those in others. The object is rather to show how Maryland made the first halting steps away from a society in which class, kinship, and friendship determined status toward one in which rewards might more closely approximate ability. In 1776, such an objective was merely a glimmer on the horizon.

This undertaking, though difficult, should produce a useful study of the steps to independence on the shores of the upper Chesapeake.

NOTES

1. See Charles A. Barker's "Proprietary Rights in the Provincial System of Maryland: Proprietary Policy," *Journal of Southern History*, II (1936), pp. 43-68; "Proprietary Rights in the Provincial System of Maryland: Proprietary Revenues," ibid., pp. 211-231; "Maryland before the Revolution: Society and Thought," *American Historical Review*, XLVI (1940–1941), pp. 1-20; Charles A. Barker, *The Background of the Revolution in Maryland* (New Haven: Yale University Press: 1940). For the purposes of this study, "Chesapeake" refers to the colonies of Virginia and Maryland, and northern or upper Chesapeake to Maryland alone.

2. R. E. and B. K. Brown, *Virginia, 1705-1786: Democracy or Aristocracy?* (East Lansing, Michigan: Michigan State University Press, 1964), p. 301; see also his *Middle-Class Democracy and the Revolution in Massachusetts, 1691-1780* (Ithaca. N. Y.: Cornell University Press, 1955); and D. J. Boorstin, *The Genius of American Politics* (Chicago: University of Chicago Press, 1953), pp. 66-98.

3. John Cary, "Statistical Method and the Brown Thesis on Colonial Democracy with a Rebuttal by Robert E. Brown," *William and Mary Quarterly,* Series 3, XX (1963), pp. 251–252.

4. Cary, "Statistical Method," pp. 263–264; Chilton Williamson's Review of Brown and Brown, *Virginia, Journal of Southern History,* XXXI (1965), pp. 98–99.

5. J. T. Lemon and G. B. Nash, "The Distribution of Wealth in Eighteenth-Century America: A Century of Change in Chester County, Pennsylvania, 1693–1802," *Journal of Social History,* II (1968), pp. 1–24; J. A. Henretta, "Economic Development and Social Structure in Colonial Boston," *William and Mary Quarterly,* Series 3, XXII (1965), pp. 75–92; J. T. Main, *The Social Structure of Revolutionary America* (Princeton, N. J.: Princeton University Press, 1965); Kenneth Lockridge, "Land, Population, and the Evolution of New England Society, 1630–1790," *Past and Present,* #39 (1968), pp. 62–80.

6. See reviews of *Middle-Class Democracy* by R. P. Stearns, *William and Mary Quarterly,* Series 3, XIV (1957), pp. 100–103; G. R. Taylor, *American Quarterly,* VIII (1956), pp. 387–388; Carl Bridenbaugh's review of *Virginia* in *American Historical Review,* LXX (1965), pp. 472–473; Brown's rebuttal in Cary, "Statistical Method," pp. 266–267; J. R. Pole, "Historians and the Problem of Early American Democracy," *American Historical Review,* LXVII (1961–1962), pp. 627–628.

7. R. N. Lokken, "The Concept of Democracy in Colonial Political Thought," *William and Mary Quarterly,* Series 3, XVI (1959), pp. 569–570; C. M. Kenyon, "Republicanism and Radicalism in the American Revolution: An Old Fashioned Interpretation," *William and Mary Quarterly,* Series 3, XIX (1962), pp. 157–163.

8. A. Ranney and W. Kendall, *Democracy and the American Party System* (New York: Harcourt, Brace and World, 1956), pp. 1–39, especially pp. 23–39. For a more detailed definition of what he calls "populistic democracy," see R. A. Dahl, *A Preface to Democratic Theory* (Chicago; University of Chicago Press, 1956), pp. 34–62.

9. Pole, "Historians," pp. 626–646; R. Buel, "Democracy and the American Revolution: A Frame of Reference," *William and Mary Quarterly,* Series 3, XXI (1964), pp. 165–190; J. T. Main, "Government by the People: The American Revolution and the Democratization of the Legislatures," *William and Mary Quarterly,* Series 3, XXIII (1966), pp. 391–407.

10. J. Lemisch, "The American Revolution Seen from the Bottom Up," in B. J. Berstein, ed., *Towards a New Past: Dissenting Essays in American History* (New York: Pantheon Books, 1967), pp. 3–45, quote p. 19; J. Lemisch, "Jack Tar in the Streets: Merchant Seamen in the Politics of Revolutionary America," *William and Mary Quarterly,* Series 3, XXV (1968), pp. 371–407; J. Lemisch, "Listening to the 'Inarticulate': William Widger's Dream and the Loyalties of American Revolutionary Seamen in British Prisons," *Journal of Social History,* III (1969–1970), pp. 1–29; S. Lynd, *Anti-Federalism in Duchess County, New York* (Chicago: Loyola University Press, 1962); S. Lynd, "The Mechanics in New York Politics, 1774–1788," *Labor History,* V (1964), pp. 225–246. An extensive criticism of the consensus school is in J. P. Diggins, "Consciousness and Ideology in American History: The Burden of Daniel J. Boorstin," *American Historical Review,* LXXVI (1971), pp. 99–118.

I

HIS LORDSHIP'S COLONY

It has been a fine poor man's country, but now it is well peopled, the lands are all secured, and the harvest for such is now over. The Lands are mostly worked by the landlord's negroes, and, of consequence, white servants, after their bondage is out, are strolling about the country without bread.

Joseph Mosley, S. J., 1772

2

THE STRUCTURE OF POLITICS

For faithful service and continued friendship to himself and his father, King Charles I rewarded Sir George Calvert, first Baron of Baltimore, with a patent of land encompassing the upper half of the Chesapeake Bay. Sir George died before the grant could be consummated, so the charter was issued to his son, Cecilius Calvert, second Lord Baltimore, in June 1632. The document made Lord Baltimore and his heirs landlords of a vast tract, with the authority to govern and dispose of the land on such terms as they should see fit. In effect, the lord proprietor was a constitutional monarch restricted only by the requirements that the laws of the colony must be in harmony with those in England and that the proprietor could not enact laws nor levy taxes without the consent of the freemen of the province or their deputies. Because of the medieval characteristics of His Lordship's charter, limitations were placed upon political development in the colony which were in marked contrast to provisions in the fundamental laws of other British North American settlements.

The Calverts intended their palatinate to materially enhance their dignity, their fortune, and the prestige of the family. This it was doing one hundred and twenty years later when Frederick Calvert, sixth Lord Baltimore, dispatched a new lieutenant-governor to rule the province in his name.

It was a long passage from London. Capt. Nicholas Coxen and the crew of the *Molly* found few summer winds to hasten the voyage of Horatio Sharpe, Rev. Matthias Harris, and John Ridout. It took nearly twelve weeks to travel from England to Annapolis. Upon his arrival, Sharpe was joyously received by the citizens and, after presenting his credentials to Benjamin Tasker, Sr., president of His Lordship's Council, he issued a proclamation notifying the citizens of his assumption of the governorship. From the time of his landing on August 10, 1753 until the opening of the General Assembly in early October, the new governor, his chaplain Mr. Harris, and his secretary Mr. Ridout were entertained and feted by Maryland's leading families. At one such function it was reported that "His Excellency tarry'd 'til the breaking up of the Ball, at Twelve o'Clock." The colony's gentry were willing to bear the expense of burning candles to such a late hour in order to provide the finest reception for Lord Baltimore's "Governor and Commander-in-Chief." It was not until October that the realities of Maryland politics were revealed to the neophyte governor in the Assembly's deliberations.[1]

Governor Sharpe, like his predecessors, found that Maryland's peculiar charter gave unique character to the government of the colony. This feudal document gave the Lord Proprietor powers, prerequisites, and privileges unlike those ever possessed by a royal governor, or even by the sole surviving proprietors, the Penns, whose charter, granted fifty years after Calvert's, greatly curtailed these feudal powers. These proprietary rights were subject to change only at the discretion of Lord Baltimore—who was not likely to make substantive changes.

The proprietor possessed extensive powers. He could and did create offices, appoint and direct officials, sell and grant land, and run his colony in almost any manner he desired so long as it was not displeasing to the monarchy. He was *ex officio* governor of the province, but he usually designated a lieutenant-governor to serve in his place. This latter official served as chief executive and military commander of the colony. The lieutenant-governor had an absolute veto over legislation, although his power was seldom exercised since the Upper House of the Assembly usually did his bidding. Among his prerogatives was the power to postpone and to call sessions of the Assembly, as well as to dismiss that body and call for new elections when he thought it prudent to do so.

Equally important in provincial governance was the secretaryship of the province, a London-based office which Cecilius Calvert, uncle of the last Lord Baltimore, used to tighten the reins of provincial control. For the period under discussion, the profligate Frederick Calvert, sixth Lord Baltimore, was proprietor, 1751–1771; his illegitimate son, Henry Harford, succeeded him, 1771–1776. The lieutenant-governors were Horatio Sharpe, 1753–1769, and Robert Eden, 1769–1776, and the secretaries were Cecilius Calvert, 1751–1767, and Hugh Hammersley, 1767–1776.[2]

The principal administrative organ of Maryland was His Lordship's Council of about ten members, appointed by the governor on the advice of the proprietor. This body served not only as a sort of governor's cabinet but also as the Upper House of the Maryland Assembly. Membership was generally restricted to great landholders who cooperated with the government. Among those serving in the period under discussion were three Dulanys, two members of the Tasker, Plater, Goldsborough, Lee, and Bordley families, and one member of the Calvert, Chamberlaine, Lloyd, Thomas, Ogle, Key, and Fitzhugh families.

Councilors also received the most lucrative public offices to insure their loyalty to the proprietor. For example, Col. Edward Lloyd III served as councilor, 1743–1770, as well as Naval Officer of Oxford, Eastern Shore Treasurer, Rent Roll Keeper for the Eastern Shore, and His Lordship's Agent and Receiver General. George Plater III, councilor, 1771–1776, was also Naval Officer of the Patuxent; and Daniel Dulany, the younger, councilor, 1757–1776, held among his many offices those of Attorney General, Commissary General, and Deputy Secretary of Maryland. While these offices may not sound particularly important to the modern reader, almost all of them required the collection of fees, a percentage of which was retained by the collector. As the province grew in population and wealth, these offices became more and more lucrative since the fee rates remained the same while the number of collections increased.[3]

The whole structure of Maryland government below these high public offices was calculated to cultivate loyalty to the proprietor because of the financial and social privileges that could be conferred by appointment. There were no elected county officials. The acceptance

ley had accepted the attorney generalship and the post as Annapolis naval officer, cried out, "So flys away burning glowing Patriotism!" The only reason Ringgold felt that the younger Daniel Dulany was not in the proprietary camp was that Dulany demanded a higher price for his services than the Governor would deliver. Ringgold expressed the general attitude, and perhaps the general rationalization, of those not serving in a public capacity when he wrote: "The solid satisfaction, the self-approved consciousness, arising from true and real patriotism, from a life well spent in rectitude and real service to the country, must be worth much more than the mistaken tinsel of Honour, attending what we call, our high stations here."[10]

There were some limitations on the appointive power. Provincial law denied non-ecclesiastical appointive public office to anyone who had been a resident of the province for less than three years. Another custom required anyone holding an Assembly seat to resign it upon such an appointment and run for re-election to see if the electorate wanted a placeman as its representative.[11]

As we have already noted, there were elective offices in the province. These fell into two categories: delegates to the Lower House of Assembly and vestrymen in the parishes of the established Church of England. By far the more prestigious of these positions was that of assemblyman.

To understand the nature of democracy in Maryland one must understand the electoral process in the province by which such men were chosen. In 1715, when Maryland was a royal colony, the Assembly passed new and important election laws which served as the basis of electoral procedure until the Revolution. Elections were held at the county court houses, where the county's freemen with 50 acres of land or a "visible estate" of £40 sterling cast *viva voce* ballots for four county delegates. The law also prescribed compulsory attendance of electors at all elections, although this requirement was not strictly adhered to. Delegates had to meet the same property requirements as the electors.[12]

These restrictions were considerably in excess of franchise requirements in neighboring Virginia. The Old Dominion allowed suffrage to white adult males having an improved freehold of 25 acres and/ or leaseholds of the same size on terms of one or more lives. The difference between a 25-acre and a 50-acre plantation allowed many Virginians the franchise who would not have the same right in Maryland. For instance, the quitrent debt books for Prince George's and Talbot counties in 1756 and 1771 list 119 private landholdings of 49 acres or less. Of this number, 67, or 57 percent, were freeholds of between 25 and 49 acres. Assuming a similar proportion existed elsewhere, a significant portion of Maryland's small farmers were excluded from the suffrage who would not have been excluded in Virginia. Any tenant expecting to vote in His Lordship's colony had to have at least a £ 40 sterling "visible estate."[13]

When the proprietary government returned to power in 1716, the Maryland Houses of Assembly re-enacted the 1715 royal statute. Two new provisions prohibited sheriffs from candidacy in the delegate contests and provided a penalty of 100 pounds of tobacco for missing an election without a good excuse. A supplementary election law of 1718 allowed by-elections in case of the death or removal of a delegate, and prohibited Roman Catholics from voting by requiring them to take oaths to which they could not swear in good conscience.[14]

The city of Annapolis was the single exception to these electoral restrictions. A royal charter of 1708 granted the capital the right of incorporation with an elected council, a board of aldermen and a mayor. The ten city councilmen constituted the only popularly-elected officials in the colony save the delegates and vestrymen. Of interest in Annapolis were the liberal franchise requirements allowed by the charter. To qualify, one had to own a city lot with a house thereon, or be a resident of the city having a visible estate of £ 20 sterling, or be a free tradesman having served five years at any trade in the city and be a resident thereof. These liberal property requirements were similar to ones granted to Virginia's urban centers.[15] They applied only to a community which reached a maximum population of 1,500 and which constituted about two-thirds of one percent of the colony's populace.

As the electoral law of 1715 prescribed, "the safest and best rule for this Province to follow in Electing such Delegates and representatives is the precedents of the proceedings in Parliaments in England as near as the Constitution of this Province will Admitt." Certain British traditions also applied to Maryland elections, such as denying the franchise to those under 21 and requiring the voter to have paid his taxes within twelve months of election day and to be a natural born citizen of the United Kingdom. Such traditions were subject to change by the provincial assembly. The property requirement was one of the changes wrought by Marylanders. An old British statute confined the franchise to 40–shilling freeholders, i.e., landowners who received 40 shillings a year in rental value or income from their holdings. Maryland's provision of £ 40 visible estate gave the vote to non-landholders, in contrast to British law.[16]

Unlike the findings of Robert and Katherine Brown in their study of Virginia, there is little reason to believe, and no evidence to support the idea, that Maryland's tenant farmers could vote if they held a lifetime lease on 50 acres or more. Not a single voting list has been uncovered in the vast Maryland archives held by the Hall of Records. Thus no one has been able to prove or disprove the statement that unqualified persons voted. Keeping in mind the highly centralized nature of colonial Maryland government and the tendency towards litigation and legalisms that characterized her citizens, there is some evidence to support a rather rigid enforcement of suffrage restrictions in His Lordship's colony. Probably the best evidence that voting restrictions were observed during the relatively placid colonial period is that in the midst of the turmoil of the summer of 1776, the Constitutional Convention was able to secure, albeit with some opposition, elections under the proprietary code requirements.[17]

In denying the suffrage to aliens, Romanists, and the propertyless, the design was to confine the vote to those with the greatest stake in maintaining the status quo. Maryland electoral law "was drafted in the conviction that efficiency, honesty, and harmony in government rested, in the last analysis, upon a salutary degree of homogeneity of interests, opinions, and fundamental loyalists—religious, ethnic, and class."[18]

Election procedure followed the legal prescriptions. The governor issued writs of election to each sheriff, who then called the county justices together so that they might set a date of election for their county. The sheriff then posted notices of the forthcoming polling "in the most public places of his Bailiwick," the parish churches and the local taverns. There was little formal campaigning time. The county court usually called for the election to begin from ten days to three weeks after its initial meeting. Thus in 1754 the Frederick County court met on November 11 to call for an election on December 3, and that of Prince George's met on May 4, 1773, to call for an election on the 24th.[19]

On election day, the county court convened and each elector came before the sheriff, the court, and the clerk to announce his vote. The clerk recorded and counted all votes in front of the court and witnesses. After the balloting, an indenture or warrant of election was drawn and was signed by the sheriff, the justices, and several electors certifying the winning candidates. This warrant was then sent to the capital to be opened at the next session of Assembly.[20]

The customary short notice and the difficulties of transportation made it inconvenient for electors to come to the court house to vote. Imagine how the electors in Hagerstown and Georgetown must have felt upon receiving notice only a few days before the election day of polling to take place in distant Frederick. So also were the voters of upper Anne Arundel County and western Baltimore County sorely pressed to make a single election day.

For greater convenience, polls were often held open for several days. Usually they remained open only a day or two, but if a candidate could show cause, and many did, voting might continue for over a week—undoubtedly to the delight of the local tavernkeeper. The 1758 poll in Frederick took six days to complete. Anne Arundel's for 1767 lasted thirteen days. Two years later the Lower House admonished Baltimore sheriff Daniel Chamier for closing the polls when he "had good reason to believe that a Number of Persons were on their way" to the court house.[21]

The election code not only allowed each county to send four delegates, but also gave the city of Annapolis the right to send two. The city elections conformed to the pattern of those in the counties. After the Mayor's Court (consisting of the mayor and aldermen) selected the date, the clerk posted notices of the forthcoming event in public places. The mayor presided over the election. Unlike the sheriff, the mayor could be a candidate for delegate, a fact which led to disputed elections when the mayor contested the right of his opponent's supporters to vote.[22]

The nomination and election process was similar in both Chesapeake colonies. Although the exact means of nomination is not apparent from existing records, one does find indications of considerable backstage maneuvering by the gentry prior to balloting. Before the 1745 Kent County contest, Stephen Bordley, an Annapolis merchant, urged his relatives in the county to use their not inconsiderable influence in favor of Matthias Harris against incumbent James Calder. Councilor Lloyd urged James Hollyday to enter the Queen Anne's lists in 1758. Even Cecilius Calvert tried to influence a 1756 Annapolis campaign from London. Their common tactic was simple. Because the voter normally gave deference to the opinions of his social superiors, the art of winning an election depended upon securing the right combination of influential supporters. During the election, a few men of consequence spoke in the candidate's behalf as the voters gathered at the court house just before the ballots were cast. All candidates appear to have been pre-selected, and there is no evidence of surprise nominations at the polling places.

The depth of the deferential attitudes may in part be seen in the sermons of the popular rector of St. Thomas Parish, Baltimore County. The Rev. Thomas Cradock often spoke of an ordered society divided between "the *meaner,* and ... the *higher,* Classes of People." Each element of such a society had his obligations to the whole. His congregation learned how the true Christian "shews deference to his superiors, is open clear and friendly with his equals, [and is] easy of access to Inferiors." The prevalence of this ideological construct affected political as well as social conduct. Thus, Stephen Bordley knew his brother John and his cousin Thomas had "always a large share in the Elections for" Kent County, and he was undoubtedly not surprised when their solicitations in Harris' behalf were successful. In urging James Hollyday to run, the squire of Wye House was expected to—and did—back his candidate at the Queen Anne's County hustings. Hollyday did not win in 1758, but he won the next three elections before joining his mentor on the Council. Similarly, Secretary Calvert expected Stephen Bordley to actively champion, the proprietary candidates in Annapolis, since Bordley had just received two lucrative public appointments.[23] There can be little doubt that the control exercised by the gentry over the nominating and campaigning processes seriously affected popular participation in the political system.

Experienced politicians only occasionally received an electoral challenge. In one such instance, two political novices could give very little opposition to their veteran opponents in the 1754 Assembly race in Prince George's County. The most notable challenge came in the 1764 Annapolis representative contest. Charles Carroll, barrister (1723–1783), gave his considerable support to Samuel Chase (1741–1811), antiproprietary candidate, against Dr. George Steuart, conservative incumbent, who held a previously unbeatable proprietary seat from the capital. Promising reformation of the city administration and renovation of the decaying port of Annapolis, Chase received the backing of local tradesmen and artisans. These men organized parades and demonstrations complete with the bands, banners, and ballyhoo characteristic of the most spirited American election contests. Chase's campaign and subsequent victory was so unique that it left a lasting impression upon young Charles Willson Peale, who was about to embark on a career as one of the great artists of early America.

But these were rare exceptions to the general rule that little or no opposition was present. In 1773, Benjamin Galloway noted with astonishment: "There are ten Candidates for Kent County!" With such a multiplicity of aspirants for the four positions, Galloway's brother-in-law, Thomas Ringgold, Jr., expected the election to be a "Farce" from which he foresaw "no small Entertainment." Even in the Annapolis contest Carroll and Chase did not try to take over the entire slate. While Chase sought Steuart's seat, conservative Walter Dulany easily won re-election to the city's other Assembly post. The result of this general absence of opposition was that men were returned to the Lower House time after time until they declined to run, resigned, or died.[24]

There were, however, some issues and some defeats. In the 1751 elections in Queen Anne's County and the 1754 elections in St. Mary's, Prince George's and Frederick counties, for example, the major issue was anti-Catholicism. Chase's Annapolis campaign issue concerned the degree of proprietary control over that town, normally a "rotten borough" for the establishment. By 1773 any close association with the proprietor was suspect, and this forced Anthony Stewart, an Annapolis merchant, to withdraw since "a strong suspecion was entertained of his political principles and court connexions."[25]

Electioneering involved more than behind-the-scenes maneuvering, election day speeches, and a few real issues. Candidates willingly "treated" electors before and after balloting in a convenient tavern. This method of influencing the vote was so common that in 1768 the Lower House prohibited any person from giving "any money, meat, drink, entertainment, or provision, or [making] . . . any promise, agreement, obligation or engagement . . . in order to be elected." Nonetheless the practice continued. When notice of its repetition was brought before the Assembly, the voters evidenced their approval of the tactic. In Charles County, Robert Henley Courts pleaded the illegality of the election of Francis Ware and Josias Hawkins because of their "treating." The Lower House invalidated the election and a new one was called to fill the two empty seats. "Treating" was obviously enjoyed by the Charles County electors, who again returned Ware and Hawkins to the Assembly.[26]

The practice of herding supporters to the polls in groups was not uncommon. Henry Hall, Jr. (1727–1770) reported how the "magistrates," the county justices, of Prince George's County "Commit[ted] [w]hole Companies at once" during the 1754 balloting. The same is indicated in a disputed 1769 Baltimore County election where persons were known to be arriving, presumably in numbers large enough to switch the vote. Finally, the way men from various sections of Anne Arundel, Baltimore, and Prince George's counties came in groups loyal to particular leaders at the time of the *Peggy Stewart* affair shows that such groupings around prominent men continued into the late colonial period. Secretary Calvert charged that the county justices deliberately used their positions to court the favor of prospective voters by refusing to require bond for witnesses and accused persons, thereby allowing them to skip trial. The magistrate hoped to gain the thanks of those whom he freed and expected repayment "by a Choice as a Member of the Lower House." This magisterial factor and the economic influence of some great planters over their neighbors was undoubtedly the basis of most such groupings. A few often-elected men like John Hall of the Vineyard (1729–1797) could become indifferent about the necessity of such electioneering techniques and write their backers: "I am willing to serve the people if they are pleased to choose me . . . but please make no great stir or noise about the matter."[27]

Besides the regular elections for the Assembly which occurred in 1754, 1758, 1761, 1764, 1767, 1771, and 1773 in the period under discussion in this book, there were annual elections to the vestry of the established church.

In 1702, an act establishing the Church of England passed the Assembly and met with royal approval. The act prescribed the use of the *Book of Common Prayer* in its services and gave liberty of worship to all Protestant dissenters. It did not discriminate against such non-Anglicans except by requiring that they pay the necessary parish taxes. The vestry consisted of six lay vestrymen, two lay wardens, and the rector, who served in an *ex officio* capacity. Their duties included appointing tobacco inspectors for the parish, overseeing the morals of the laity, supervising the upkeep of the church and its properties, and maintaining public records of birth, death, and marriage. Vestrymen served for three years and wardens for one. Consecutive election to the vestry was uncommon. Elections were held each Easter Monday at the parish churches in each county. At this time the tax-paying freeholders of the parish, regardless of religious affiliation, elected the vestrymen and wardens, the latter of whom were directly responsible for church finances.[28]

Voting for vestrymen was more restricted than for assemblymen, since only those freeholders paying the poll tax could vote. The vestries tried to be strict about such elections. St. Paul's Parish, Prince George's County (1751) and St. Paul's Parish, Queen Anne's County (1763) disqualified two otherwise duly elected vestrymen because they lacked a freehold. When sundry non-freeholding parishioners offered to vote in the 1770 election in St. Anne's Parish, Annapolis, they were disqualified. However, one did not need to be an Anglican to serve on the vestry of the Church of England. In 1751, John Beall, Jr., received enough votes to join the vestry of St. John's Parish, Prince George's County. This election of a Presbyterian to the governing body of another denomination was objected to by the Rev. Henry Addison and the rest of the vestry, but the Council forced them to accept Beall as a member.[29]

The Rev. Jonathan Boucher considered vestry elections a vital ingredient in the colony's politics. One might doubt the validity of this upon learning several common aspects of such elections. Easter Monday 1759 found only five voters and one vestryman at the St. Paul's, Prince George's County, election. The vestry of All Faiths Parish, St. Mary's County, discharged George Burroughs, who "was infamous for drunkenness, profane swearing, fighting etc., and unfit to discharge the duties of vestryman," only to see him returned to that body by the electorate. Col. William Hopper, a former vestryman, probably achieved the lowest marks for good behavior. On February 9, 1762, at one of the best attended vestry meetings in colonial history, the Rev. Alexander Malcolm and his Queen Anne's County vestry chastised Colonel Hopper and Miss Jane Brown for six years of illicit cohabitation. Despite these blotches on vestry service and its importance, evidence presented later will indicate that it was often a prerequisite to election to the Lower House.[30]

Such was the government of the Chesapeake province. Controlled by a dissolute absentee proprietor, based upon a charter with feudal characteristics, there was little latitude for popular government to attempt to cope with the growing economic, social and political problems of the eighteenth century. As Maryland grew more diverse and sophisticated, the House of Calvert failed to supply the necessary progressive leadership. The end of the colonial period saw the emergence of a sharp conflict between those associated with the proprietary establishment and its many profitable offices and those elected officials of the Lower House and the vestries. A look at the provincial charter, the patronage system, and the electoral process shows the structure of Maryland politics in the Age of George III to have been more like that of Britain than is normally ascribed to colonial America.

NOTES

1. *Maryland Gazette,* August 16, August 23, September 6, September 13, 1753.

2. N.D. Mereness, *Maryland as a Proprietary Province* (New York: Macmillan, 1901), pp. 153–173; C. A. Barker, "Proprietary Rights in the Provincial System of Maryland: Proprietary Policy," *Journal of Southern History,* II (1936), pp. 55–56.

3. Mereness, *Maryland,* pp. 174–193.

4. W. Eddis, *Letters from America* (London: 1792), October 19, 1769, p. 24; C. A. Barker, *The Background of the Revolution in Maryland* (New Haven: Yale University Press, 1940), pp. 125–127, quote 153.

5. J. Boucher, *Reminiscences of an American Loyalist, 1738-1789*, J. Bouchier, editor (Boston: Houghton Mifflin, 1925), p. 54; C. Carroll to C. Carroll of Carrollton, October 28, 1772, "Extracts from the Carroll Papers," *Maryland Historical Magazine*, XIV (1919), p. 361.

6. J. High, "A Facet of Sovereignty: The Proprietary Governor and the Maryland Charter," *Maryland Historical Magazine*, LV (1960), p. 80; J. High, "Reluctant Loyalist: Governor Horatio Sharpe of Maryland, 1753-1769" (Ph.D. dissertation, University of California at Los Angeles, 1951), pp. 223–225.

7. Barker, *Background*, pp. 126–127; P. H. Giddens, "Governor Horatio Sharpe and His Maryland Government," *Maryland Historical Magazine*, XXXII (1937), p. 172. For a detailed analysis of the seventeenth century court system, which had similar importance in the following century, see P. G. Miller, "The County Court System of Maryland: Genesis, Evolution, and Significance" (M. A. thesis, Georgetown University, 1963).

8. February 17, 1772, Eddis, *Letters*, p. 125; B. W. Bond, "The Quit Rent in Maryland," *Maryland Historical Magazine*, V (1910), p. 358n; Giddens, "Governor Sharpe," pp. 165–166; for wage rates, see Tables 7 and 8 in D. C. Skaggs, "Democracy in Colonial Maryland, 1753-1776" (Ph.D. dissertation, Georgetown University, 1965), pp. 127–130. All monetary figures subsequently used herein will be in Maryland's current money, and not in pounds sterling, unless specifically noted in the text.

9. "Sermon Preached on the Occasion of the Death of Edward Lloyd Esquire," Lloyd Papers, Maryland Historical Society, n.p.; L.C. Wroth, "A Maryland Merchant and His Friends in 1750," *Maryland Historical Magazine*, VI (1911), p. 240; H. Sharpe to W. Sharpe, May 2, 1756, *Archives of Maryland*, VI, pp. 400–401; H. Sharpe to C. Calvert, December 15, 1764, *Archives of Maryland*, XIV, p. 186; H. Sharpe to Baltimore, July 13, 1756, *Archives of Maryland*, VI, p. 451.

10. C. Carroll to Carrollton, November 2, 1770, "Extracts," *Maryland Historical Magazine* (1918), p. 69; Carroll to Carrollton, October 6, 1759, Kate M. Rowland, *The Life of Charles Carroll of Carrollton*, 2 vols. (New York: G. P. Putman's Sons, 1898), I, p. 39; T. Ringgold to J. Hollyday, June 5, 1756, G. T. Hollyday, "Biographical Memoir of James Hollyday," *Pennsylvania Magazine of History and Biography*, VII (1883), p. 438; see also "A Voter," *Maryland Journal*, August 20, 1773; "A Planter," *Maryland Gazette*, June 24, 1773; "A Voter," *Maryland Gazette*, October 21, 1773.

11. Mereness, *Maryland*, pp. 188–190, 213–214.

12. *Archives of Maryland*, XXX, pp. 270–274.

13. R. E. Brown and B. K. Brown, *Virginia, 1705-1786: Democracy or Aristocracy?* (East Lansing, Mich.: Michigan State University Press, 1964), pp. 129–134. For landholding figures, see Appendices I and II in Skaggs, "Democracy in Colonial Maryland," pp. 284–345.

14. *Archives of Maryland*, XXX, pp. 617–622; XXXIII, pp. 287–289.

15. E. S. Riley, *"The Ancient City"*: *A History of Annapolis, In Maryland, 1649–1887* (Annapolis: Record Printing Office, 1887), pp. 85–89; Mereness, *Maryland,* pp. 420–422; Brown & Brown, *Virginia,* pp. 129–130.

16. *Archives of Maryland,* XXX, p. 270; C. Williamson, *American Suffrage from Property to Democracy, 1760–1860* (Princeton: Princeton University Press, 1960), pp. 5, 9.

17. Brown & Brown,, *Virginia,* pp. 129–131; *Proceedings of the Convention of the Province of Maryland, Held at the City of Annapolis, on Wednesday the Fourteenth of August, 1776 (Annapolis, [1776]),* pp. 2–6, 12, 23.

18. Williamson, *American Suffrage,* p. 19.

19. "Writ of Election," in Frederick County Court Papers, 1757–1763, Maryland Hall of Records; Frederick County Court Records, 1753–1758, Maryland Hall of Records, p. 721; Prince George's County Court Records. Maryland Hall of Records, XXXI, p. 552.

20. Baltimore County Indenture of Election, 1773, Gilmore Papers, Maryland Historical Society, III, p. 99; *Maryland Gazette,* February 13, 1752; Mereness, *Maryland,* pp. 212–213. The actual voting process in Maryland was undoubtedly much like that described in C. S. Sydnor, *Gentlemen Freeholders: Political Practices in Washington's Virginia* (Chapel Hill: University of North Carolina Press, 1952), chap. 2.

21. *Maryland Gazette,* October 5, 1758, December 3, 10, 17, 1767; *Archives of Maryland,* LXII, pp. 12, 14, 56, 75–77.

22. Annapolis City Records, Maryland Hall of Records, 1753–1767, I, pp. 39–40; II, pp. 38, 172, 245.

23. D. C. Skaggs, "Thomas Cradock's Sermon on the Governance of Maryland's Established Church," *William and Mary Quarterly,* Series 3, XXVII (1970), p. 648; Thomas Cradock, Sermon on Patience, Heb. 6:12, Maryland Diocesan Archives; S. Bordley to T. Bordley, November 18, 1745, S. Bordley to M. Harris, November 18, 1745, S. Bordley to J. Bordley, November 20, 1745, Bordley Letterbook, 1740–1747, Maryland Historical Society, pp. 128–132; *Archives of Maryland,* XLIV, vii, p. 63; E. Lloyd to J. Hollyday, September 7, 1758, Hollyday, "Biographical Memoir," p. 439; C. Calvert to S. Bordley, December 16, 1756, Bordley-Calvert Collection, Maryland Historical Society; H. Sharpe to C. Calvert, July 10, 1764, *Archives of Maryland,* XIV, p. 165.

24. H. Hall, Jr., to S. Galloway, November 5, 1754, Galloway, Maxcy, Markoe Papers, Library of Congress, I; *Maryland Gazette,* November 21, 1754, November 29, 1764; T. Ringgold to S. Galloway, May 23, 1773, B. Galloway to J. Galloway, May 27, 1773, Galloway, Maxcy, Markoe Papers, Library of Congress, XII; H. W. Sellers, "Charles Willson Peale, Artist-Soldier." *Pennsylvania Magazine of History and Biography,* XXXVIII (1914), pp. 261–262.

25. P. Hemsley to H. Hollyday, February 23, 1752, Maryland Colony and Revolutionary Papers, Duke University Library; H. Sharpe to C. Calvert, March 12 and May 22, 1755, *Archives of Maryland,* VI, pp. 178–208; *Maryland Gazette,* November 28, 1754, May 20, 1773 (quote); see also P. Hughes to H. Sharpe, June 13, 1769, *Archives of Maryland,* XIV, pp. 562–563.

26. *Archives of Maryland,* LXI, pp. 417–418; LXIII, xvi, pp. 102–103.

27. H. Hall, Jr., to S. Galloway, November 5, 1754, Galloway, Maxcy, Markoe papers, Library of Congress, I; *Archives of Maryland,* LXII, pp. 56, 75–77; J. Galloway to ——, October 20, 1774, "Account of the Destruction of the Brig 'Peggy Stewart,' at Annapolis, 1774," *Pennsylvania Magazine of History and Biography,* XXV (1901), pp. 249–251; A. Hamilton to J. Brown & Co., October 31, 1774, "The Letterbooks of Alexander Hamilton, Piscataway Factor," R. K. MacMaster and D. C. Skaggs, editors, *Maryland Historical Magazine,* LX (1966), pp. 318–319; J. Hall to J. Hall of W. River, December 13, 1776, T. J. Hall, *The Hall Family of West River and Kindred Families* (Denton, Md.: Rue Publishing Co., 1941), p. 62; C. Calvert to S. Bordley, December 16, 1756, Bordley-Calvert Collection, Maryland Historical Society.

28. *Archives of Maryland,* XXIV, p. 265; A. Clem, "The Vestries and Local Government in Colonial Maryland," *Historical Magazine of the Protestant Episcopal Church,* XXXI (1962), pp. 220–222; S. Ervin, "The Established Church of Colonial Maryland," *Historical Magazine of the Protestant Episcopal Church,* XXIV (1955), pp. 237–240.

29. St. Paul's Parish, Prince George's County, Vestry Proceedings, Maryland Hall of Records, p. 159; St. Paul's Parish, Queen Anne's County, Vestry Proceedings, Maryland Hall of Records, pp. 6-7; St. John's Parish, Prince George's County, Vestry Proceedings, Maryland Historical Society, pp. 121–122; *Archives of Maryland,* XXVIII, pp. 512–513. F.M.M. Beall, *Colonial Families of The United States* (Washington, D. C.: Charles Porter & Co., 1929), p. 125, is the only source for the identification of this particular John Beall (b. 1674), one of several men of the same name living in the county at that time.

30. St. Paul's Parish, Prince George's County, Vestry Proceedings, Maryland Hall of Records, p. 194; H. J. Berkley, "Early Records of the Church and Parish of All Faiths, St. Mary's County, 1692—1835," *Maryland Historical Magazine,* XXX (1936), pp. 28, 29, 30, 32; St. Paul's Parish, Queen Anne's County, Vestry Proceedings, Maryland Hall of Records, pp. 444, 445-447. See also G. E. Hartdagen, "The Anglican Vestry in Colonial Maryland: Organizational Structure and Problems," *Historical Magazine of the Protestant Episcopal Church,* XXXVIII (1969), pp. 349–360; G. E. Hartdagen, "The Vestry as a Unit of Local Government in Colonial Maryland," *Maryland Historical Magazine,* LXVII (1972), pp. 363–388.

Chapter

3

DEMOGRAPHIC AND ECONOMIC DEVELOPMENTS

Any attempt to describe a colony stretching from the wetlands of the lower Eastern Shore to the Great Appalachian Valley of Frederick County as a coherent economic and social unit is doomed to failure and error. The Chesapeake Bay itself undoubtedly dominated life in His Lordship's province, but it was demographic and economic diversity that characterized the region, and this lack of uniformity affected the political situation.

Maryland's growing, heterogeneous population rose from 153,000 in 1752 to 228,000 by the eve of revolution. Approximately 25 percent of these were slaves, 5 percent free blacks, and 65 percent white freemen. In 1775, the colony ranked fourth in population behind Virginia, Massachusetts, and Pennsylvania.

The population became increasingly more concentrated on the Western Shore. In the two decades before the Declaration of Independence, the percentage of population west of the bay rose from 53 percent to 62 percent. In the decade 1760–1770, the counties of the Eastern Shore (that portion of the colony east of the bay) and lower Western Shore showed a slowing down or an absolute decline in population growth, while other counties displayed increases of nearly 20 percent.

Recovering from a population decline caused by the Great War for the Empire, Frederick County (which at this time included the western third of the province) jumped a phenomenal 54 percent in the last ten years of colonial rule[2] (see Table 1).

The migrant nature of Maryland's population resulted in a loss of political equality among the colony's citizens. Because each county, regardless of its size, had four delegates, the inequality of population in the various counties led to a malapportionment of the Assembly seats which particularly affected the residents of Baltimore and Frederick counties.

After 1748 both Eastern and Western Shores had seven counties, and this balance continued in 1773 when Harford County was created from eastern Baltimore County, and Caroline County was carved from Dorchester and Queen Anne's counties. When one looks at the populations of the two counties (see Table 2) from which these two new jurisdictions came, it becomes apparent that there was no need for the new Eastern Shore county except to maintain some sort of regional balance in the Assembly. At this time, vast and populous Frederick County seemed to cry for greater political representation. In fact, the addition of Caroline County unbalanced even further an already inequitable situation of popular representation in the Lower House. With an equal number of counties on each shore, only the seats from the town of Annapolis tipped the balance ever so slightly to the Western Shore.[3]

The proprietary government alternated in its attitude toward new counties. In 1755, Lord Baltimore proposed a new county for the territory beyond what is now Cumberland, but Governor Sharpe opposed the idea on the grounds that it was not settled enough to support the expense of a court system. Secretary Calvert opposed the creation of new counties by dividing the old ones in 1760 "because every Division by increasing the Number of Delegates, increases the number of opponents to the Government." A new proprietor and secretary, in addition to increased pressure for some aid to populous Baltimore County, where the legislature was petitioned annually by citizens wanting the county seat in Joppa or Baltimore Town, resulted in the creation of Harford County, and its Eastern Shore twin, Caroline, in 1773.[4]

TABLE 1

COUNTY POPULATION GROWTH, 1755–1775[1]

County	1755	1765	1775
Eastern Shore			
Cecil	7,800	9,300	8,950
Kent	10,430	11,740	12,440
Queen Anne's	12,000	14,300	11,800
Caroline	– – –	– – –	7,810
Talbot	8,200	10,600	9,000
Dorchester	11,750	12,000	10,100
Somerset	8,500	9,800	13,000
Worcester	10,125	9,550	11,800
Total	78,805	77,290	87,900
Western Shore			
St. Mary's	11,254	12,500	13,200
Calvert	5,800	7,885	8,430
Charles	13,050	15,665	18,020
Anne Arundel	13,050	16,000	19,130
Prince George's	13,000	16,000	18,400
Baltimore	18,000	20,000	21,000
Harford	– – –	– – –	12,600
Frederick	13,969	13,800	30,000
Total	88,123	102,750	140,880

[1] A. E. Karinen, "Numerical and Distributional Aspects of Maryland Population, 1631–1840," pp. 122–137.

TABLE 2

COMPARISONS BETWEEN THE TWO SHORES[1]

Year	Population		Ratio
	Eastern	Western	Western to Eastern
1755	78,805	88,123	1.12 to 1
1765	77,295	102,750	1.32 to 1
1775	87,900	140,880	1.60 to 1

Years	Assembly Seats		Ratio
	Eastern	Western	Western to Eastern
1748–1773	28	30	1.07 to 1
1773–1776	32	34	1.06 to 1
1776–1789	32	44	1.38 to 1

[1]Karinen, "Numerical," pp. 111–137.

As Table 2 shows, the addition in 1776 of two western counties (Montgomery and Washington), and the allowance of two delegates from the city of Baltimore, partly remedied the maldistribution of Assembly seats. This division of the old Frederick County into three parts came as the result of local political action, and not from any desire on the part of citizens from other parts of Maryland for such a change. While there is no indication of a conspiracy on the part of the Eastern Shore delegates to insure equality where none should have existed, the evidence of inaction suggests that the earlier creation of additional western counties may have been curtailed by them.[5]

This discrimination was more severe than the figures in Tables 1 and 2 indicate. Because all blacks, whether slave or free, were disfranchised, and because the Negro population was concentrated more in some counties than in others, white citizens in counties where there were fewer blacks were seriously discriminated against in political influence in comparison to their fellow freemen in the other counties. In southern Maryland (Calvert, Prince George's, Anne Arundel, and St. Mary's counties), Negroes constituted approximately half of the total population. On the central Eastern Shore (Queen Anne's and Kent counties) slaves accounted for between 40 to 45 percent of the total. In these six counties the growing of tobacco was the principal economic occupation. The harvest of wood products (shingles, barrel staves, and others) necessitated the use of significant numbers of blacks on the lower Eastern Shore. There, in Dorchester, Somerset, and Worcester counties, approximately 30 to 40 percent of the population was black. In the rest of the province the average was below 25 percent, with populous Frederick County having only one percent in involuntary servitude.[6]

The peculiar geographic and demographic position of the counties with a high concentration of blacks placed their residents on the horns of a dilemma when revolution broke out. A particularly outspoken demand for social equality might bring about consequences that would drastically alter the positions of members of the races. Any naval operations against the province (particularly when coupled with a call to arms to loyalist blacks) would find the colony's "black belt" most vulnerable. Undoubtedly these factors influenced the essential political conservatism and loyalism that flared up on the Eastern Shore during the Revolutionary years.

If the potential for change affected the political climate of the "black belt" counties towards conservatism, urbanization demanded modifications in other regions. One cannot escape the fact that Maryland was a predominantly rural province which did not achieve a single community, in the urban definition of 2,500 always used by the Bureau of the Census, until Baltimore Town reached that status in about 1765. That community on the Patapsco was growing at an exceptionally rapid pace, probably more rapidly than any other place in colonial British America. Of importance as local entreports were Chestertown in Kent County, and Easton (or Talbot Court House) in Talbot County. Their populations were small, but they served as the nucleus for the settlement of leading merchants, tradesmen, and lawyers. Furthermore, the leading religious denominations usually had congregations in such communities, with the result that they were more important as cultural centers than the mere population figures indicate. The colonial capital of Annapolis on the Western Shore was a small community, but it was the center of political life and was linked with the rest of the province by the easy communication that the bay offered. A description of the colonial Chesapeake as a "sylvan Venice" indicates the unifying rather than the divisive influence of the bay's waters. The backcountry communities of Frederick and Hagerstown served as commercial, political, and social centers in the late colonial period and rivaled, if not exceeded, Annapolis in population. (See Table 3 for population figures.) A series of small communities like Georgetown, Bladensburg, Piscataway, Port Tobacco, Benedict, Upper Marlboro, Queen Anne, Elkton, Oxford, and Vienna served as collecting points for the export of various products and the location of small mercantile houses operated by either local merchants or factors for British firms.[7]

TABLE 3

URBAN POPULATION IN MARYLAND[1]

City	1750	1760	1770	1780
Annapolis	800	1000		1500
Baltimore	200	1200	3600	5700
Chestertown		800		
Easton		600		
Frederick	1000	1000		1700
Hagerstown				1600

[1] Karinen, "Numerical," pp. 159–163.

The rise of these communities was attributable to a number of factors: among them were (1) the tobacco inspection act of 1747, which centralized the grading of tobacco at one point within each parish, which usually served as a concentration point for tobacco traders; (2) the development of plantations above the fall line, which made commercial transfer points at the tidewater-fall line juncture a necessity; and (3) the growing specialization of certain economic tasks, which brought about a degree of concentration at a convenient place.

Thus, while urbanization was relatively modest in the colonial period, it reflected a social change occurring in the colony—a change which necessitated some modification of the political order. Annapolis, with its two delegates, was decidedly over-represented in the Assembly when compared with the counties, the least populous of which—Caroline—had nearly 8,000 people in 1775. By 1770, on the other hand, Baltimore Town deserved at least as many delegates as Annapolis, if not more. No indication of either proprietary or "country" party concern for these citizens exists until the Baltimore revolutionaries, like the backcountry men of Frederick County, presented the Constitutional Convention of 1776 with a *fait accompli* concerning their independent political status.

The settlement of Frederick County and the rise of the urban centers at Baltimore, Frederick, Hagerstown, and Georgetown reflected an important economic transformation of economic and social life on the upper Chesapeake. Nowhere was this more significant than in the rush to settle the Monocacy and Concocheague valleys of Frederick County. Scotch–Irish, English, and Germans migrated there, seeking financial rewards in the lush soils especially adapted for grain and forage crops. These settlements, as Aubrey C. Land noted, were suited for an entirely different type of culture from that of the Tobacco Coast of the tidewater. Daniel Dulany, the elder (1685–1753), saw his great opportunity in this area and quickly pressed for its development after 1744. German and Scotch-Irish farmers coming from the inhabited regions of Pennsylvania saw the same possibilities, as did numerous English settlers from the lower Potomac valley. The dangers created by the French and Indian War kept the frontier population at 14,000 in the 1755–1765 decade. But the next ten years saw rapid settlement in what are now Frederick, Montgomery, Washington, and Carroll counties, so that by 1775 there were some 30,000 persons in the area and significant urban centers had developed at Frederick and Hagerstown.[8]

The growth of the backcountry required a seaport, and Baltimore filled this need because of its easy ability to tap commerce along the Philadelphia road, which ran up the Appalachian valleys to the Pennsylvania city. Baltimore's wealth was enhanced by the extensive flourmilling industry along Jones Falls which prepared the backcountry grain for markets in the West Indies and southern Europe. Baltimore also became the center of a growing iron industry. The first of its profitable smelting enterprises came in 1715 when a group of British iron-masters, merchants, and investors established the Principio Company. Under the skillful direction of Stephen Onion and

Thomas Russell, Sr., this firm grew until it owned upwards of 30,000 acres of land (from which to draw timber needed to make charcoal for its furnaces) and over 100 slaves. At least as large was the Baltimore Ironworks Company founded in 1731 by a group of Maryland's most influential citizens—Daniel Dulany, the elder, Benjamin Tasker, Sr., Dr. Charles Carroll, Charles Carroll, Esq., and Daniel Carroll. This firm owned 30,000 acres of Anne Arundel and Baltimore timberland, employed a large number of slaves, servants, and freemen, and built an operation which Barrister Carroll claimed exported bar iron that both in price and quality was "not in the Least Inferior" to that of Sweden. By 1756, six ironworks owned 46,269 acres of Baltimore County lands. In 1758, Maryland and Virginia exported 3,448 tons of pig iron and 341 tons of bar iron. Even though competition from Pennsylvania and New York furnaces cut this quantity in subsequent years, Maryland apparently had the largest share of the colonial iron industry.[9]

The beginnings of the change from a tobacco-oriented society to one in which cereal grain and smelting production played important roles created little response in the political life of the colony. A recognition of the contributions of the German settlers, who scorned the use of slaves and worked the land themselves, lay in the future. The rise of grain and forage farming in the west, and the emergence of milling and iron industries and a large urban seaport on the northern Chesapeake, worked a significant change in the economic life of Maryland.[10]

While population trends and economic power moved northward and westward, the center of social and political influence remained in the tidewater homes of tobacco planters and the drawing rooms of Annapolis. Although we have already looked at the changing aspects of Maryland's economy with the rise of the grain trade in Frederick County and the Eastern Shore, and of the ironworks on the upper reaches of the bay, the basic commodity of the region was still the tobacco leaf. To understand the politics of the colony, one must, perforce, understand the tobacco economy, which underwrote the political system.

The rise of the Chesapeake region into what Arthur Middleton has called the "Tobacco Coast" was the result not merely of geographic features like soil fertility and rainfall, but was primarily due to the peculiar contour of the bay with its hundreds of rivers, creeks, and inlets. These allowed easy transportation of the heavy hogsheads of tobacco to the waiting vessels ready to take the crop to European markets.[11]

On the eve of the break with England, Maryland and Virginia annually produced some £ 900,000 sterling worth of tobacco, which constituted 75 percent of the total value of their exported products. Maryland's 38,963,000-pound tobacco export of 1771 constituted approximately one-third of that produced in British America. This was consistent with the usual percentage of the total of the American crop exported from His Lordship's province. The rapid expansion of the tobacco trade in the eighteenth century sustained three types of marketers. Along the Potomac valley there grew up a series of factoring stations operated by storekeepers sent by Glasgow firms, which dominated the trade. On the bayshore, individual planters sold directly to London merchant houses on a commission basis. An increasingly larger commercial group was the American merchants. The Bordleys, Galloways, Hancocks, Johnsons, Lees, Luxes, Platers, Purviances, Ridgleys, Ringgolds, and Wests constituted a new element in the mercantile picture.

Whether merchant-planters or independent merchants, they represented a growing continental commercial class desiring a greater share in the economic affairs of the province. For the planter, they provided a new option in the marketing of crops. It is important to note that from this group of mostly self-made men and families came many of the most ardent revolutionaries.[12] Hence, despite the growing trade in grain, iron, and wood products, tobacco was the most important ingredient in the provincial economy for each class of merchant.

Whatever the crop, there can be little doubt that the pervasiveness of agriculture as the basic form of livelihood meant that all had a common bond with the soil. All could converse on the universal topics of the husbandman—fertility of the soil, necessity of rainfall, rotation of corps, commodity prices, and methods of cultivation, storage, and transportation. The difference between the great planter and the tenant was the size of the agricultural operation with which he was concerned—his stake in society. The great question concerning economic equality was the degree to which it was held and the opportunity those in the lower economic brackets had of rising to the top. To make such an inquiry, one must first understand the distribution of property in the colony—for land in such a community was the *sine qua non* of political and economic status.

In order to make a detailed analysis of landholding in colonial Maryland, four representative counties have been chosen for detailed investigation: Baltimore, Prince George's, Queen Anne's, and Talbot. There are several reasons for this particular selection. First, their governmental records, such as quitrent Debt Books, parish vestry proceedings, Prerogative Court Records, and other such sources, are virtually complete. Second, in most cases a considerable number of primary documents, such as private letters, records, and speeches, are available. Third, secondary material, such as genealogical data, county and local histories, and other studies which add detail and insight, are abundant. Fourth, these counties in several ways give one a broad survey of the state as a whole with its many diverse elements. They show the development of older (Talbot and Queen Anne's) and more recently settled (Baltimore and Prince George's) regions of the colony. They represent differing approaches to the sale of tobacco—Talbot using the consignment system, Prince George's the factoring method, and Baltimore mostly local mercantile firms. Baltimore also gives a look at a county which had a growing urban area as well as a quickly developing backcountry filling with German and Scotch-Irish immigrants who cultivated corn and wheat rather than the traditional tobacco crop. Baltimore also had a considerable number of milling and iron manufacturing industries. All four give a good cross section of the religious and ethnic diversification of Maryland.

From an analysis of such data in these counties, it becomes apparent that the economic welfare of Maryland's ordinary citizens may have been below that found elsewhere in British America. Only about 40 percent of the white freemen owned land. Land ownership in these representative counties became increasingly more restrictive in the years under investigation. As Table 4 indicates, some 44 percent of the white adult freemen owned land in these counties in 1756. By 1771, the percentage of landowners to freemen dropped to 37 percent (see Table 5). In all cases except Baltimore County, where the sale

TABLE 4

PERCENTAGE OF WHITE ADULT FREEMEN WHO WERE LANDOWNERS, 1756[1]

County	Total Pop. 1756	Adult Freemen 1756	Land- owners 1756	% Land- owners
Baltimore	18,000	2,400	1,096	45.7
Prince George's	14,500	1,934	752	38.9
Queen Anne's	11,500	1,533	780	50.9
Talbot	8,500	1,133	451	39.8
Total	52,500	7,000	3,079	44.0

[1] The population statistics for Tables 4 and 5 are taken from Karinen, "Numerical and Distributional Aspects," pp. 115-130. The number of adult freemen is derived from the assumption that 20 percent of the population was adult male and that one-third of these were either slaves or servants. The number of landowners is derived from the quitrent Debt Books for these counties for 1756 and 1771 (1769 in the case of Queen Anne's County where the 1770 and 1771 records are missing) located in the Maryland Hall of Records, Annapolis. Tables 4 and 5 were previously published in D. C. Skaggs, "Maryland's Impulse Toward Social Revolution, 1750–1776," *Journal of American History* LIV (March, 1968), p. 772.

TABLE 5

PERCENTAGE OF WHITE ADULT FREEMEN WHO WERE LANDOWNERS, 1771

County	Total Pop. 1771	Adult Freemen 1771	Land- owners 1771	% Land- owners
Baltimore	28,000	3,733	1,531	41,0
Prince George's	18,400·	2,453	775	31.6
Queen Anne's	13,800	1,840	813	44.2
Talbot	11,500	1,533	419	27.3
Total	71,700	9,560	3,538	37.0

of lots in Baltimore Town affects the statistics, the size of the median farm holding (between 157 to 209 acres) rose in the period. These figures do not indicate that the small planter was becoming a larger one, but that land was steadily falling into the hands of the larger planters.

The median landholding was around 200 acres. This figure is in direct conflict with the 1913 findings of Clarence Gould showing several county averages varying from 250 to 475 acres. In using the mean instead of the median, Professor Gould allowed his figures to become distorted. He found the 1756 Talbot County average to be some 329.5 acres, in contrast to the median for the same year of 199 acres. Such a difference is a direct result of his methodology. The use of an average instead of a median caused such huge landholdings as the 12,884-acre operation of Edward Lloyd III to have an adverse effect on the validity of his figures.[13]

Not only were Gould's estimates of the typical acreage holdings too high, but his estimate that approximately half of the colony's planters owned land was also excessively high.

Assuming that the population of Prince George's County was 18,400 in 1771 (one has little reason to doubt the conclusion of geographer Arthur Karinen in this matter), and assuming that 20 percent of the population was adult male (a generally accepted figure used by colonial demographers), and also assuming that a third of the population was in servitude at the time (as contemporary accounts indicate), one learns that the county had some 2,453 freemen and only 775 freeholders. This means that less than a third of the white freemen in the county held land, even should one count all the women landowners as men. This estimate shows a remarkable discrepancy with the figures presented by Professor Gould for Maryland, and is in sharp contrast with the high figures presented by Professor and Mrs. Brown for both Massachusetts and Virginia. A similar statistical inquiry into the other three counties of our sample shows that an equally small percentage of the white male population held land. In all, it is apparent that landownership was not as widespread in the future Old Line State as previous studies have indicated and as the Browns would like to postulate.[14]

The avenues to economic opportunity in landholding were becoming increasingly restrictive. Population was rising at a much faster rate than land-ownership. In Talbot County, 1756–1771, the population increased 32.29 percent, while the number of freeholders *declined* 7.10 percent. In Queen Anne's, the population rose 20.00 percent and the number of land-owners rose only 4.23 percent; Prince George's population increased 26.89 percent, while its number of freeholders rose only 4.45 percent. Baltimore County's population rose an astonishing 55.55 percent in the period, while its number of landowners increased only 39.69 percent. Moreover, entry into the small landholding class declined in two of the counties, remained static in a third, and rose due to the development of town lots in Baltimore Town in the fourth (see Table 6). There were half as many men owning one to 49 acres in Queen Anne's County in 1769 as there had been 13 years earlier. It was becoming increasingly difficult for a man with limited capital to enter into the landholding class.

The rate of declining landownership varied in the counties surveyed. In the older, Eastern Shore counties of Queen Anne's and Talbot, the rate of decline in landowners was one-and-a-half and three times, respectively, as fast as in Baltimore. Prince George's County saw landownership decline at a rate almost twice that of Baltimore. Both the urbanization and the frontier situation of this latter county allowed a somewhat greater opportunity than existed elsewhere.

Contemporary statements validate the conclusion arising from these figures. A large proportion of the population was in the small planter and tenant class. Using the pseudonym "George Meanwell," one large land and slave owner of Prince George's County wrote of "the honest industrious Planter, who has but a small Portion of Property; and the no less honest, but more poor and laborious one, who rents Land . . . who to be sure, make a great Part of our People."[15] Table 6 reinforces this statement with statistics. On the whole, Marylanders of the late colonial period were in modest circumstances as far as "real" property was concerned.

In this golden age of Chesapeake culture, His Lordship's province was faced with a growing number of landless peasants in an agricultural society. Most persons were in want of the chance to rise above a mere grubbing for a living. Maryland was hardly the land of opportunity usually depicted for colonial America.

TABLE 6

DISTRIBUTION OF LANDOWNERSHIP, 1756 AND 1771[1]

County No. Acres	Baltimore			Prince George's			Queen Anne's			Talbot		
	% Land-holders (N=1096) 1756	% Land-holders (N=1531) 1771	% Change 1756-1771	% Land-holders (N=742) 1756	% Land-holders (N=775) 1771	% Change 1756-1771	%'Land-holders (N=780) 1756	%'Land-holders (N=813) 1769	% Change 1756-1771	% Land-holders (N=451) 1756	% Land-holders (N=419) 1771	% Change 1756-1771
1-49	5.01	7.90	+120.00	5.50	5.80	+ 9.76	5.51	2.70	-48.84	6.87	5.01	-22.26
50-99	16.23	18.41	+ 57.54	11.45	9.41	-14.12	15.12	12.66	-12.71	14.63	14.55	- 7.58
100-149	20.80	20.57	+ 38.16	20.08	20.51	+ 6.71	19.09	19.80	+ 8.78	18.40	17.42	-12.05
150-199	9.30	9.60	+ 44.12	10.37	10.58	+ 6.49	12.17	11.93	+ 2.11	10.19	10.75	- 2.17
200-249	9.67	9.40	+ 35.85	11.05	11.75	+10.98	11.79	12.66	+11.96	10.86	11.21	- 4.08
250-299	4.92	4.76	+.35.19	7.54	5.16	-28.57	5.76	6.76	+22.22	7.09	3.81	-50.00
300-399	7.75	7.70	+ 38.82	9.29	10.06	+13.04	10.00	9.96	+ 3.85	8.42	11.93	+31.58
400-499	5.93	5.42	+ 27.69	5.66	5.80	+ 7.14	5.64	6.02	+11.36	6.65	7.63	+ 6.67
500-599	4.83	3.46	0.00	5.12	6.19	+26.32	3.33	4.05	+26.92	4.21	3.81	-15.79
600-999	6.47	6.40	+ 38.03	6.87	7.09	+ 7.84	5.64	6.64	+22.73	5.98	7.15	+11.11
1000-1499	1.09	2.28	+191.67	3.23	3.09	+ 0.00	2.17	3.69	+76.47	3.54	2.60	+32.25
1500 & over	7.84	4.04	- 27.91	3.77	4.51	+25.00	3.84	3.07	-16.67	3.10	4.05	+21.43
Total Owners	100.00	100.00	+ 39.69	100.00	100.00	+ 4.45	100.00	100.00	+ 4.23	100.00	100.00	- 7.10

Quartile	Baltimore 1756 - Acres - 1771		Prince George's 1756 - Acres - 1771		Queen Anne's 1756 - Acres - 1769		Talbot 1756 - Acres - 1771	
1st Quartile	1-100	1-92	1-100	1-100	1-100	1-103	1-100	1-100
2nd Quartile	100-186	92-157	100-200	100-204	100-190	103-200	100-199	100-209
3rd Quartile	187-410	157-347	200-393	205-360	190-343	200-381	200-385	210-399
4th Quartile	411-20590	348-22520	394-12884	361-12797	344-7143	382-7326	386-12648	400-11928

[1] All data are compiled from the holdings listed in the quitrent Debt Books for these counties for 1756 and 1771 (1769 in the case of Queen Anne's County where the later records are missing) Maryland Hall of Records.

Of course, this does not indicate that suffrage was not widespread, since one did not have to own land to enjoy the franchise. One had only to possess a visible estate of £ 40 sterling to do so. So it becomes necessary to find out whether a large number of the freemen held personal property —"visible estates"—of such valuation.

As the search for the size of the median estate was facilitated by the magnificent set of Debt Books for these two counties available at the Maryland Land Office, so the quest for determining the size of the typical personal property estate is facilitated by the Prerogative Court Records at the Maryland Hall of Records. The Inventories in these records allow one to learn the size of the personal property estate of each freeman or freewoman who died in the province. Of course, one must first determine what is a "visible estate." If such is the value of personal property less all the debts against it, then most of the colony's population was disqualified.

If, on the other hand, as this author believes, "visible estate" means only the property the assessor could *see,* excluding the debts against it, then a much larger portion of the population possessed the franchise. (There is no eighteenth-century or modern definition of "visible estate" to be found.) Of those personal estates of non-landowners appearing in the Talbot County Inventories, nearly 39 percent were valued at less than £ 66.13.4, the current money equivalent of £ 40 sterling. Of the 323 freeman estates assessed in the county between 1753 and 1773, approximately 29 percent were not qualified to vote because of insufficient estate (see Table 7). A study of similar records for Baltimore County produced almost identical statistics.[16] An additional six percent of the landowners were not qualified to vote because they did not have the requisite 50 acres of land, and a further eight percent were denied the franchise because of their Roman Catholicism. Thus, at the very least, between 33 and 40 percent of Maryland's white freemen were disfranchised.

This conclusion can be confirmed from another direction. Only 55 percent of the non-freeholders listed in the Baltimore and Talbot county inventories were qualified because they had sufficient personal estate. If this figure is projected over the four representative counties, and if the estimate of 7,000 adult freemen therein in 1756 is valid, then 2,156 of the 3,921 non-landowners were qualified. If to this figure we add the 94

TABLE 7

TALBOT COUNTY PERSONAL ESTATES , 1753–1773[1]

Currency Value £	Non-landowners 1756 or 1771	Landowners 1756 or 1771
0–66	81	11
67–99	30	10
100–149	27	16
150–199	25	14
200–299	14	17
300–399	8	1
400–499	7	4
500–599	11	20
1,000 & over	6	21
Totals	209	114

[1]Based on the data compiled from the Prerogative Court Records, Inventories, Talbot County, Maryland Hall of Records, 1750–1773.

percent of the 3,079 landowners possessing the requisite 50 acres we can account for 2,956 more qualified voters for a total of 5,112. Of this number approximately eight percent must be subtracted because their Catholicism disqualified them. This decreases the number of voters by 409 to 4,703, or 69 percent of the freemen. If one uses the 1771 figures and the same methodology, the number so qualified drops to just less than 64 percent.[17]

Actually, the number of qualified voters was probably less than is indicated by these percentages. First, because the figures from the quitrent Debt Books and Prerogative Court Records include many women and a few businesses which did not possess the franchise, and second, because many freemen died without any property worthy of an inventory, one can conclude that the percentage of eligible voters was less than 60 percent. This is corroborated by a commentator of 1776 who claimed that the election requirements of the convention era, which by this time allowed Roman Catholic voting, excluded at least half of the freemen from the suffrage. Philip A. Crowl estimated that the broadened franchise requirements of the 1776 constitution permitted only 55 percent of the white male freemen to vote in 1790.[18]

These Baltimore and Talbot County figures support another theory of Maryland life already referred to in this study—that there were nearly twice as many landless freemen as freeholders.

One should not be led to believe from the figures that considerable personal property was inherited, as such was not the case. Over a third of these Talbot Countians (over half of the non-landowners) possessed estates of less than £ 100 currency. This means they lived a meager existence. They had no slaves, ate off wooden dishes, possessed extremely limited amounts of clothing and household furniture, and owned very few farm animals and tools.

Their diet consisted of an alternation of mush and milk or molasses and hominy with wild fowl and fish. Outside the cider season, their principal drink was water; in fact, the lack of hard liquor was one of the leading complaints of the poor. Viewing the hard but honest life of the lower classes, English novelist Edward Kimber (1719–1769) was reminded of "the Golden Age, the Times of ancient Frugality and Purity."[19]

The typical freeman was like the Susquehanna ferryman Dr. Alexander Hamilton described in 1744 in his *Itinerarium*. When the family sat down to their "homely dish of fish without any kind of sauce," they "had no cloth upon the table, and their mess was in a dirty, deep, wooden dish which they evacuated with their hands, cramming down skins, scales, and all. They used neither knife, fork, spoon, plate, or napkin because, I suppose, they had none to use."[20]

The high incidence of poverty in colonial Maryland is confirmed by the Prerogative Court Records. Of the 209 non-freeholders dying in Talbot County from 1753–1773 in possession of any personal estate at all, some 37, or nearly 18 percent, had estates of less than £ 33. This was the current money equivalent of the £ 20 sterling legal definition of poverty in the colony.[21] Assuming that all the slaves and servants were in this same category, this means half the colony's population was in want. Comparing this with Franklin Roosevelt's lament about one-third of the nation being ill-fed, ill-clothed, and ill-housed, one begins to realize just how deprived many of the colonists must have been.

Studies directed by Professor A. C. Land of the University of Georgia, relative to the impoverished state of many Maryland colonists,[22] only reinforce this author's conclusions. Too much time has been spent admiring the splendors of Wye House, Mt. Clare, Whitehall, and Tulip Hill, which were decidedly not typical of the time.

This abject poverty is no better illustrated than in the letters of the Rev. Joseph Mosley, S. J. In St. Mary's County in 1759 he found the people "to be very poor, and not to be compared in riches to the rest of our colonies." Eleven years later, when stationed on the Eastern Shore, he wrote touchingly of "poor, miserable, abandoned families, in poverty, want and misery."[23]

Poverty was closely intertwined with the large indebtedness of the typical colonist. The estate of Capt. James Lloyd II (1716–1768) of Talbot County showed some £ 2,435.18.8 in 322 "sparate" or collectible debts owed the late planter, and an additional 200 "desparate" or uncollectible debts valued at £ 496.4.2.

If Captain Lloyd's economic power was amply illustrated by these figures, that of his cousin, Col. Edward Lloyd III (1711–1770) of Wye House was even greater. Colonel Lloyd's "Bond Book" and ledgers contain loans made to several hundred Marylanders, mostly on the Eastern Shore. At his funeral the minister felt the need to comment on how to "the honest and industrious poor, he was helpful and charitable, and where he judged the Objects proper, even liberal and genteel. Finally, to the many poor people that had Dealings with him, he shewed much Lenity and Forbearance; not harassing them with vexatious Lawsuits, but having patience with them, till they should pay the Debt." To Henry Callister, the eulogy was all too charitable. He compared the squire of Wye House with a beast of the Apocalypse from whom only "the ingrossers & monopolizers of the Tobacco trade are qualified to buy & sell." By every evidence Colonel Lloyd held significant economic power in his section of the province.[24]

On the Western Shore indebtedness involved significant numbers of planters and merchants. Charles Carroll of Annapolis estimated in

1762 that he had some £ 24,230 out at interest. The small Glasgow firm of James Brown & Co. had in its Prince George's County stores in 1775 a planter indebtedness amounting to over £ 500 in store goods, £ 9,600 currency, £ 1,000 sterling, and 20,000 pounds of tobacco. The estate of Frederick County merchant-planter Joseph Chaplin showed some 55 debts, amounting to £ 1,251, owed to it in 1768.[25]

Illustrative of the size of such debts was the estate of Philemon Hambleton, Sr., a Talbot planter. Owner of nearly 900 acres, the value of his personal property was £ 1,050. Of this wealth, however, nearly £ 356 were in debts owed to such gentry as Matthew Tilghman, James Dickinson, William Goldsborough, and Colonel Lloyd. Over a third of his personal property was indebted. Among smaller planters the percentage of indebtedness was higher than that of Hambleton. In fact, the property of some planters was overvalued by the appraisers in order to cover all obligations upon it. To be sure, this tissue of debt involved relations with creditors in London and Glasgow. But the small planter and artisan had most of his credit relations with domestic planter-moneylenders, who subsidized much of the economic development of the region.[26] Surely one of the most important consequences of such an arrangement was the effect it had upon the debtor's political independence from his creditor. In a deferential society this must have been significant.

Although the burden of debt was heavy, an equally serious problem was the rising incidence of tenancy in the colony. This came as the result of two major circumstances: the concentration of land ownership in fewer hands and the unavailability of new lands, especially new land suitable for tobacco farming. An expanding population in this agricultural society, and the need of the large landowners to cultivate as much land as possible in order to pay the quitrent, were also contributing factors. (The quitrent payments required that most land be put to productive use rather than have it remain a liability to the owner.) Leasing did not become common in the province until the third decade of the eighteenth century when both proprietary and private manors began to let out numerous acres. The monetary return to the owner from such a practice was not great, but it did allow him to pay the quitrent, and it increased the value of his property by bringing more woodland into cultivation. The other option was to use an overseer system to cultivate the tobacco crop. Such a system gave greater returns, but it involved a considerably greater investment in slaves and indentured servants, an investment many felt they could not afford or would rather put into land.[27]

To the end of the proprietary period, wealth in the colony was ascertained in landholdings. We have already noted the tendency in Baltimore, Prince George's, Queen Anne's and Talbot counties for land to be concentrated in the hands of fewer persons. After the Proclamation of 1763, land prices in the more settled areas rose significantly. Land which Fr. Joseph Mosley bought for £ 1.10.0 an acre in 1765 sold for £ 6 or £ 7 an acre less than ten years later. The 1765 prices were 200 to 300 percent higher than those of 1725. In the period under discussion, land prices were sufficiently high to discourage the wide distribution of property among the non-landholding citizens. The sole source of new land in the colony lay in the Frederick County frontier area.[28]

As long as there was sufficient good unpatented land, the rate of tenantry was low. After 1720, leasing became more common. It was not until the 1740s that the Piedmont area of lower Frederick County came under cultivation. Previously, speculation in land by holding it until the price rose had been risky, since it required considerable capital investment and the continued payment of quitrents while the property went undeveloped. Never before in the colony's history had investors been enabled to secure large numbers of lessors before the frontier receded. Now such an opportunity arose with the immigration of Germans who could secure only limited title to the land, who knew little about patenting procedures, and who had little aversion to becoming tenants. This influx played directly into the hands of a small group of speculators who were able to bring the tenant and the land together.[29]

These speculators may be divided into three groups: those directly in the proprietary camp as high officeholders and favorites; those wealthy Marylanders not currently involved with the proprietary, but who had secured extensive holdings of their own; and those few who are not known to have any direct relationship with the gentry or the proprietor.

Of this first group the most significant was Daniel Dulany, the elder, and his family. Dulany's operations began in 1744 when he first saw the economic opportunities inherent in the backcountry. Dulany patented some 58,000 acres in Frederick County. Among other proprietary favorites involved in this speculation were John Morton Jordan, Dr. Upton Scott, Benjamin Tasker, Sr., Stephen Bordley, Benedict Calvert, Edmund Jenings, George Plater II, John Ridout, and Gov. Horatio Sharpe. One must not exclude Lord Baltimore, holder of 148,000 acres of manor and reserve lands in this county alone.[30]

The second group claimed Charles Carroll of Annapolis as its greatest leader. He patented about 47,000 acres. It included such well-known gentlemen as Dr. Charles Carroll and his son Charles Carroll, barrister, Thomas Ringgold, Jr., Samuel Chase, Thomas Johnson, Jr. Joseph Chaplin, James Brooke, Samuel Galloway III, Henry Darnall III, and Richard Snowden. Of all the men in these two groups, only Chaplin and Johnson lived in Frederick County. Most of the rest lived in Anne Arundel or Prince George's Counties. This was absentee ownership on a large scale.[31]

In the last group were a few of the non-gentry class, such as Lancelot Jacques and Stephen Onion, manufacturers; Jonathan Hager, immigrant; and Thomas Cresap, a frontiersman. The largest speculator in this group, Hager, held 12,000 acres, most of it in the vicinity of the city bearing his name.[32]

Thirteen men owned some 250,000 acres constituting 21 percent of the total patented land in Frederick County. In addition to this were the vast holdings of the Lord Proprietor.[33] There can be little doubt that such large-scale engrossment of land, combined with the small size of the western end of the province, limited the amount of economic opportunity on the frontier. On the whole, landownership in Maryland seemed to be a classic example of the rich getting richer.

Still, one must not discount the fact that opportunity was available to those possessing education and ability. There is no better case in point than that of Valerious Duchart. A Lorraine Huguenot, Duchart immigrated to Maryland in 1754, rented land in Baltimore County, and opened an inn. Before his accidental death some two years later, he acquired an estate valued at £ 400. While it seems apparent that Duchart brought some funds with him, he prospered mostly through his own ingenuity and ability in the two succeeding years.[34]

The prosperity of men like Duchart, Hager, and Cresap should not, however, lead one to believe that such achievement was common, or, for that matter, easy. One young Scotsman, indentured to a Charles County merchant, put it succinctly: "I have heard of several people by marrying advantageously . . . come from nothing to something but I have heard two [sic] of more whose predecessors have been along while in the Country and yet are in straiting enough circumstances."[35]

Documentation of those in "straiting circumstances" was the subject of an exhaustive study by Professor Land. By the 1750s over half the population dying with any estate at all had a value of less than £ 100 currency. This meant that most of the colony's population enjoyed at best what Land calls a "rude" living. The road to financial success and social prestige required one to "marry advantageously" or receive financial support from a variety of economic enterprises that were out of the reach of either the small planter or the tenant. The great planters became such by being land speculators, manufacturers, merchants, money-lenders, lawyers or office-holders. In fact, most of the truly "great" planters found themselves engaged in at least several, if not all, of these occupations.[36]

Examples of "rags to riches" career patterns were not uncommon in eighteenth-century Maryland. When examined at close range, however, one finds few native Marylanders rapidly climbing the socioeconomic ladder. Daniel Dulany, the elder, Robert Morris, the elder, Anthony Bacon, Dr. Alexander Hamilton, Dr. Charles Carroll, Richard Henderson, Dr. David Ross, Jonathan Hager, Drs. Henry and John Stevenson, and Stephen West all received their education and/or their initial financial backing outside the colony. These immigrants had few colonial rivals of similar stature who could boast of a transformation from poverty or moderate status to wealth in one generation.[37]

If mobility is to occur in a society with an expanding population base, the number of positions throughout the hierarchy must be continually increased. In colonial Maryland, such an increase did not occur. The economic system was based upon landownership, while the number of available acres for newly patented land diminished to the vanishing point. Only further subdivision of landholdings would allow large numbers to participate as freeholders. But this did not happen.

Instead, land continued to be concentrated in the hands of larger planters who either leased it or cultivated it with slaves. The Maryland yeomanry declined as a segment of the population in the late colonial period.

Upward mobility was further decreased by the fact that outside influences limited the opportunity to advance in the mercantile trade or in governmental service. British merchants sent over their own men to occupy positions in the province instead of employing colonials. His Lordship utilized his vast powers of patronage for the benefit of his British favorites and thus diminished the colonists' opportunity to rise in the civil or ecclesiastical service. Certain restrictions due to social attitudes and the lack of education opportunity, to be discussed later, also contributed to this lack of vertical mobility.

Both demographic and economic development of the last quarter century of the colonial period thus strongly influenced the degree of political equality in provincial Maryland. Population distribution, both geographic and racial, allowed many citizens a degree of political leverage not given to others. The weight of a vote in Baltimore and Frederick counties was reduced by malapportionment of the Lower House of the Assembly. The tidewater region unwittingly or deliberately discriminated against the faster growing Piedmont area with its higher indices of freeholding, white population, and social mobility. *Viva voce* voting, combined with the traditional deference of the lower classes to the gentry, may also have inhibited many who might have disagreed with their creditors, justices, or neighbors over political issues and personalities.

The declining percentage of Marylanders able to move into the freeholding class illustrates a severe limitation on political opportunity in a society which expected each political participant to have a landholding stake in it. Land prices rose astronomically in the more settled counties and great speculators accumulated large tracts of the choicest western lands. The rise of tenantry indicates that the scarcity of land forced the decline of an independent yeomanry. One finds that the average provincial was poor and that only two-fifths of the white freemen owned land. Penury simply disqualified many from voting. At very best, perhaps two-thirds of the white male freemen could vote. Probably only about half of them really were entitled to the franchise.

The continued high levels of poverty among both native-born and immigrant colonists was a reflection of the restrictions which the system imposed upon upward social movement. Thus, while such mobility occurred, the tightening of opportunity meant that political equality was becoming more limited than it had been. The idealized picture of the free, happy yeomanry painted by some colonists and historians does not apply to Maryland. Is it a realistic picture elsewhere in the Southern colonies?

NOTES

1. A. E. Karinen, "Numerical and Distributional Aspects of Maryland Population, 1631–1840" (Ph. D. dissertation, University of Maryland, 1958), pp. 108–111; E. B. Mathews, *The Counties of Maryland: Their Origins, Boundaries, and Election Districts* (Baltimore: Johns Hopkins University Press, 1907), p. 421; J. M. Wright, *The Free Negro in Maryland, 1634–1860* (Columbia University Studies, Series XCVII, New York, 1921), pp. 14–16; E. B. Greene and V. G. Harrington, *American Population Before the Federal Census of 1790* (New York: Columbia University Press, 1932), pp. 125–126.

2. Karinen, "Numerical," pp. 139–140.

3. *Archives of Maryland*, LXIV, pp. xxx–xxxii.

4. H. Sharpe to C. Calvert, January 5, 1756, *Archives of Maryland*, VI, pp. 335–336; Calvert to Sharpe, March 17, 1760, *Archives of Maryland*, IX, p. 381; *Archives of Maryland*, LXIV, pp. xxx-xxxi.

5. The division of Frederick County into three parts is described in B.C. Steiner, *Western Maryland in the Revolution* (Johns Hopkins University Studies, Series XX, Baltimore, 1902), pp. 8–9.

6. Karinen, "Numerical,"pp. 159–163; U.S. Department of Commerce and Labor, Bureau of the Census, *Heads of Families at the First Census of the United States taken in the Year 1790: Maryland* (Washington, D. C.: Government Printing Office, 1907), p. 9.

7. Karinen, "Numerical," pp. 159–163; Joseph Scott, *A Geographical Description of the State of Maryland and Delaware* (Philadelphia: Kimber, Conrad & Co., 1807), pp. 117, 141–142.

8. A.C. Land, *The Dulanys of Maryland* (Baltimore: Maryland Historical Society, 1955), pp. 179–181; Karinen, "Numerical," pp. 133–135.

9. C.P. Gould, "The Economic Causes of the Rise of Baltimore," in *Essays in Colonial History Presented to Charles McLean Andrews by His Students* (New Haven: Yale University Press, 1931), pp. 225–251; H. Whitely, "The Principio Company," *Pennsylvania Magazine of History and Biography*, XI (1887), pp. 63–68, 190–198,

228–295; K. Johnson, "The Genesis of the Baltimore Ironworks," *Journal of Southern History,* XIX (1953), pp. 157–179; C. Carroll, bar. to A. Bacon & Co., December 3, 1763, "Letters of Charles Carroll, Barrister," W.S. Holt, editor, *Maryland Historical Magazine,* XXXIII (1938), p. 385; U.S. Department of Commerce, Bureau of the Census, *Historical Statistics of the United States: Colonial Times to 1957* (Washington, D.C.: Government Printing Office, 1960), pp. 762–763; Debt Books, Baltimore County, 1756, Maryland Hall of Records.

10. R. H. Shryock, "British Versus German Traditions in Colonial Agriculture," *Mississippi Valley Historical Review,* XXVI (1939), pp. 39–54; J.A. Gagliardo, "Germans and Agriculture in Colonial Pennsylvania," *Pennsylvania Magazine of History and Biography,* LXXXIII (1959), pp. 192–218; P. H. Giddens, "Trade and Industry in Colonial Maryland, 1753–1769," *Journal of Economic and Business History,* IV (1932), pp. 512–538; D. Klingaman, "The Significance of Grain in the Development of the Tobacco Colonies," *Journal of Economic History,* XXIX (1969), pp. 268–278; D. Klingaman, "The Development of the Coastwise Trade of Virginia in the late Colonial Period," *Virginia Magazine of History and Biography,* LXXVII (1969), pp. 26–45.

11. A. P. Middleton, *Tobacco Coast: A Maritime History of Chesapeake Bay in the Colonial Era* (Newport News, Va.: The Mariners' Museum, 1953), pp. 34, 93–132.

12. J. M. Price, "The Economic Growth of the Chesapeake and the European Market, 1697–1775," *Journal of Economic History,* XXIV (1964), pp. 496–511; J. M. Price, "The Rise of Glasgow in the Chesapeake Tobacco Trade, 1707–1775," *William and Mary Quarterly,* Series 3, XI (1954), pp. 179–197; J.H. Soltow, "Scottish Traders in Virginia, 1750–1775," *Economic History Review,* XII (1959), pp. 83–98; Middleton, *Tobacco Coast,* pp. 39–41; U. S. Department of Commerce, Bureau of the Census, *Historical Statistics,* pp. 761, 765, 767. For the rise of the domestic merchants, see Oxford Port Record Book, 1760–1773; Annapolis Port Record Book, 1758–1774; "The Autobiography of Robert Gilmor," Gilmor Papers; Bordley Letterbooks; Purviance Papers; Ridgley Account Books; Wallace, Johnson, and Muir Letterbook, Maryland Historical Society; and Thomas W. Griffith, *Annals of Baltimore* (Baltimore: W. Wooddy, 1824), pp. 30–60. The interrelationships of the three types of commercial systems may be seen in "The Letterbooks of Alexander Hamilton, Piscataway Factor," R. K. MacMaster and D. C. Skaggs, editors, *Maryland Historical Magazine,* LXI (1966), pp. 146–166, 305–328; LXII (1967), pp. 135–169.

13. C. P. Gould, *The Land System in Maryland,* 1720–1765 (Johns Hopkins University Studies, Series XXXI, Baltimore, 1913), pp. 77–82. V.J. Wyckhoff, "The Sizes of Plantations in Seventeenth Century Maryland," *Maryland Historical Magazine,* XXXII (1937), pp. 331–339 gives an interesting account of land grants, which tends to put the typical early colonial Maryland plantation under 250 acres.

14. Karinen, "Numerical," pp. 15–16, 115–117, 127–128; R. E. Brown, "Democracy in Colonial Massachusetts," *New England Quarterly,* XXV (1952), p. 302; R. E. Brown, *Middle-Class Democracy and the Revolution in Massachusetts, 1691–1780* (Ithaca, N. Y.: Cornell University Press, 1955), p. 408; Tables 4 and 5, above.

15. *Maryland Gazette,* April 5, 1753.

16. *Archives of Maryland,* XXX, pp. 270–274; K. L. Behrens, *Paper Money in Maryland,* 1727–1789 (Johns Hopkins University Studies, Series XLI, Baltimore, 1923) pp. 50–56; Prerogative Records, Baltimore and Talbot County Inventories, 1750–1773, Maryland Hall of Records. The relative stability of the colony's currency was due to its £ 25,000 sinking fund in Bank of England stock.

17. Personal estate figures are based on the author's investigation of the Prerogative Court Records, Baltimore and Talbot County Inventories, 1750–1773, Maryland Hall of Records; population figures come from Tables 2 and 3.

18. "Watchman," *Maryland Gazette,* August 15, 1776; P. A. Crowl, *Maryland During and After the Revolution: A Political and Economic Study* (Johns Hopkins University Studies, Series LXI, Baltimore, 1943), pp. 35–36.

19. E. Kimber, *Itinerant Observations in America, Reprinted from the London Magazine, 1745-6* (Savannah, Ga.: J.H. Estill, 1878), pp. 32, 34.

20. A. Hamilton, *Gentlemen's Progress: The Itinerarium of Dr. Alexander Hamilton, 1744,* C. Bridenbaugh, editor (Chapel Hill: University of North Carolina Press, 1948), p. 8.

21. See Table 7.

22. Schonfeld & Wilson, "Value of Personal Estates," *Maryland Historical Magazine,* LVIII (1963), pp. 333–343; J. P. Moore, "The Landed Gentry of Maryland: A Study of Their Political Influence on Colonial Society, 1700–1710," (M.A. thesis, University of Maryland, 1964), *passim;* A.C. Land, "Economic Base and Social Structure: The Northern Chesapeake in the Eighteenth Century," *Journal of Economic History,* XXV (1965), pp. 639–654; A. C. Land, "The Planters of Colonial Maryland *Maryland Historical Magazine,* LXVII (1972), pp. 109–128.

23. J. Mosley to his sister, September 1, 1759, September 8, 1770, "Letters," *Woodstock Letters,* XXXV (1906), pp. 40, 52.

24. "Bond Book," Lloyd Ledger, 1770–1774," "Lloyd Ledger, 1770–1791," and "Sermon Preached on Occasion of the Death of Edward Lloyd Esquire," Lloyd Papers, Maryland Historical Society; Prerogative Court Records, Inventories, Talbot County, Maryland Hall of Records, VI, 714–729; H. Calister, "Interpretation of Revelation, 13: 17–18," (c. 1755), Ethan Allen Collection, Maryland Diocesan Archives.

25. C. Carroll to Carrollton, January 9, 1764, "Extracts," *Maryland Historical Magazine,* XII (1917), p. 27; Glassford & Co. Records, Library of Congress, CXLII, 1–16; "A List of Bonds and notes Due to the Estate of Joseph Chaplin, Late of Frederick Co.," Joseph Chaplin Papers, Duke University Library.

26. Prerogative Court Records, Inventories, Maryland Hall of Records, Liber 69, folio 226; Land, "Economic Base;" pp. 639–654; J. M. Price discusses the debt issue in "Capital and Credit in the Chesapeake Tobacco Trade, 1750–1775," in V. B. Platt and D. C. Skaggs, editors, *Of Mother Country and Plantations: Proceedings of the Twenty-Seventh Conference in Early American History* (Bowling Green, Ohio: Bowling Green State University Press, 1971), pp. 7–36 as does Land in his "Comment," pp. 37–41.

27. Sharpe to Baltimore, October 22, 1766, *Archives of Maryland,* XIV, pp.

335–336; Gould, *Land System,* pp. 65–78; R. B. Harley, "The Land System in Colonial Maryland" (Ph. D. dissertation, State University of Iowa, 1948), pp. 179–181; P.H. Giddens, "Land Policies and Administration in Maryland, 1753–1769," *Maryland Historical Magazine,* XXVIII (1933), pp. 142–171.

28. J. Mosley to his sister, October 3, 1774, "Letters, " *Woodstock Letters,* XXXV (1906), p. 236; Gould, *Land System,* p. 61.

29. Gould, *Land System,* pp. 82–87; Harley, "Land System," pp. 147–149.

30. Land, *Dulanys,* pp. 172–185; Harley, "Land System," pp. 160, 245, 260; High, "Reluctant Loyalist," pp. 228–230, 252.

31. Harley, "Land System," pp. 160, 260; R. B. Harley, "Dr. Charles Carroll—Land Speculator, 1730–1755," *Maryland Historical Magazine,* XLVI (1951), p. 106; Neil E. Strawser, "The Early Life of Samuel Chase" (M.A. thesis, George Washington University, 1958), pp. 80–81, 92–93.

32. Harley, "Land System," pp. 166–167; Barker, *Background,* pp. 139– 141; L. C. Wroth, "The Story of Thomas Cresap, A Maryland Pioneer," *Maryland Historical Magazine,* IX (1914), pp. 1–37.

33. Harley, "Land System," pp. 166, 181.

34. *Archives of Maryland,* LVI, pp. 517–518.

35. Chancery Record, #34, pp. 68–69, Maryland Hall of Records.

36. Land, "Economic Base," pp. 639–654; A. C. Land, "Economic Behavior in a Planting Society: The Eighteenth-Century Chesapeake," *Journal of Southern History,* XXXIII (1967), pp. 469–485.

37. Land, *Dulanys;* J. C. Morton, "Stephen Bordley of Colonial Annapolis," (Ph. D. dissertation, University of Maryland, 1964); L. B. Namier, "Anthony Bacon, M.P., an Eighteenth-Century Merchant," *Journal of Economic and Business History,* II (1929–1930); Hamilton, *Gentlemen's Progress;* R. B. Harley, "Dr. Charles Carroll—Land Speculator, 1730–1755," pp. 93–107; B. Sollers, "Jonathan Hagar, the Founder of Hagarstown," *Society for the History of Germans in Maryland Report,* II (1888), pp. 17–30. For Morris, see J. Banning, *Log and Will of Jeremiah Banning (1733–1798)* (New York?: Privately printed, 1932), n.p. Henderson and Ross, both Scotsmen, were partners in the Frederick Forge, Debt Books, Frederick Co., 1771, f. 25; Land Records, Frederick Co., Liber J, ff. 793–815; Wills, Montgomery Co., Box 3, folder 90, Maryland Hall of Records. On the Stevenson brothers, Scotch-Irishmen, see *Maryland Journal,* May 20, July 15, 1783, March 23, 1785, Wills, Baltimore Co., Box 21, folder 51, Maryland Hall of Records; on West, see *Maryland Gazette,* August 27, 1761; E. G. Bowie, *Across the Years,* in *Prince George's County* (Richmond, Va.: Garrett and Massie, 1947), p.764. Declining social mobility is noted in the late seventeenth century in R. R. Menard, "From Servant to Freeholder: Status Mobility and Property Accumulation in Seventeenth-Century Maryland," *William and Mary Quarterly,* Series 3, XXX (1973), pp. 37–64.

Chapter

4

A COLONIAL SOCIETY

Several aspects of Maryland society significantly affected the degree of political equality in the province. The conditions of former servants and slaves, the opportunity for educational advancement, the religious heterodoxy, and the ethnic diversity contributed to a situation that adversely affected social mobility. The social system was, therefore, an important factor in determining the degree of political equality.

Along the Chesapeake shores, the buying and selling of indentured servants was as common as the buying and selling of tobacco. Reliance on the latter resulted in the utilization of forced labor systems to meet the demand for the sotweed. While slavery has concerned scholars for more than a century, the largest number of colonial immigrants were either indentured or convict servants; in fact, over half of the Chesapeake colonists initially emigrated under one of these procedures. Adding the Negroes, probably four-fifths of colonial American families began life in the New World under some form of voluntary or involuntary service. Since bonded servitude was particularly important as a source of labor for the Chesapeake colonies, it becomes important to examine the degree of economic opportunity available to such servants after their tenure was completed.[1]

There is little doubt that the conditions under which they lived as servants were deplorable. An excellent description of their life came from the pen of Elizabeth Spriggs, indentured to Richard Cross of Baltimore. She wrote her father in London that what she suffered was "beyond the probability of you in England to conceive." She worked night and day, often cleaning the stables, had "scarce anything but Indian Corn and Salt to eat and that begrudged," went "almost naked [with] no shoes nor stockings to wear," slept on the ground with only a blanket, and found her services rewarded with a yell from her master, "you Bitch you do not halfe enough," and a whipping.[2] Edward Kimber, an English novelist, described in his *Adventures of Mr. Anderson* the mistreatment of several Maryland indentured servants who "endured all the miseries of subjection." Like Miss Spriggs, Kimber's hero found "many Neagroes are better used" than servants.[3]

Many were so distressed by these conditions that they fled their masters. A survey of the advertisements for runaway and captured servants indicates the degree of dissatisfaction, and the number of runaway servants rose during the late colonial period. In 1749–1759, 70 former servants were sought; fifteen years later the number was 120 for a two-year period, and 82 were sought in 1771 alone. Of 556 servants advertised for in the years 1749, 1750, 1754, 1755, 1759, 1760, 1764, 1765, 1769, and 1770, only 21 were females. In almost all cases they were accompanied by one or more men. Whether this means that women were reluctant to escape, were unable to do so because the society did not allow unchaperoned women at large, were better treated, or were not considered worth the cost of an advertisement is debatable. The list of more than 30 occupations most often mentioned these: carpenters, farmers, shoemakers, tailors, and blacksmiths. About half of the total number of runaway servants were advertised as having some skilled or semi-skilled occupation.

If these notices reflect some indication of the difficulty of circumstances under which various servants labored, then the iron works and the shipyards were the least desirable places of work. The various ironmasters of Baltimore, Anne Arundel, and Frederick counties, and shipbuilders like Patrick Creagh of Annapolis and Samuel Galloway of West River, most frequently sought the return of their servants. Many of these departures were not the result of rash decisions of the immature. Nearly half of the runaways were in their twenties, three-fifths were in their thirties, a tenth were teenagers, and an equal proportion were age 40 or over. The ages ranged from 14 to 70.[4]

Freedom from servitude brought little alteration in living conditions. At the height of the colony's pre-Revolutionary prosperity, Father Mosley, a Jesuit missionary, wrote that Maryland "has been a fine poor man's country, but now it is well peopled, the lands are all secured and the harvest for such is now over. The Lands are mostly worked by the landlords' negroes, and, of consequence, white servants, after their bondage is out, are strolling about the country without bread."[5] Governor Sharpe reinforced Father Mosley's conclusion when he wrote Gen. Thomas Gage in 1765 referring to the Acadian neutrals' desire to leave the colony: "Could they on very moderate Terms procure Lands to settle on and cultivate for the Support of their Familys (which are in general pretty large) [they] would not I believe be anxious to remove, but as Vacant Lands are not now to be procurred here, and the want of Employment at times reduces them to Distress, It would I think be an Act of Charity to suffer them to go where they may provide more easily for their Support."[6]

Wages for these landless agricultural workers were relatively low and seasonal in character. They fluctuated almost in direct proportion to the price of grain. When grain prices dropped radically during the Townshend Duties embargo (1769–1770), the price of farm labor fell to its lowest point— £ 0.1.1 per day "for reaping" in Frederick County. Farm wages usually included provision for one meal a day and possibly a pint of rum per man for those employed at the daily rate. For longer periods of employment, board and room were also included.

Non-farm wages rose to their greatest heights during a building boom of the early 1770s. Normally the artisans did not receive provisions for daily work or for board and room in longer periods as the agricultural workers did. They did receive board and room when working outside the community of their residence.

All except the Scottish factors and their employees received their wages in current money. These factors were almost alone in earning enough to become substantial citizens. The most common labor—work in the fields at harvest time—was a condition of temporary employment rarely allowing a man to become solvent enough to emerge as a landowner.[7]

Some wages and some occupations could bring one out of obscurity. Anglican Jonathan Boucher used his education, his parish taxes, and his tutoring fees to achieve considerable economic status and to marry into the Addison family. Daniel Dulany, the elder, used his education and his friendship with his master, George Plater I, to elevate himself into a position bringing proprietary favor. Charles Carroll (1660–1720), immigrant progenitor of the wealthiest branch of this family, combined his education with proprietary support to secure great wealth for his descendants. The most striking similarity of these individuals is that they had British, not American, educations.

If education was a key to success in the colony, one might ask, why did the colonists not provide a good school system? The answer is that they tried, although rather unsuccessfully. There were usually three choices for an education in colonial Maryland—the publicly supported "free schools" in each county; private schools, usually religiously sponsored; and private education outside the colony, usually in Europe.[8]

In 1696, the Assembly chartered two "free schools" to be erected in Annapolis and Oxford and to be supported by taxes. The first of these, the King William School in the capital, opened its doors in 1701. School reform laws of 1715, 1717, 1720, and 1723 authorized a school in each county to be supported in part by taxes levied on all Irish Catholic servants and Negroes imported into the colony. Even though the master was to get £ 20 a year in addition to the use of 50 acres of pasture and 50 acres of woodland, the whole system collapsed. The Lower House finally acknowledged the experiment to be a failure in 1750—the result of insufficient funds, poorly qualified masters, small attendance, and inadequate facilities. Subsequent attempts at reform by combining these schools into multi-county districts (such as the creation of Eden School for Somerset and Worcester counties and Charlotte Hall for St. Mary's, Charles, and Prince George's counties) failed to solve the problem. The general verdict on the system was that of Andrew Burnaby in 1760: "the education of youth is but little attended to."[9]

The largest number of schools in the colony were the private ones. These consisted of tutoring at individual plantations and formal schools operated by clergymen, usually with some church support. The Anglican clergy operated the largest number of these church schools. Most prominent among such educators were the Reverends John Gordon of Talbot County, Charles Lake of Anne Arundel, Jonathan Boucher, Alexander Williamson II, William Brogden, and John Eversfield of Prince George's, Thomas Bacon of Talbot and Frederick, and Thomas Cradock of Baltimore.[10]

Of the Presbyterian schools, the most important were those operated by the Rev. Samuel Finley (later president of Princeton) and his brother the Rev. James Finley in Cecil County, as well as the Somerset Academy established in 1767 in the county of that name, which employed such Princetonians as Luther Martin and Hugh Henry Brackenridge as teachers. Under the direction of Thomas Schley, the German Reformed congregation at Frederick was operating a school by 1748.[11]

Roman Catholic schools like Bohemia Manor in Cecil County operated *sub rosa,* since their existence violated the 1704 law regulating the growth of "Popery." Their demise, however, seems to have been more the result of the death or departure of the principal teacher rather than of Protestant opposition. This conclusion concerning the Catholic schools applies equally to those operated by Protestants. Educational institutions surviving the colonial period had public support, like the King William School or Charlotte Hall. The rest died a natural death with the demise or departure of their founders.[12]

By far the most creative Maryland schoolmaster of the colonial period was the Rev. Thomas Bacon. The Anglican rector received support for a Charity School for boys in Talbot County in 1754. When he moved to wealthy All Saints parish in Frederick County, he backed a plan for itinerant masters to tour the county to help the "Numbers of Poor Planters and Farmers and their children, by being taught to read, write and join with Propriety and Decency in the several Parts of divine Service." Bacon did not stop with this novel idea. He proposed that the Associates of Dr. Bray, an English humanitarian society, support a school for 30 Negro children of the parish in order that they might be taught to read, be instructed in Christian morality, and learn some basic household trades. Finally, he asked his vestry to endorse a school in Frederick for the German children of the area so that they might learn how to read and write in English and thereby promote "a further Harmony and Union between us and the Dutch, both in religious and civil matters." None of Bacon's proposals reached fruition. They represent the concepts of a man far advanced for his time, who was probably the greatest humanitarian of colonial Maryland. [13]

Equally important, perhaps in some ways more so, were the educational facilities offered in the counting houses of the merchants and on the quarterdecks of the Chesapeake trading vessels. Here such men as Walter and Dennis Dulany received their training. Openings were at the invitation of the merchant or captain and were probably much like that offered by merchant-planter Stephen West of the Woodyard in 1772. "I hope you take Care to give your little boy good Schooling," he wrote John Hall of West River before volunteering to take the child at the age of 12 or 14 into his Upper Marlboro mercantile establishment, "if he is a good boy and desires it. [14]

Education outside the colony was common for children of the gentry. John Beale Bordley sent his sons Thomas, Matthias, and John to Eton for their education. James Jones Wilmer, son of a Kent County assemblyman, studied at St. Paul's School, London, before matriculating at Christ Church College, Oxford. St. Omer in Flanders received many sons of wealthy Catholics. Many other students went to the new Philadelphia Academy for training. [15]

All collegiate education was obtained outside Maryland. The province tried to establish a college (1761–1763), but the Lower House and the proprietor became so entangled over financing the plan that it failed to pass. Many went to William and Mary College; the more affluent sailed to England where Oxford, Cambridge, and the Inns of Court received them. Of the 98 native colonial Americans educated at the two British universities, 11 were Marylanders. These included Anglican rectors such as Henry Addison and James Jones Wilmer and lawyers such as Dulany, the younger, Charles Carroll, barrister, John Hammond, Philip Thomas Lee, and Lloyd Dulany. Studying at the Inns of Court for their legal education were the Dulanys, Carroll, Hammond, Lee, and a host of others like James Hollyday, Robert Goldsborough, Edward and Richard Tilghman, Stephen and Thomas Bordley, and William Paca. The group represented an impressive array of talent. [16]

What the colonists wanted from their education was best expressed in Boucher's sermon "On American Education," written for the 1773 opening of the Charlotte Hall school. The "Tory priest," often depicted as the symbol of reaction, called for a good Christian master who taught the classics in moderation, instructed his pupils in Christian morality, and used a curriculum containing practical subjects such as business, military science, agriculture, science, and government. As a man who devoted much of his life to the education of American youth, Boucher knew what the colonists wanted and needed from the education system. The work of the two Anglican clergymen, Boucher and Bacon, represented the finest tradition of the eighteenth century in meeting the educational needs of all citizens. They never suggested that education should be limited to a particular economic or social group nor that schooling be restricted to a particular religious denomination. They never so much as hinted that education was something to be denied because of race. Whatever Boucher's ideas on government, his concepts of education were certainly in the vanguard of liberal thought.[17]

But a system based almost entirely on private rather than public schooling was an expensive matter. This becomes apparent when one finds the elder Daniel Dulany sending only two of his four sons to England to be educated, and John Beale Bordley and Charles Carroll, the immigrant, having sons die while the boys were in Europe for their education. Only the rich could afford such expenses and hazards.[18]

The success or failure of this educational system has received mixed judgments. Joseph T. Wheeler estimated that it succeeded in making 60 percent of the free whites literate.[19] Contemporary opinion, as seen in the estimation of Burnaby, in the continued agitation in the Assembly for reforms, in the desire for change exhibited in the writings of Parsons, Bacon and Boucher, and in the necessity or desire to send one's children outside the colony for an education, indicated that many colonists believed both public and private education had failed. They certainly did not provide the children of the poor with the educational opportunities necessary to rise socially and economically. One searches in vain for a master who pushed the bright son of a poor family into college. The system produced a brilliant elite group which was able to use its educational privileges to continue a social system that sustained its position.

Another class of people merits comment. Although free Negroes and mulattoes (a distinction that was quite important in the eighteenth century) constituted only five percent of the population of the colony, they represented a unique problem resulting from the racial stigma attached to slavery. On the whole, Maryland slaves received no worse treatment than those elsewhere in British dominions; probably they were better off than their brethren in the sugar islands, and perhaps they were better off than some indentured servants. Boucher claimed they "were not upon the whole worse off nor less happy than the labouring poor in Great Britain." Nevertheless, a New Englander like Ebenezer Hazard found the slave system incongruous with the ideals professed by the revolutionaries. "It is astonishing," he wrote in 1777, "that Men who feel the Value and Importance of Liberty as much as the Inhabitants of the southern States do that of their own, should keep such Numbers of the human Species in so absolute Vassalage." This conflict of ideals became an important one in post–1776 Maryland, and by the time of the Civil War nearly half of the state's Negroes were free.[20]

It is obvious from the number of free Negroes in colonial Maryland that many colonists felt aversion to slaveholding and freed their own slaves. The Society of Friends, foremost in championing manumission, lost many members over this issue. Many Quakers, however, did free a considerable number of slaves. Boucher urged the education and gradual emancipation of the slaves. There must have been others like John Gibbs of Queen Anne's County who, upon his death in 1747 freed his 18 Negroes and bequeathed them his extensive personal and real estate. Quaker James Berry of Talbot County also freed his slaves and then hired them to work his farm lands. Berry was an active abolitionist before and after the Revolutionary period.[21]

The life of a freedman was undoubtedly a hard one. Berry reputedly used his ex-slaves more cruelly in their freed capacity than he ever did when they were his property. A study of the daily wages paid during the late colonial period indicates that the income of freedmen ran considerably below that of their white equivalents. Still, one does find some cases where they enjoyed status equal to that of many whites. The records of the Glasgow firm of Simson, Baird & Company show that their Piscataway store in Prince George's County carried an account with one "Benjamin Brown, free mallatoe." Brown was a frequent customer of the store and marketed tobacco which he may have raised himself. Charles Ridgely & Company of Baltimore had an account with "Negro Sabo," apparently a freedman, who regularly worked for Mr. Ridgely and bought goods in his establishment. "Negro Jehu" owned 131 acres in Baltimore County in 1771.[22]

No case has been found showing that Negro freemen desired to vote. Although there was no legal prohibition against such voting, it is doubtful whether any free colored man could have voted without having his ballot contested, a contest that would have found its way into the large number of court records available for the colony. One must conclude that another 5 percent of the colony's people found the franchise out of their grasp.

Besides the differences in status resulting from servitude and the largely unchallenged racial barriers, the growth of political equality in the colony was peculiarly limited by religious heterodoxy. In colonial British America, probably only New York, New Jersey, and Pennsylvania displayed greater religious diversification.

The available figures indicate that a substantial portion of the population was at least nominally Anglican. No other denomination had greater universality of dispersion throughout the Chesapeake basin and none had more clergy. With considerable justification, the Rev. Nelson W. Rightmyer argues that the established church enjoyed remarkable support from the laity, as witnessed by new church buildings, repairs to older ones, and expansions which entailed additional taxes. All this occurred despite the incompetence of many priests, the excessive size of parishes, and the oppressive nature of the taxation system. Toward the end of the colonial period, the emergence of a strong Methodist Society within Maryland Anglicanism brought a serious threat to church unity, which bore fruit in the post-revolutionary years.[23]

Anglicanism receives considerable attention in subsequent chapters of this study. Of more interest at this point are several other denominations lacking in the support afforded the established church by public taxation and official sanction.

The membership of the Roman Church varied, by its own estimates, between 4,000 to 10,000 communicants, with approximately an equal number of non-communicant members. This means that between eight and ten percent of the population was of that faith. The next group in order of size was probably the Presbyterians, mostly of Scot and Scotch-Irish descent, who had congregations of some importance in Prince George's, Baltimore, Cecil, and Somerset counties. This group was split by conflicts between its "Old Light" and "New Light" branches, resulting from the revival preaching of the Great Awakening. The Society of Friends had meetings on both shores, with its strongest center probably the Tread Avon Meeting of Talbot County. Serious conflicts within the Society over slavery, a growing affluence which tended to numb piety, and the Anglican establishment, caused a relative decline in Quaker strength during the eighteenth century from what had been an influential religious and economic position. There were few Baptists, and German Reformed congregations near Frederick and Hagerstown comprised fewer than 100 families in 1748. It is doubtful whether any of these Protestant dissenter groups equalled the Catholic membership, although definite estimates of their numbers cannot be made.[24]

Excessive proprietary favoritism received by the colony's Roman Catholics was one of the causes of Maryland's revolution in 1689. The Protestant majority took advantage of proprietary indecision at the time of the Glorious Revolution to seize provincial government in the name of the crown. In the next quarter century a series of laws limited the free exercise of Catholicism. The most notorious of these penal codes was the 1704 "Act to prevent the growth of popery" which restricted the occupational status of Catholics and prohibited any exercise of the rites of the Roman Church in the province. Queen Anne suspended this latter provision of the act, and in 1707 the Assembly concurred by allowing such rites to be performed in private family dwellings. Further limitations came in 1716 when Governor John Hart backed a law preventing Catholics from holding public office by requiring them to deny belief in the doctrine of transubstantiation. This test oath was also imposed on all prospective electors; thus Catholics lost the franchise. This was the high watermark of anti-Catholicism in Maryland and, although none of these laws was repealed in colonial times, after 1716 the degree of enforcement was the principal issue.[25]

Several incidents influenced the course and the severity of anti-Catholicism in Maryland. Among these were the Popish Plot of 1678–1681, the revocation of the Edict of Nantes in 1685, the Jacobite Rebellions of 1715 and 1745, and the long series of wars for empire between England and Catholic France in the eighteenth century. Despite all of these factors, toleration of Catholics and Catholicism in England and Maryland was considerable. The last English Catholic to be persecuted for his religion was Oliver Plunkett, Archbishop of Armagh in Ireland, during the Popish Plot affair. There were no convictions in colonial Maryland for violating the province's mild penal codes—mild when compared with those of England.[26]

Roman Catholics, both lay and cleric, acknowledged that there was little persecution. Between 1717 and 1750 the Maryland Jesuits and their flock were, as one group of laymen wrote, "undisturbed and, tho' deprived of our Rights and Priviledges, enjoyed peace & Quiet." The total strength of Maryland Catholicism remained almost constant between the Glorious and the American Revolutions. Anglican Commissary Thomas Bray estimated a twelfth of the population to be Romanist in 1700, and Governor Sharpe found a thirteenth part of the colony of that faith six decades later. There is absolutely nothing to confirm the statement of Msgr. John Tracy Ellis that colonial Catholics were not allowed "to emerge from the catacombs in which the penal codes had managed to bury them." There was no burial of Maryland Catholicism, although certainly it can be said that the faith did not increase in relative size after it was stripped of its former social, economic, and political importance. Considering the status of their religious brethren in any Catholic nation, Maryland Protestants showed remarkable toleration of the "Papists" in their midst.[27]

The 1750s brought the last anti-Catholic outbursts to the province. Lighting the fires of religious prejudice were the continuing quarrel between the Protestant and Catholic branches of the Carroll family, the appointment of a Catholic to public office, the bringing of the Acadian "neutrals" to the Chesapeake, and the ongoing war with France.

The first of these disturbances came in 1750 when Charles Carroll of Annapolis, Esquire (called "Squire Carroll" hereafter), asked Dr. Charles Carroll to account for his half of the trusteeship of the estate of James Carroll, of which they had both been trustees since the latter's death in 1729. The physician, an Anglican convert, countered by claiming possession of the entire estate, since under the 1704 law neither a recusant (Squire Carroll) nor a priest (the now-of-age heir to the estate, Fr. James Carroll) could act as executor. An opinion of the younger Dulany, Commissary General of the province, favored the Catholic Carrolls, so the chirurgeon took his case to the Assembly, of which he was a member. Here Doctor Carroll's Committee on Grievances reported out a bill to put the stringent English penal codes into effect in Maryland. Squire Carroll, enraged by this affront to his dignity, nailed Dulany's opinion and a statement of his own to the Assembly's door, whereupon the Assembly voted a resolution condemning this action and committing the squire to the county jail. The sheriff released him at the end of the session, but young Marylanders like Henry Hollyday and Philemon Hemsley took great delight in seeing this powerful man laid "by his Heels."[28]

A jail term did not terminate Squire Carroll's opposition to the doctor. According to his opponent, the squire forced London merchants to deny any credit to Doctor Carroll's son, then a student at the Middle Temple. The doctor complained to a merchant, William Black, transferred his account to John Hanbury & Co., and told his son how "the whole Popish Interest have Levelled their Artillery Ag[ains]t me and are strongly Associated with the Government." The doctor lost his attempts to control the estate of Father Carroll, and thus the Society of Jesus received the 2,000-acre White Marsh plantation, the largest single Jesuit gift in colonial British America.[29]

The embittered physician used his Assembly influence to attack his antagonists. His committee charged that Squire Carroll, "a powerful Papist, before and at the late Elections, did endeavour to influence many Electors in Anne Arundel, Prince George's, and Frederick Counties, by treating, writing, and other artful Means." Shortly thereafter in 1753 the Lower House passed a resolution designed to insure that all voters take the prescribed test oaths before voting. This seems to indicate that the restrictions of 1716 were not being adhered to. Instructions to voters of Prince George's County in 1754 indicate that Romanists or their sympathizers participated in the election. These Protestant voters instructed their delegates to support vigorous anti-Catholic legislation. Similarly, a meeting of Anglican clergy noted several violations of the 1704 code and urged prosecutions. Essayists in the *Maryland Gazette* warned how that "horrid Religion, which patronized Perjury, Rebellion, Murder, Parricide, and whatever Crime can advance their Church, and enslave the world" was attempting to take over the province.[30]

In the midst of this intra-family feud and the French and Indian War, Protestant voices of moderation still cried out. When the Rev. Thomas Chase (1703–1779) proposed radical persecution of Catholics at a 1753 meeting of Anglican clergy, the Rev. Thomas Bacon admonished him by noting that to urge the state to prosecute was an admission of their own failure and would leave them open to public ridicule. While he felt the current laws necessary for public safety, he wanted the "Conscience free and unrestrained" and could "not agree in the Expediencey of our calling upon them [the civil government] to carry the English Penals laws into Execution, or to create new Penalties at this Time." Daniel Dulany the younger also urged moderation, and a survey by the county courts found no Catholic support for the French in the war.[31] Festered by Braddock's defeat, rumors of Catholic collaboration with the French, and the continued presence of Henry Darnall III in public office, the open wound of anti-Catholicism nonetheless remained a sore upon the body politic.

Darnall was probably the most nominal Protestant convert that ever existed. Educated at St. Omers in France, as were many children of wealthy Catholics, he supposedly left his family's faith when he took the test oaths. Nevertheless he was not known to have entered a Protestant church in his life; his wife heard Mass in the family home, and his sons went to St. Omers. Discontent over this matter continued until 1761, when it was discovered that Darnall had embezzled £ 2000 as Naval Officer of the Patuxent. This forced his brother, John, and his cousin, Squire Carroll, to absorb the loss because they held the performance bond for his services in the office. Darnall's defalcation caused him to retire in disgrace from the public scene. Nonetheless, this whole issue, which involved at least indiscretion on the part of the proprietary, helped fan the flames of religious prejudice at a time when the coals were already hot.[32]

With the deposit of 913 Acadian neutrals on the Chesapeake in 1755, more fuel was added to the fire. Despite the comfort offered by Henry Callister and Parson Bacon, agitation against the Acadians increased. Councilor Lloyd felt they should be named prisoners-of-war, confined, and not allowed to run free to corrupt his slaves by leading them to believe the French would emancipate them.[33]

Anti-Catholicism became a factor in the 1754 elections, causing the defeat of Philip Key in St. Mary's County and the refusal of Daniel Dulany to run in Frederick County. Prince George's electors urged their delegates to support a long series of laws designed to dispossess the Jesuits of their estates (the large White Marsh plantation was of especial importance to the county's voters since it was located there), to prohibit the foreign education of Catholic youths, and to disqualify their fellow countian, Darnall, and other suspected Catholics from holding public office.[34]

The delegates quickly acted on the urgings of their constituents. Bills to confiscate Jesuit estates, to prohibit the admission of Jesuits to the colony, to stop the sending of children to foreign "Popish" seminaries, and to enact the English penal codes in Maryland, passed the Lower House only to encounter disapproval in the upper chamber. Finally, an act placing a double tax on the property of Catholics received the approval of both houses and of the governor. At this point, Squire Carroll and other wealthy landholding Romanists rose in rage against Sharpe. Petitions went to council, governor, proprietor, and King in an effort to have the law disallowed. Carroll went to England to secure relief. Finding none, he journeyed to France hoping to secure a grant for Maryland Catholics in Louisiana. Rebuffed again, he was still determined to leave Maryland. Two things discouraged him: the death of his wife in 1761 after a lingering illness, and the continued disapproval of the scheme by his son, Charles of Carrollton.[35]

It was the younger Carroll who saw that no matter how odious religious persecution might be, it was preferable to civil persecution. The relatively mild persecution of Maryland Catholics was chosen in preference to life under any Catholic monarch, for Carroll knew "of no Catholic country where that great blessing of civil liberty is enjoyed." Social prestige as well as civil liberty was an important factor in their staying. Private correspondence and public records indicate that adherence to the Roman Church carried no social stigma. Gentlemen of the great Catholic families like the Digges, Darnalls, Neales, and Carrolls received the appellation "esquire." Roman priests were listed in most records as "Reverend" along with the clergy of various Protestant sects. Of about 12 percent of the patented land owned by Catholics, approximately 10 percent was in the hands of the Jesuits. Thus, when Antonio De Ulloa, first Spanish Governor of Louisiana, invited Maryland Catholics to his colony, only a few Acadians accepted. The blessings of civil liberty, property, and prestige were too dear to forego.[36]

Meanwhile, the governmental and popular attitudes towards the Catholics changed. Lord Baltimore, who supported the anti-Catholic activities of Governor Sharpe earlier, forbade unneeded restrictions by 1759. Prosecution against a Jesuit for attempting to convert a spinster to Catholicism was dropped for lack of evidence. The appointment of the younger Dulany to the Council in 1757 pleased Squire Carroll, who had long admired this man of moderation. In Baltimore, Catholics taught school without prosecution, in open violation of the law. English Jesuits reported to the Vatican in 1763 that Maryland's penal laws "are rarely put into execution and usually there is a sort of tacit toleration" in the province. During and shortly after the last French war, the Jesuits expanded their missionary activities in Anne Arundel, Harford, Frederick, and Talbot counties. Finally, in 1766, the Rev. James Ashby, S. J., built the church of St. Francis Xavier in St. Mary's County in open violation of the 1707 law allowing services only in private homes.

There appears a direct relationship between the threat of French victory and the degree of persecution directed against this religious minority. As the tide of battle turned, so also did the tide of persecution ebb.[37]

While no immediate governmental action threatened them, Romanists always sensed the penal laws poised like a sword of Damocles over their heads. Whatever the degree of their participation in politics before the war, the last conflict with France and its concurrent outbursts of anti-Catholicism had a sobering effect upon them. Not until the eve of revolution did they emerge from this quiescent political condition. A Frenchman noted that only the Catholics kept out of public arguments over the Stamp Act. Fr. Joseph Mosley told his sister that a "Clergyman's call has little to do with civil broils and troubled waters; the fisherman never chooses to fish in muddy or disturbed water." When, after the Peace of Paris, the Holy See directed Bishop Oliver Briand of Quebec to journey to Maryland and Pennsylvania, he declined to do so on the advice of Fr. Ferdinand (Steinmeyer) Farmer, who felt such a trip would arouse latent antagonism already stimulated by the possibility of an Anglican bishop in America. And it was Carroll of Carrollton who noted that his security and that of his coreligionists lay not in the popularly-elected Lower House but in the governor and Council. Only there were they sure that popular prejudice might be successfully resisted.[38]

Probably no group faced a more awesome choice on the eve of the Revolution than did this Catholic minority. The undemocratic elements in the government protected their lives and property. They had no assurance that a popular government would be as tolerant; in fact, based on past experience, they had every reason to fear otherwise. It was this choice between a tolerant proprietary paternalism and a possibly intolerant republicanism that Charles Carroll of Carrollton made when he took up his pen against Daniel Dulany (the man who had backed toleration just a few years before), the governor, and the whole proprietary establishment in 1773. As the lay leader of Maryland's Catholics, the task of guiding Catholicism through the next few delicate years lay on his small shoulders, and on those of his cousin, Fr. John Carroll, their spiritual leader.[39]

The largest and most potent of the dissenting Protestant groups was the Presbyterian Church. Organized by Francis Makemie on the southern Eastern Shore, Maryland Presbyterianism spread to the Potomac Valley and upper Chesapeake in the early eighteenth century. The total number of congregations was small, the tenure of many clergy short, and the geographic region under a minister's supervision large. The Rev. Hugh Henry, Princeton graduate of 1748, led congregations at Wicomico Church in Salisbury, Rehobeth Church on Pocomoke River, Somerset County (1751–1762), Buckingham Church in Berlin, Worcester County (1751–1758), and Manokin in Princess Anne (1758–1762). The Rev. Jacob Ker succeeded him at Manokin and Wicomico and occasionally visited Rehobeth (1764–1795). Along with such extensive jurisdictions, the minister often conducted a school. Teachers included Charles Tennent of Worcester County, Samuel and James Finley of Cecil County, and Luther Martin and Hugh Henry Brackenridge of Somerset County.[40]

In most areas, relative harmony prevailed between members of the established and the dissenting churches. On the Eastern Shore, however, religious partisanship displayed, according to one contemporary, a "narrow, persecuting & inveterate spirit."[41] The depth of this rivalry was revealed in the loyalist versus patriot outbursts of the late 1770s.

Probably because they constituted many of the first settlers in the region, the Presbyterians apparently were among the largest landholders of Somerset and Worcester counties. In a reversal of what is usually considered their social role, the Anglicans were relegated to the lower strata of society. In the late colonial period, however, the size, if not the prestige, of the Presbyterian congregations was diminished by an influx of highly competent and vigorous Anglican clergy. An account of the tenure of the Rev. John Harris, Presbyterian Minister at Snow Hill and Pitts Creek in Worcester County, noted that the size of these congregations, due to "removals by Death, and other ways," diminished to the point where "the few who remain, are so disper'd, and loaded with taxes, both from Church and State, as to acknowledge themselves incapable of affording him." In 1771, these two congregations, the first being the oldest Presbyterian Church in America, became vacant. The "excessive love of spirituous Liquors" attributed to the Rev. Charles Tennent of Buckingham Church in Berlin, Worcester County, did not improve clerical reputations in that area.[42]

Thus, at a time when Anglican laity in the region of southern Maryland and Delaware were making vigorous efforts to reform clerical morals and expand church membership, the Presbyterians were confronted with internal discord and declining membership. In this context, the full implications of the Coventry Parish controversy of the late 1760s (which is discussed fully in chapter 6) becomes more significant.[43]

While exact figures regarding landholding by the various religious groups on the southern portion of the Eastern Shore are not available, no doubt exists regarding the ability of such Anglican clergy as John Bowie, Rector of Worcester Parish (1744–1801) and John Scott, Rector of Stepney Parish (1745–1784), both native Americans, to lead the lower socioeconomic elements in opposition to independence. The churchmen raised a flag emblazoned "GR" in honor of their king during a brief uprising in 1776–1777. William Eddis felt "a Dispute between the Churchmen & the Dissenters had given Rise to this Commotion." According to General William Smallwood, many of the insurrectionists made "Religion a Cloak for their nefarious Designs." Eddis described the principal purpose as being an opposition to "the vindictive Republican Spirit of their Presbyterian Neighbours."[44]

At least one observer felt the greatest accomplishment of the "civil war" (the American Revolution) was a "general toleration & indeed, almost a total change, in opinions in regard to religious sentiments"—a change from embittered rivalry between sects to an attitude where "every one is permitted to serve his Creator in a manner most conformable to his reason."[45] How much influence the differences in religious beliefs or economic status had on the choice of loyalism or patriotism may not be ascertainable, but Col. Jeremiah Banning made acute observations on the consequences of the Revolution upon subsequent religious conflict.

By all indications, Anglicans, Catholics, and Presbyterians constituted a vast preponderance of the total church membership in the colony. Quakerism declined rapidly in the eighteenth century, and Lutheran and German Reformed congregations constituted a small force for political change. For the latter groups, their status as aliens in British America was more important than their religious affiliation.

According to the 1790 census, which has been broken into national origins of heads of households on the basis of surnames, the ethnic distribution for Maryland was: English, 65 percent; Scottish, 8 percent; Ulster Irish, 6 percent; southern Irish, 7 percent; German, 12 percent; and a sprinkling of others. Of the original states, Maryland had the largest percentage of southern Irish (mostly Catholic) citizens, and was second only to Pennsylvania in the percentage of population of German origins. Only New York, New Jersey, and Pennsylvania had more heterogeneous populations.[46]

Facing discrimination on the basis of their national origin were the German immigrants. An understanding of their status can be obtained only through an understanding of British naturalization procedures.

Prior to 1740 there were two methods of naturalization in British America—either by letters of patent of denization issued by the King or by special act of Parliament. These cumbersome procedures gave a person property rights but not political rights. In fact, a law passed in 1700 excluded all alien-born persons, whether naturalized or not, from public office. As any British electoral law not specifically changed by the Maryland Assembly was applicable to the colony, this measure denied the Germans the rights of full political citizenship. However, since the Hanoverian kings, the Penn and Calvert proprietors, and Pennsylvania and Maryland land speculators wanted the Germans to come, they did all they could to encourage immigration.

As the influx of Germans reached tidal wave proportions in the third decade of the century, agitation for legislation to help these immigrants arose. Finally, Parliament passed a general naturalization act in 1740 allowing foreigners (Catholics excepted) who inhabited an American colony for seven years or more all the rights of natural-born citizens save that of holding public office. This satisfied those Germans who merely wanted economic gain and neither cared about nor desired a place in representative government.[47]

The Maryland Germans, however, were eventually to demand more political rights—unsuccessfully, as a result of several circumstances. As early as 1753, a bill for the "Naturalization of foreigners coming into this Province" was in a Lower House committee. In 1758, the lower chamber approved such a bill, but the Upper House rejected it despite the pleas of the younger Daniel Dulany (1722–1797). When the Lord Proprietor agreed with the principle of such a novel law, the upper body passed the measure in 1760, only to have it blocked in the Lower House by an unacceptable amendment excluding Romanists from certain provisions relative to land titles. The net result was stalemate through 1763, when both sides dropped the issue.[48]

Actually, the political aspects of the problem lay dormant until an immigrant decided to pursue a political career. This came in 1771 when Jonathan Hager, the most ambitious German-American of the period, received enough votes of fellow Frederick County freemen for an Assembly seat. The Lower House, in a quandary, voted 24 to 23 that Hager be declared ineligible for membership on the basis of the parliamentary acts previously mentioned. Realizing that Hager could make significant contributions to the Assembly, the two houses broke a deadlock of two decades and passed a naturalization bill allowing foreign-born citizens the right to hold public office. A re-elected Hager then took his seat.

One might suppose that the question was settled, but it was not, primarily because of one of the peculiarities of colonial Maryland politics. For several years, the anti-proprietary forces in the colony had claimed that the 1702 law establishing the Church of England was illegal, since it was approved by the governor after the death of King William III, from whom he had received his appointment. The "popular" faction in the Assembly contended that the act was void, even though the royal governor had acted in good faith because he did not know of the king's death. The same thing happened again. Frederick Calvert, Sixth Lord Baltimore, died before the Assembly passed the 1771 naturalization bill, and Governor Eden signed it without knowing of His Lordship's death. The anti-proprietary faction was caught in a dilemma. They could not allow the naturalization act to become law if they opposed the establishing act on the same technicality. Similarly, the Upper House could not pass a second naturalization act, since it would thereby concede the whole establishment issue to the lower chamber. After some deliberation and delay during the 1773 session, the Lower House declared Hager's seat vacant. The enraged Governor Eden could do nothing about this action, because the house had the sole right to determine the eligibility of its members.[49]

Thus, by the end of the colonial period another large minority group felt the hand of political discrimination. One cannot ignore the German immigrants simply because they were not active in politics. Certainly it took time for them to develop a man of Hager's political abilities. But in those affairs where these prohibitions did not exist, such as the protest groups which arose prior to the Revolution, a number of Germans, such as Jacob Funk, Jacob Weller, Henry Kootz, Andrew Rench, and Christian Ohrendorff, participated. The fact that the Pennsylvania Germans constituted an active political force indicates that, given the chance, those in Maryland could have done the same. It took the origin of extra-legal political agencies in the few years before the Revolution to allow these citizens a change at self-government. Prof. Dieter Cunz, the leading authority on this ethnic group, reported that the "revolutionary cause was the vehicle upon which the Germans rode into the previously forbidden territory of local and state politics." Like the Catholics, this predominantly Protestant group faced political disfranchisement during the colonial period and represented another instance of the frustration of democracy in the colony.[50]

Within provincial society, a number of social elements found themselves among the underprivileged. Servants and former servants, Negro freedmen, Roman Catholics, and German immigrants all suffered some form of political discrimination resulting from their peculiar social status. The educational system certainly opened few doors of upward mobility for the mass of Maryland's free white populace. The number of persons involved in this less-than-equal situation necessitated a restructuring of the social system should a major political upheaval occur. How to maintain some semblance of the social fabric in a period of political change was one of the most difficult tasks facing the colonial leadership.

NOTES

1. E. I. McCormac, *White Servitude in Maryland, 1634–1820* (Johns Hopkins University Studies, Series XXII, Baltimore, 1904); R. B. Morris, *Government and Labor in Early America* (New York: Columbia University Press, 1946), Part II; A. E. Smith, *Colonists in Bondage: White Servitude and Convict Labor in America,* 1607–1776 (Chapel Hill: University of North Carolina Press, 1947). For the origins of the indentured servant system on the Chesapeake, see E. S. Morgan, "The First American Boom: Virginia 1618 to 1630," *William and Mary Quarterly,* Series 3, XXVIII (1971), pp. 169–198; E. S. Morgan, "Slavery and Freedom: The American Paradox," *Journal of American History,* LIX (1972–1973), pp. 16–29.

2. E. Spriggs to J. Spriggs, n.d., High Court of the Admiralty Records, Public Record Office Transcripts, Class 30, Vol. 358, Library of Congress, cited in J. H. High, "Reluctant Loyalist: Governor Horatio Sharpe of Maryland, 1753–1769," (Ph.D. dissertation, UCLA, 1951), pp. 27–28.

3. E. Kimber, *The History of the Life and Adventures of Mr. Anderson* (London: W. Duren, 1754), *passim,* quote 34; W. G. Milne, "Glimpse of Colonial America:

As Seen in an English Novel of 1754," *Maryland Historical Magazine,* XLII (1947), p. 249. See also J. Mosley to his sister, June 5, 1772, "Letters of Father Joseph Mosley, 1756–1786," E. I. Devitt, editor, *Woodstock Letters,* XXXV (1906), pp. 53–54.

4. *Maryland Gazette,* 1749, 1750, 1754, 1755, 1759, 1760, 1764, 1765, 1769, 1770, 1771. The author is indebted to the following Bowling Green State University students for their assistance in compiling these data: Larry J. Busdeker, James Lane, Wayne Olsson, Robin Reid, and Neil Weiser.

5. J. Mosley to his sister, June 5, 1772, "Letters," *Woodstock Letters,* XXXV (1906), p. 54.

6. H. Sharpe to T. Gage, June 29, 1765, Gage Papers, William L. Clements Library, vol. 39.

7. Fc the Annapolis building boom of the 1770s, see R R. Beirne, "William Buckland, Architect of Virginia and Maryland," *Maryland Historical Magazine,* XLI (1946), pp. 199–218. For wages, see Tables 7 and 8 in D. C, Skaggs, "Democracy in Colonial Maryland" (Ph.D. dissertation, Georgetown University, 1965), pp. 127–130.

8. L. J. McCormick, *Church-State Relationships in Education in Maryland* (Washington: Catholic University of America Press, 1942), pp. 1–44, gives the best survey of educational policy in the colony; B. Sollers, "Education of Colonial Maryland," in B. C. Steiner, *History of Education in Maryland* (U. S. Bureau of Education, "Circular of Information No. 2, 1894," Washington, 1894), pp. 13–38, is not of the same caliber.

9. *Archives of Maryland,* XXXII, 109–111; "Maryland in 1773," *Maryland Historical Magazine,* IV (1907), pp. 359–360, N. D. Mereness, *Maryland as a Proprietary Province* (New York: Macmillan, 1901), pp. 137–145; C. P. McMahon, "A Note on the Free School Idea in Colonial Maryland," *Maryland Historical Magazine,* LIV (1959), pp. 149–152; D. R. Randall, "Notes on a Colonial Free School in Anne Arundel County, With Side Lights Upon the Early Education of Johns Hopkins," *Maryland Historical Magazine,* XVIII (1923), pp. 251–254; Sollers, "Education," in Steiner, *History,* pp. 25–26, 37–38; A. Burnaby, "Travels Through the Middle Settlements in North America in the Years 1759 and 1760" in J. Pinkerton, *A General Collection of the Best and Most Interesting Travels in All Parts of the World,* XIII (London: Longman, 1812), p. 726; L. J. Hienton, "The Free School in Prince George's County, 1723–1774," *Maryland Historical Magazine,* LIX (1964), pp. 380–391.

10. "Eighteenth Century Maryland as Portrayed in the 'Itinerant Observations' of Edward Kimber," *Maryland Historical Magazine,* LI (1956), pp. 334–335; Sollers, "Education," in Steiner, *History,* pp. 33–36; L. L. Bowie, "The Reverend John Bowie, Tory," *Maryland Historical Magazine,* XXXVIII (1943), p. 142; E. D. Gutridge, "Saint Paul's Church, Rock Creek Parish, Washington, D.C.," *Historical Magazine of the Protestant Episcopal Church,* XIX (1950), p. 150.

11. G. Johnston, *History of Cecil County, Maryland* (Elkton, Md.: The Author,

1881), pp. 278–285: R. B. Clark, "Washington Academy, Somerset County, Maryland," *Maryland Historical Magazine* XLIV (1949), pp. 200–203; H. Harbaugh, *The Life of the Rev. Michael Schlatter* (Philadelphia: Lindsay & Blakiston, 1857), p. 177; D. Cunz, *The Maryland Germans: A History* (Princeton: Princeton University Press, 1948), pp. 68–69.

12. W. C. Repetti, "Catholic Schools in Colonial Maryland," *Woodstock Letters,* LXXXI (1952), pp. 123–134. Among the earlier authors ascribing the fall of these Catholic schools to Protestant opposition are: M. A. (Ray), *American Opinion of Roman Catholicism in the Eighteenth Century* (New York: Columbia University Press, 1936), p. 161; McCormick, *Church-State,* pp. 7–8; E. I. Devitt, "History of the Maryland-New York Province, IX: Bohemia Mission of St. Francis Xavier, Cecil County, Maryland," *Woodstock Letters,* LXIII (1934), pp. 2–19.

13. "Thomas Bacon to the Vestry of All Saints Parish," *Maryland Historical Magazine,* VI (1911), pp. 271–272.

14. S. West to J. Hall, January 2, 1772, William Henry Hall Papers, Duke University Library.

15. E. B. Gibson, *Biographical Sketches of the Bordley Family of Maryland* (Philadelphia: Henry B. Ashmead, 1865), p. 79; "Memoirs of the Rev. James Jones Wilmer," J. H. Pleasants, editor, *Maryland Historical Magazine,* XIX (1924), pp. 220–228; Mereness, *Maryland,* p. 145.

16. *Archives of Maryland,* LVIII, pp. lv–lviii, 344–345; "Marylanders at Oxford and Cambridge before 1776," *Maryland Historical Magazine,* XXXVII (1942), pp. 335; J. T. Wheeler, "Reading Interests of the Professional Classes in Colonial Maryland," *Maryland Historical Magazine,* XXXVI (1941), p. 282.

17. J. Boucher, *A View of the Causes and Consequences of the American Revolution; in Thirteen Discourses, Preached in North America Between the Years 1763 and 1775; With an Historical Preface* (London: G. G. and J. Robinson, 1797), pp. 152–201. See also Thomas Cradock's sermon "On Education," Maryland Diocesan Archives.

18. A. C. Land, *The Dulanys of Maryland* (Baltimore: Maryland Historical Society, 1955), pp. 150, 153–154, 166–169, 185, 217–219; Gibson, *Biographical,* p. 79; Wheeler, "Reading," p. 282.

19. J. T. Wheeler, "Books Owned by Marylanders, 1770–1776," *Maryland Historical Magazine,* XXV (1940), p. 353.

20. Giddens, "Governor Sharpe," pp. 58–60: "Ebenezer Hazard's Travels Through Maryland in 1777," Fred Shelley, editor, *Maryland Historical Magazine,* XLVI (1951), p. 50; J. Boucher, *Reminiscences of an American Loyalist, 1738–1789,* J. Bouchier, editor (Boston: Houghton Mifflin, 1925), p. 97; "Eighteenth Century Maryland," *Maryland Historical Magazine,* LI (1956), pp. 327–328; J. M. Wright, *The Free Negro, in Maryland, 1634–1860,* (Columbia University Studies, Series XCVII, New York, 1921), pp. 14–16.

21. J. R. Kelly, *Quakers in the Founding of Anne Arundel County, Maryland* (Baltimore: Maryland Historical Society, 1963), pp. 83–92; Boucher, *A View,* pp 40–42; Report of St. Peter's Parish, Talbot County, 1797, Ethan Allen Collection,

Maryland Diocesan Archives, p. 2; L. H. Gipson, *The British Empire Before the American Revolution,* 14 vols. (New York: A. A. Knopf, 1936 – 1969), II (2d ed.), pp. 65– 66.

22. Report of St. Peter's Parish, Talbot County, 1797, Ethan Allen Collection, Maryland Diocesan Archives, p. 2; Glassford & Co. Records, Library of Congress, XXII, p. 88; Ridgely Account Books, Maryland Historical Society, XX, p. 241; Debt Books, Baltimore County, 1771, fol. 67, MLO.

23. N. W. Rightmyer, *Maryland's Established Church* (Baltimore: The Church Historical Society for the Diocese of Maryland, 1956), pp. 109–112; for the rise of Methodism, see the "William Duke Journal, 1774–1776," and Report of St. Peter's Parish, Talbot Co., 1797, p. 3, in the Ethan Allen Collection, Maryland Diocesan Archives.

24. J.D.G. Shea, *History of the Catholic Church in the United States,* 4 vols. (New York, 1886– 1892), I, p. 449, II, pp. 52, 257; L. J. Heinton, "Presbyterian Beginnings in Prince George's County, Maryland," *Journal of the Presbyterian Historical Society,* XXXIX (1961), pp. 30– 42; J. H. Gardner, Jr., "Presbyterians of Old Baltimore," *Maryland Historical Magazine,* XXXV (1940), pp. 244– 245; R. P. Davis, "Beginnings of Presbyterianism in Makemieland to 1788: A Study of the Early History of the Presbyterian Church in Somerset, Worcester, and Wicomico Counties, Maryland" (M.T. thesis, Union Theological Seminary, Richmond, Va., 1941), pp. 109 – 138; Johnston, *History,* pp. 278–279, 284– 285; "Minutes of the Third Haven or Tread Avon Friend's Meeting: Talbot County, Maryland," compl. A. E. Burns, 5 vols., typescript (Baltimore: The Compiler, 1940?); Kelly, *Quakers,* pp. 83– 92; Harbaugh, *Schlatter,* pp. 154,   176– 77, 204, 244; N. H. Maring, "A Denominational History of the Maryland Baptists (1742– 1882)" (Ph.D. dissertation, University of Maryland, 1948), p. 1 – 12.

25. M. G. Kammen, "The Causes of the Maryland Revolution of 1689," *Maryland Historical Magazine,* LV (1960), pp. 293-333; D. M. Moran, "Anti-Catholicism in Early Maryland Politics: The Protestant Revolution," *Records of the American Catholic Historical Society of Philadelphia,* LXI (1950), pp. 213 – 236; T. O. Hanley, "His Excellency's Council: Maryland, 1715–1720," *Records of the American Catholic Historical Society of Philadelphia,* LXXIV (1963), pp. 137– 150; *Archives of Maryland,* XXVI, pp. 340– 341; *Archives of Maryland,* XXVII, pp. 146–148; *Archives of Maryland,* XXX, pp. 612– 617.

26. M.D.R. Leys, *Catholics in England, 1559– 1829: A Social History* (London: Longmans, Green, 1961), pp. 98–125; C. E. Martin, "The Legal Aspect of the English Penal Laws," *Records of the American Catholic Historical Society of Philadelphia,* XLI (1930), pp. 129–161.

27. T. Hughes, *History of the Society of Jesus in North America, Text,* 2 vols. (London: Longmans, Green, 1917– 1919), II, p. 438; "Petition of Sundry Roman Catholics Against the Imposition Upon Them of a Double Tax as a Discrimination Against Their Religion," *Maryland Historical Magazine,* V (1910), p. 57; Moran, "Anti-Catholicism," p. 233; H. Sharpe to Baltimore, December 16, 1758, *Archives of Maryland,* IX, p. 316; J. T. Ellis, "Catholics in Colonial America," *American Ecclesiastical Review,* CXXXVI (1957), p. 266. For opinions similar to those of Msgr.

Ellis concerning the status of Catholics in Maryland, see (Ray), *American Opinion,* pp. 58–60; on the opposite side is B. E. Steiner, "The Catholic Brents of Colonial Virginia: An Instance of Practical Toleration," *Virginia Magazine of History and Biography,* LXX (1962), pp. 387–409.

28. Hughes, *History,* II, p. 495, 529–535; H. Hollyday to P. Hemsley, June 12, 1751, & Hemsley to Hollyday, February 23, 1752, Maryland Colony & Revolutionary Papers, Duke University Library.

29. Dr. Carroll to W. Black, May 8, 1752, to C. Carroll, bar., May 15, 1753, to J. Hanbury, July 8, 1754, "Extracts from the Account and Letter Books of Dr. Charles Carroll of Annapolis," *Maryland Historical Magazine,* XXVI, quote 51, XXVII, pp. 218–219, 224; Hughes, *History,* II, p. 495.

30. *Archives of Maryland,* L, pp. 54, 177–178; *Maryland Gazette,* November 14 & 28, 1754; [Thomas Bacon], "Proceedings of the Parochial Clergy," *Maryland Historical Magazine,* III (1908), pp. 373–374.

31. [Bacon], "Proceedings," pp. 369–370; D. Dulany, "Military and Political Affairs in the Middle Colonies in 1775," *Pennsylvania Magazine of History and Biography,* III (1879), pp. 27–28; *Archives of Maryland,* XXXI, pp. 47–49, 54, 71–72, 80, 81, 85–89, 245–246; Sharpe to Baltimore, December 16, 1758, *Archives of Maryland,* IX, p. 318.

32. P. H. Giddens, "The French and Indian War in Maryland," *Maryland Historical Magazine,* XXX (1935), p. 304; *Archives of Maryland,* L, pp. ix, 51–54; LII, pp. xviii–xix, 356–360; LVI, pp. lv–lviii, 484–486, 490–492. On Darnell, see T. O. Hanley, *Charles Carroll of Carrolltor.: The Making of a Revolutionary Gentleman* (Washington: Catholic University of America Press, 1970), pp. 14, 85, 163, 265.

33. Gipson, *British Empire,* VI, pp. 304–307; E. Lloyd III to J. Hollyday, December 9, 1755, G. T. Hollyday, "Biographical Memoir of James Hollyday," *Pennsylvania Magazine of History and Biography,* VII (1883), pp. 433–435.

34. H. Sharpe to C. Calvert, March 12, May 22, 1755, *Archives of Maryland,* VI, pp. 178, 208; *Maryland Gazette,* November 28, 1754.

35. Hughes, *History,* II, pp. 535–544; *Archives of Maryland,* L, pp. xii–xiii, LII, pp. xxiv–xxv, 427–430, 441–449; H. Sharpe to J. Sharpe, October 10, 1756, *Archives of Maryland,* VI, pp. 496–497; same to W. Sharpe, July 6, 1757, *Archives of Maryland,* IX, p. 46; "Papers Relating to the Early History of the Maryland Mission. III— The Penal Laws," *Woodstock Letters,* X (1881), pp. 8–10; E. H. Smith, *Charles Carroll of Carrollton* (Cambridge: Harvard University Press, 1942), pp. 38–41, 50–51; K. M. Rowland, *The Life and Correspondence of Charles Carroll of Carrollton,* 2 vols. (New York: G. P. Putman's Sons, 1898), I, pp. 42–43; Hanley, *Charles Carroll,* pp. 38–51, 67–72.

36. Carrollton to C. Carroll, January 1, 1761, "Extracts from the Carroll Papers," *Maryland Historical Magazine,* X (1915), pp. 331–332; S. G. Reges, "A Spanish Governor's Invitation to Maryland Catholics," *Maryland Historical Magazine,* LXI (1965), pp. 93–98; Johnston, *History,* pp. 263-264.

37. C. Calvert to H. Sharpe, December 23, 1755, Sharpe to Calvert, May 27, 1756,

Calvert to Sharpe, April 7, 1757, Sharpe to Calvert, December 26, 1757, Sharpe to Baltimore, December 16, 1758, Calvert to Sharpe, March 30, 1759, *Archives of Maryland,* VI, pp. 323, 419-420, 439-540; IX, pp. 117, 315-317; LVI, p. 526; Carrollton to C. Carroll, February 13, 1761, "Extracts," *Maryland Historical Magazine,* X (1915), p. 335; S. Bordley to C. Carroll, July 16, 1757, Bordley Letterbook, 1756-1759, Maryland Historical Society, p. 35; Carroll to Bordley, December 15, 1757, Bordley-Calvert Collection, Maryland Historical Society; "An Account of the Condition of the Catholic Religion in the English Colonies of America," *Catholic Historical Review,* VI (1924), p. 522; J. Mosley to his sister, October 14, 1766, "Letters of Father Joseph Mosley, 1757-1786," E. I. Devitt, editor, *Woodstock Letters,* XXXV (1906), pp. 48-51; E. W. Beitzell, "Newtown Hundred," *Maryland Historical Magazine,* LI (1956), p. 130; E. A. Ryan, "Sketch of St. Aloysius' Parish, Leonardtown, Maryland." *Woodstock Letters,* LXXVI (1947), pp. 325-326; P. G. Gleis, "German Catholic Missionaries in Maryland During the Eighteenth Century," *Society for the History of Germans in Maryland Report,* XXVI (1945), pp. 33-36.

38. Carrollton to C. Carroll, December 10, 1759, to same, September 16, 1760, *Maryland Historical Magazine,* X (1915), pp. 246, 328; "Journal of a French Traveler in the Colonies, 1765," *American Historical Review,* XXVII (1921), p. 73; J. Mosley to sister, August 15, 1775, "Letters," *Woodstock Letters,* XXV (1906), p. 238; P. Guilday, "The Priesthood of Colonial Maryland," *Woodstock Letters,* LXIII (1934), pp. 186-187; (Ray), *American Opinion,* pp. 268-269, "Jesuit Missions in 1773," *Catholic Historical Review,* II (1916), pp. 316-317.

39. (Ray), *American Opinion,* pp. 313-315; Hanley, *Charles Carroll,* pp. 222-260; [John Carroll], *An Address to the Roman Catholics of the United States* (Annapolis: Frederick Green, 1784).

40. Davis, "Beginnings of Presbyterianism," pp. 113-130; Heiton, "Presbyterian Beginnings," pp. 30-42; Gardner, "Presbyterians," pp. 244-245; Johnston, *History,* pp. 278-279, 284-285.

41. Banning, *Log & Will,* n. p.

42. Davis. "Beginnings of Presbyterianism," pp. 117-120.

43. Men like Charles Ridgely of Dover, Delaware, worked hard to expand Anglicanism on the Delmarva Peninsula. Ridgely to C. Inglis, October 31, 1766, John W. Lydekker, *The Life and Letters of Charles Inglis* (London: Society for Promoting Christian Knowledge, 1936), p. 68. The impact of SPG missionaries like Inglis on the region emerged in 1767 when the Conventry vestry requested the appointment of the Rev. Dr. Thomas B. Chandler, SPG missionary in New Jersey, to their vacancy. Vestry to Sharpe, January ?, 1767, *Archives of Maryland,* XIV, pp. 363-369.

44. Eddis to Eden, July 23, 1777, PRO, CO 5/722, I, 10-11, Library of Congress; Smallwood to T. Johnson, March 14, 1777, Brown Books, II, f. 2, Maryland Hall of Records; Bonds of John Scott, August 29, 1776, October 15, 1776, J. Dashiell to Smallwood, April 2, 1777, Exec. Papers, Box II, ff. 63-78, Box VII, f. 17, Maryland Hall of Records.

45. Banning, *Log & Will,* n.p.

46. American Council of Learned Societies, "Report of Committee on Linguistic

and National Stocks in the Population of the United States" in *Annual Report of the American Historical Association for the Year 1931,* 3 vols. (Washington, D.C., 1932), I, p. 124.

47. B.C. Steiner, *Citizenship and Suffrage in Maryland* (Baltimore: Cushing & Co., 1895), p. 18; C. Start, "Naturalization in the English Colonies of America," *Annual Report of The American Historical Association for 1893* (Washington, D. C., 1894), pp. 359-360; *The Statutes at Large from the Magna Charta to . . . 1761,* D. Pickering, editor, 24 vols. (Cambridge, England: Joseph Bentham and others, 1762-1769), X, pp. 12-13, William III, c. 2(1700), XVII, 13 Geo. II, c. 7 (1740); A.H. Carpenter, "Naturalization in England and the American Colonies," *American Historical Review,* IX (1904), pp. 288-303.

48. H. Sharpe to Baltimore, May 2, 1754, *Archives of Maryland,* VI, p. 52; Sharpe to C. Calvert, June 4, 1759, *Archives of Maryland,* IX, pp. 341-342; L, p, 211; LII, pp. 344,421, 424; LVI, pp. lxiii-lxvi, 56- 59, 90, 225; LVIII, pp. lxvi, 248, 259, 304- 305, 354- 375.

49. *Archives of Maryland,* LXIII, pp. 92-93, 100, 107, 174-175, 238, 369; LXIV, pp. 22-23, 436. B. Sollers, "Jonathan Hager, the Founder of Hagerstown," *Society for the History of Germans in Maryland Report,* II (1888), pp. 17-30, gives the traditional account of the Hager case, but it leaves out the Lower House's rejection of the German in the 1773 session; this account is followed, despite its limitations, in modern studies such as Cunz, *Maryland Germans,* pp. 83-84.

50. Cunz, *Maryland Germans,* pp. 124-125, 133-135, quote 134; W. S. Hanna, *Benjamin Franklin and Pennsylvania Politics* (Stanford, Calif., Stanford University Press, 1964), pp. 46-48.

5

POLITICIANS AND POLITICAL THOUGHT

Despite the heterogeneous nature of Maryland society, the colony's politicians were selected primarily from a small and exclusive group. In no way did their backgrounds approximate the economic and social diversity of the upper Chesapeake. Their political thought revolved around the ideals of eighteenth century whiggism: stake-in-society franchise requirements, elite leadership, and ordered society. It was they who would confront the growing restlessness brought on by the multiplicity of social and economic interests. To understand their reaction, one must understand them.

To British observers, Maryland, like most colonies, was democratic. They perceived the typical provincial as a rough hewn "buckskin" who should never grace the councils of an English borough, much less the House of Commons. While sojourning in the colony in 1744, William Black described the Maryland Lower House as containing "Nothing but a confus'd Multitude, and the Greater part of the meaner Sort, Such as make Patriotism their Plea, but Preferment their Design." A decade later Governor Sharpe noted that the Assembly seats were filled in "too many Instances of the lowest Persons at least men of small fortunes no Soul & very mean Capacities." He described certain individuals, like the long-time delegate Henry Wright Crabb, as "an ignorant overbearing Inhabitant of Frederick County." Cecilius Calvert reflected the same attitude when he wrote in the *London Chronicle* that assembly-men consisted "for the most part" of those "such as are fit Tools for Demagogues to work with." Secretary Calvert so believed this that he proposed as early as 1754 to insure proprietary control of the Assembly by using the vast patronage opportunities as plums for those who showed the greatest anti-proprietary tendencies.[1]

In a letter of March 17, 1760, Cecilius Calvert formally laid out his scheme for ending the dissidence in the lower chamber. To him it seemed "extreamly easy, with the several advantages this Government has, to prevent for the future that Turbulent & Malevolent Spirit in the Lower House of Assembly . . . without leaving it in the Power of any Individual amongst them either for Motives of Interest, Avarice or Ambition, to disturb its operation." He proposed to do this "by throwing out a Sop in a proper manner to these Noisy animals." His "sop" consisted of such county offices as sheriff, farmer of the quitrents, deputy commissary, and deputy surveyor. All of these, he held, possessed incomes that were "considerable to the Middling sort of people, of whom the Lower House is composed, and might gain a great Majority of that House by being properly applyed amongst them, their Brothers & Sons." The gratitude supposedly resulting therefrom would divide the opponents of the government and insure proprietary control of the Assembly.[2]

The governor could not believe what he read. After seven years in the colony, which Calvert never visited, Sharpe became somewhat better acquainted with the political situation. He objected to Calvert's proposal on grounds that (1) such a policy would run counter to the ambitions and inclinations of those already in the proprietary camp, who favored these offices for their own friends and relatives; (2) such offices as deputy surveyor and deputy commissary, which had incomes of between £ 10 and £ 50 a year, were of too little value to persuade men to give up their prestigious and more profitable assembly seats; (3) the proposal intimated that such offices would last only for the three-year periods between elections and such limited terms were not enough to make men change their political position; and (4) there were not enough offices to maintain such a system which would be "like a Hydra where three Serpents heads are fabled to have immediately sprouted in the place of one."[3] Besides, he saw a general popular discontent with the Assembly's continued negativism during the French and Indian War and looked for a new majority after the 1761 elections composed of the more moderate elements of the province. Such schemes would then be unnecessary—even unwise.[4]

The commentaries of Black, Sharpe, and Calvert about the origins of most delegates point to one important aspect of the problem. Were assemblymen part of the provincial masses?

Every indication of a survey of the officers in Baltimore, Prince George's, Queen Anne's and Talbot counties indicates that they were not. In Prince George's County, ninety-eight different men held the office of vestryman; of these, sixty-one came from the top fourth of the landowners and eighty-two from the top half. The situation was similar in Talbot where, of sixty vestrymen, forty-three were in the top quarter, fifty-five in the top half, and only one in the bottom quarter. Similar situations prevailed in Baltimore and Queen Anne's County vestries. Usually those vestrymen in the lower three-fourths of the landowners were related to persons in the upper quarter.

Among the delegates, the situation was more marked. Of twenty-one Talbot countians serving in the Lower House, seventeen were members of the top fourth of landowners, two were in the third quarter, and the other two were non-landowners in either 1756 or 1771. Of some thirteen Prince Georgian delegates, ten were in the top quarter, one in the third, and one was a non-landowner. In Baltimore County, sixteen of the seventeen delegates were among the wealthiest quarter of the landowners, while the other was in the top half. In Queen Anne's County, all twelve assemblymen serving from 1753 to 1776 were in the top group of landowners. As Table 8 indicates, three-fourths of the public offices went to that one-fourth of the gentry owning the most land.

One might think that the few who did not own land represented in these figures constituted a plebeian opening in the office-holding ranks. This was not the case. The non-landholding delegate from Prince George's was Thomas Contee, scion of one of the county's most influential families, who inherited his mother's nearly 1,000-acre estate prior to his election to the Assembly in 1771. His name does not appear on the Debt Book list of landowners because Mrs. Contee's estate had not been finally settled at the time the list was made. A similar situation accounts for the non-landholding status of the Thomas brothers, William III and Nicholas, who successively represented Talbot County from 1761 to 1776. The family's extensive acres were still in the estate of their father, William Thomas, Jr. (1705–1767), former vestryman and assemblyman himself, when the accounting of the debt books was made in 1771.

TABLE 8

LANDOWNERSHIP AND OFFICEHOLDING, 1753–1776[1]

Landholding Status	No. Delegates	No. Appointive Officers
Baltimore County		
Non-landowners 1756 or 1771	0	0
1st Quarter	0	2
2nd Quarter	0	3
3rd Quarter	1	12
4th Quarter	16	47
Prince George's County		
Non-landowners 1756 or 1771	0	5
1st Quarter	1	5
2nd Quarter	0	2
3rd Quarter	1	7
4th Quarter	10	61

TABLE 8 – Continued

LANDOWNERSHIP AND OFFICEHOLDING, 1753–1776[1]

Landholding Status	No. Delegates	No. Appointive Officers
Queen Anne's County		
Non-landowners 1756 or 1769	0	0
1st Quarter	0	0
2nd Quarter	0	1
3rd Quarter	0	10
4th Quarter	12	30
Talbot County		
Non-landowners 1756 or 1771	2	7
1st Quarter	0	1
2nd Quarter	0	2
3rd Quarter	2	6
4th Quarter	17	29

[1] Computations are based upon a comparison of the holdings listed in the quitrent Debt Books for these counties located in the MLO with the lists of delegates found in *Archives of Maryland,* L, LII, LV, LVI, LVIII, LIX, LXI, LXII, LXIII, LXIV, the ministers listed in N.W. Rightmyer, *Maryland's Established Church* (Baltimore: The Church Historical Society for the Diocese of Maryland, 1956),pp. 155–221, and the other appointive officers listed in Donnell M. Owings, *His Lordship's Patronage: Offices of Profit in Colonial Maryland* (Baltimore: Maryland Historical Society, 1953) and in the Commission Records, 1726–1786, Maryland Hall of Records. The data on vestry membership are compiled from the vestry proceedings of the parishes in the same counties; these data are then compared with the lists of landholders.

None of these men can be considered of mean estate and they were certainly not considered so by their contemporaries. Contee was a thrice-elected vestryman, a former sheriff, and a county justice before being returned as a delegate. The Thomas brothers were prominent lawyers, justices, vestrymen, and officeholders.[5] Even those whose names appear in the list of third quarter landowners can, with good reason, be counted among the wealthiest members of the community. For instance, Lloyd Buchanan, the Baltimore County delegate listed in this category, was a member of a very prominent mercantile family of Baltimore Town. He hardly represented even the middling ranks of wealth. There was, without a doubt, a high correlation between office-holding and large landholding.

The appointive offices were more widely distributed among persons of varying wealth. The close investigator will find, however, that most of the positions went to sons of the wealthy who were waiting for their patrimony. One can hardly place such non-landowners as William Bordley, Samuel Chamberlaine, Jr., and Robert Thomas of Talbot County, and Thomas Contee and Thomas Sim Lee of Prince George's, in any plebeian category. Governor Eden's shrievalty appointments of Ralph Forster and Frank Leak in Prince George's, and John Clapham in Anne Arundel, might indicate an attempt to gain greater support for the government from men of a lower financial position than was usual. But these were instances of the proprietary government at work, not of the elective democracy in Maryland.[6]

While Governor Sharpe referred to the Assembly delegates as "flaming Patriots or rather inflaming Demagogues," these were among the wealthiest demagogues in history. Historians have never doubted that a few families controlled the economic, social, and political life of the province. Paul H. Giddens observed that a "comparatively small coterie of gentlemen" bound "together by significant matrimonial alliances, . . . held the public offices, . . . controlled the legislature, . . . owned great blocks of land and numerous slaves, and many were university trained men. No finer gentleman class could be found in America." The influence of this combination of marriage, wealth, refinement, education, and office is reinforced by this study and by those of Aubrey C. Land and Charles A. Barker. There was little change in the degree of gentry control of politics between 1700 and 1770, if we accept the conclusions of John P. Moore, Robert G. Schonfeld, and Spencer Wilson, students of Professor Land.

Professor Giddens selected some 72 gentry families as those which dominated life in the province and, although one might disagree with some of his inclusions, like Callister, and his exclusions, like Beall, one has to agree that a small faction did dominate the social, political, and economic life of Maryland.[7]

Besides large landownership and intermarriage, most public officials were members of the established Anglican Church. A survey of the vestry elections in Prince George's, Queen Anne's, and Talbot counties, 1750–1776, indicates a predominance in elective offices of Anglicans who went from parish duties to those on the county level, often while still maintaining a parish office (see Appendix I). Exceptions to this rule emerge in the single election of Samuel Bowman, a Talbot County Quaker, and the several elections of Robert Jenckins Henry, son of the Rev. John Henry, Presbyterian minister in Somerset County. Henry's long support of the proprietary resulted in his elevation to the Council in 1756. Another example is George Fraser, who does not appear to have served on a Prince George's vestry. Fraser was undoubtedly an Anglican, being the son of the Rev. John Fraser, long-time rector of St. John's Parish, Piscataway. The marriages of his sisters—Anne to Allen Bowie, Susannah to George Hawkins, and Mary to William Magruder—allied the delegate with some of the largest landholding families in the county.

Many sons of the clergy enjoyed successful political careers. The Rev. Henry Hall's son, Maj. Henry Hall (1702–1756), and his grandsons, Maj. Henry Hall, Jr., and John Hall of the Vineyard, held Assembly seats from Anne Arundel County. Samuel Chase, son of Baltimore's Catholic-baiting Parson Thomas Chase, continued the same tradition.[8]

One possible exception—in addition to the Quaker Samuel Bowman— to the rule that only Anglicans served as delegates from these four counties is Josias Beall, Jr. Probably he was the son of Benjamin Beall (1704–1776) and a distant relative of Col. Ninian Beall (1625–1717). Presbyterian layman and assemblyman, 1696–1717. Many of this family were prominent Presbyterians related to the Edmonstons and Ormes, also of that faith. If we have correctly identified him, he was also a grandnephew of John Beall, the Presbyterian vestryman of St. John's Parish, Piscataway, whose election set the precedent for allowing dissenters to sit on the Anglican vestries. In This case, Josias Beall (1725—1796) was the son of Sarah Magruder, a member of one of the most vigorous Anglican families in the county. Josias' wife, Priscilla Clark, was the daughter of Thomas Clark, an immigrant from England, a fact which might also indicate that his branch of the family was Anglican, as does Josias' election as vestryman representing Prince George's Parish, Rock Creek, in 1760. Whatever the case, the man's relationship with the two major churches of the county did not hurt his political chances, for he was elected at every poll from 1758 to 1773.[9]

Of the many Quaker leaders appearing in the records of the Third Haven Meeting of the Eastern Shore, one does not find any but Bowman achieving public office, although many are of the large landholding class. Of some twenty leading Quakers in this Meeting, six were in the top quarter of Talbot County landowners, yet only Bowman occupied elective or appointive office.[10]

It becomes increasingly apparent as one examines the records of the parishes of the established church that the office of vestryman fell generally to Anglicans of the gentry. Trained in the only kind of local government available to them, and thereby having their names before the electorate of a large segment of the colony's population, many of these vestrymen moved into the Lower House. Their fathers, brothers, or in-laws often being in appointive offices, such vestrymen were often brought to the attention of influential relatives, and their successful vestry performance might cause them to be mentioned for appointive office.

Kinship seemed the dominant factor in determining most of those to receive His Lordship's most lucrative favors. The whole process could and did become circular, with one generation seeking and securing preferment for those who followed. Councilor Edward Lloyd resigned his position as Naval Officer of Oxford in favor of his cousin Samuel Chamberlaine, Sr., who in turn resigned the position for his son, Samuel, Jr. This single office remained in the family for 30 years. William Thomas III of Talbot succeeded to the Naval Officership of Pocomoke after his father-in-law, John Leeds, resigned the post. The clerkship of the Upper House and Council passed from John Ross to his son-in-law, Upton Scott. Richard Lee of Charles County succeeded his father, Philip Lee, as Naval Officer of North Potomac, and was followed into the post by his own son, Philip Thomas Lee. Councilor Benjamin Tasker, Sr. (1690–1768), brother-in-law of Gov. Thomas Bladen, father of Benjamin, Jr., and father-in-law of Gov. Samuel Ogle and the younger Daniel Dulany (1722–1797), lived to see the province's strongest concentration of appointive offices in his family, which at one time held three posts on the council.[11]

One should not be led to believe that the colony was in the iron grip of a reactionary "aristocracy" in any European sense of the word. Men with brains, luck, learning, and "gumption" might find their way to the top of the social hierarchy. There was give and take involved in the social structure of the whole colony. Yet the more one looks into the situation, the more one finds that some initial support from the Lord Proprietor was almost always necessary for the beginnings of a fortune in the province. In this category must be grouped the Carrolls, Darnalls, Dulanys, Bennetts, Bealls, Lloyds, Ogles, Platers, Ridouts, and most other wealthy Maryland families. Few fit into the pattern of men who achieved economic and political stature through other means. The exceptions to this rule are usually those attaining their initial capital through mercantile or manufacturing enterprises, like the Galloways and Ridgelys. Only in the lives of a few frontiersmen like Thomas Cresap (169?–1790) and Jonathan Hager (d. 1775) does one find men able to break through to wealth and power by other means, such as land investment, without an initial proprietary grant.

As James High pointed out recently, prominent Marylanders were bourgeois, not aristocratic, in their attitudes. They all wanted an end to the restrictions upon the expansion of free enterprise imposed by Parliament in accordance with its mercantilistic economic doctrine.[12]

Nonetheless, within this relatively homogeneous political elite there was political conflict between two groups called the "court" and the "country" parties. The term "country" given to the latter group did not denote a particular rural orientation, but rather a loyalty to the peculiar interests of the colony itself. A citizen always referred to Maryland as his "country." These groups were hardly parties in the sense that we know such organizations today. They were factions. No local political organizations existed for the sake of the party itself.

Since the landed gentry, through its exclusive nominating process, controlled all public offices, the problems that emerged were not those "between plebeian and patrician, but a question of the pride and interest of a local squirearchy opposed to the special privileges of an absentee Lord and his representatives."[13]

Membership in these factional groups was based on proprietary patronage, family alliance, and family animosities. Patronage (or the lack of it) became the leading factor behind political divisions. The Rev. Jonathan Boucher noted this division between "Placemen and their dependants" and their opponents, led mostly by lawyers, who "were instigated merely with the view of turning others out that they themselves might come in." For most of the colonial period, His Lordship's patronage power was great enough to cause a significant number of the gentry to gravitate to the party headed by the governor and his "court," as proprietary functionaries. "Patriotism," or loyalty to the country cause, could usually be extinguished with the offer of a large enough position. For example, Stephen Bordley joined the court camp, after many years as a country party assemblyman, when offered the positions of Attorney General and Naval Officer of Annapolis.[14]

While this conflict between the "ins" and the "outs" was one basis for factionalism, another was the status of family alliances. The dominant family grouping was the Tasker-Dulany-Addison tribe, whose long-time friendship was cemented by the marriage of Rebecca Tasker, daughter of Benjamin Tasker, Sr., to the younger Daniel Dulany, and of Dulany's sister Rebecca to the Rev. Henry Addison of Piscataway. The marriage of Addison's stepsister to George Plater III (1735–1792) allied the clan with one of Dulany's closest associates and the marriages of Dulany's and Addison's other brothers and sisters rounded out one of the most formidable combines within the proprietary establishment. Even Governor Sharpe, supposedly a dupe of this combine, railed against too much preferment being given this clique, which did not always follow the "court" cause.[15]

An only slightly less important family grouping, situated mainly in Queen Anne's and Talbot counties, contained the Lloyds, Tilghmans and Goldsboroughs, along with others of nearly equal importance. Allying this Eastern Shore family with the other side of the

Chesapeake were the marriages of the Protestant Carrolls to the Lloyd and Tilghman families. Doctor Carroll married Dorothy Blake, granddaughter of Philemon Lloyd I; and his son Charles Carroll, barrister, married Margaret Tilghman, daughter of Matthew and Ann (Lloyd) Tilghman.[16]

There was also a Catholic family combine composed of the intermarried Carroll, Darnall, Hill, and Brooke families. Here the genealogist is confronted with an entanglement of cousins. This is so complex that Charles Carroll of Carrollton and his cousin Archbishop John Carroll are related not so much by their common surnames as by their lineage through the Darnall family.[17]

While these are the most influential family groupings, each county had particular dominating families. Thus one finds such families as the Keys and Platers of St. Mary's, the Mackalls and Gantts of Calvert, the Hammonds and Halls of Anne Arundel, the Ridgelys and Halls of Baltimore, the Dennises of Somerset, and the Purnells of Worcester continually directing public affairs in their counties.[18]

Inter-family animosity, not any conflict about ideology, lay behind many of the colony's political alliances. Enmity between the Goldsborough and Thomas families of Talbot County fomented their continual battles for Assembly seats. Thus John Allen Thomas tried to discredit Robert Goldsborough II in the eyes of the proprietor, so that Goldsborough might not receive the attorney generalship. When Edward Tilghman lost his position as Rent Roll Keeper for the Eastern Shore, even though for incompetency, his brother, Matthew Tilghman (1718–1790), and his cousin, Edward Lloyd III, took offense and rallied to the anti-government banner.

Tilghman's removal by Governor Sharpe at the urging of Secretary Calvert and Lord Baltimore was one of the most serious political errors the proprietary made in this period. The results plagued the government until the Revolution. Similarly, animosities between the Carrolls and Dulanys were fired when Charles Carroll, Esq., suspected that the younger Dulany undercut, with a loan of money and some judicious advice, political support that squire Carroll expected from Maj. Henry Ridgely.[19]

While the court party was tightly organized around the governor and his placement, the country party was less formually drawn together.

It had no actual or titular head such as the governor. However, around such Lower House leaders as Stephen Bordley, Philip Hammond, Dr. Charles Carroll, Matthew Tilghman, Charles Carroll, barrister, John Hall of the Vineyard, and Samuel Chase, groups of men gathered who gave rather consistent support to their party.[20]

There was a considerable degree of "maverickism" as men shifted back and forth from one faction to the other. A group of court-favoring delegates like Charles Goldsborough of Dorchester County, George Plater III of St. Mary's, Thomas Johnson, Jr., of Anne Arundel, and Daniel of St. Thomas Jenifer of Charles turned to the country group before the Revolution. Likewise, James Tilghman of Talbot County and Robert Alexander of Baltimore Town went from the country position to the Loyalist side when the break came.[21]

Whatever their political differences, these were battles fought between gentlemen. Both groups were interested in maintaining the local status quo as to their privileged position. The squire, under the concept of *noblesse oblige,* supposedly represented all classes. But he did not. Instead, he followed his personal and group interests almost exclusively. These "parties" made no attempt to widen their base of support so as to include the landless, the immigrant, or the poor in their councils. Whatever their belief in mixed government, they never sought the backing of the lower classes until the Revolution.

Theirs were battles between men of the same class, men who knew each other as gentlemen, and who did not carry their animosities into the club room. The Harmony Club of Annapolis was one of several gentlemen's organizations flourishing in the period, with men of such diverse political factions as Thomas Johnson, Jr., John Brice, John Hall of the Vineyard, the Rev. Jonathan Boucher, Dennis and Walter Dulany, and Anthony and William Stewart regularly meeting together. At one such meeting the club's poet laureate, William Eddis, wrote in 1772:[22]

> While *Faction* and *Party* so madly prevail,
>   Infecting each *Rank* & Degree;
> No systems of State, shall our Councils assail,
>   Our Hearts all unbias'd & free.
> Society charms all vexations in Life:
>   While Mirth & good Humour abound

The *false Friend* is forgot: with the *dull peevish wife;*
And the *Toast* passes merrily round.

Whatever their differences, these men did not expect to engage in political activities outside their own class. They assumed leadership with the knowledge and understanding that they were expected to do so. Despite the contradictions, problems, and conflicts of their age, "the Maryland of Bordley and the Carrolls knew no order of men better able to solve those perplexities then the Bordleys and the Carrolls themselves."[23]

Within this political dualism of court and country parties, considerable divergence of opinion in political thought existed. The most conspicuous indication of this diversity came in a conflict between those of a Tory background and those with Whiggish leanings.

A most outspoken advocate of Toryism was the Rev. Jonathan Boucher (1738–1804), Virginia and Maryland schoolmaster and parson, rector of St. Anne's Parish, Annapolis, 1770–1771, and Queen Anne's Parish, Prince George's County, 1771–1775. Boucher's principles were not anti-American. He rigorously objected to the Proclamation of 1763, the Stamp Act, and the Townshend Duties. He supported the activities of the colonial assemblies in behalf of colonial rights. Not until the virtual collapse of the proprietary government did he feel called upon to condemn the course of action being followed on the Chesapeake Shores. This condemnation took place in a series of anti-revolutionary sermons preached, sometimes with a pistol on the pulpit, from his Prince George's County church.[24]

His sermon "On Civil Liberty; Passive Obedience, and Non-Resistance" best described his concept of government, which followed the Royalist tradition of Sir Robert Filmer's *Patriarcha* (1680). Men were not equal, never had been, and since the beginning of time man had copied "the fair model of heaven itself," with its obedience to superior authority, as the finest of constitutions. Boucher believed in the "patriarchal origin of government," wherein one gave blind obedience to the decision of the supreme magistrate. Liberty in such a society was the liberty one has in following the dictates of Christ, "a liberty to do everything that is right, and the being restrained from doing anything that is wrong." Passive obedience, not civil or uncivil disobedience, was the guide for the true Christian. One might object to the course of government; one might petition through his legitimate representatives for the redress of grievances; but if in the end the divinely ordained and guided magistrates rejected one's pleas, submission to that will was the only answer. This was not, the fiery rector contended, "a degrading and servile principle: it is the very reverse; and it is this superior dignity which proves its celestial origin. . . . It is the glory of Christianity to teach her votaries patiently to bear imperfections, inconveniences, and evils in government, as in everything else that is human." The greatest example of Christian charity and humility was the "patient acquiescence under some remediless evils . . . for, the only very intolerable grievance in government is when men allow themselves to disturb and destroy the peace of the world by vain attempts to render that perfect which the laws of our nature have ordained to be imperfect."[25]

Like many of his contemporaries, Boucher desired religious, political, and social conformity among the citizens of a state. He disliked the plural society emerging on the Chesapeake because such a society constituted a divisive element within the empire. Boucher deplored religious sects and political factions because they constituted a threat to the unity of church and state. He never arrived at the conclusion that a multiplicity of factions might offset one another and thus allow the constitution of a viable political system.[26]

Forced to flee to the Mother Country because of his beliefs, the Reverend Mr. Boucher undertook to inquire into a means of remedying the colonial problem. The traditional colonial government lent itself to the independence movement. In trying to insure the aggrandizement of Britain with powerful and opulent colonies, Boucher felt the royal government had failed to provide the only effectual restraint she might have put upon their eventual quest for preeminence—strong administration. The only recourse lay in providing "some Pith & Energy . . . to the executive Parts" of colonial governments.[27]

One aspect of British life that men like Boucher found missing from colonial society was a hierarchic system of church and state. Instead, the ever-perceptive William Eddis noticed that in Maryland a "republican spirit appears generally to predominate." Eddis found this to be due to the lack of an order of nobility and an ecclesiastical hierarchy which would have caused citizens "to cherish a steady adherence to monarchial principles. . . . Inattention to principles of such importance, has gradually given birth to sentiments totally repugnant to the genius of our most excellent constitution." Others observed the same phenomenon. Colonists said men like Burnaby, Boucher, and Sharpe, failed to show proper deference to their social superiors.[28]

These condescending patriarchal concepts drew strong approval from the Calverts. Secretary Cecilius Calvert's idea that the "Malevolent Spirit in the Lower House of Assembly" could be checked "by throwing out a Sop in a proper manner to these Noisy animals" who served as delegates, indicated how little he and other Britons realized what was going on in Maryland. Frederick Calvert spoke in the same patronizing manner. When colonists clung tenaciously to every concession wrung from the proprietor and tried to use these to gain more concessions, he wrote, "I will still Insist upon my rights till I see proper occasions to suspend them, and when those Occasions Cease, I will again Resume them." Agreeing with his uncle's attitudes toward the delegates, Lord Baltimore detested the provincial tribunes who "go out & Harangue the People with a cry of Liberty against the Proprietor, as if he were a Bashaw; this is licentiousness & not Liberty."[29]

The government envisioned by Boucher and the Calverts was one of paternalism, hierarchical order, uniformity of belief in matters of church and state, and obedience to one's social and political superiors. But their defense of a government created in the early seventeenth century with a then-obsolete medieval organization was bound to incite discontent among the local inhabitants who supported more modern governmental systems. Maryland's whigs were traditionally divided between those oriented toward a legalistic, constitutional, and parliamentary tradition and those believing in a natural-rights philosophy. The latter tradition was less concerned with shifting legal precedents and more at home with appeals to a higher-law concept of morality and metaphysics.

Like its other continental colonies, Maryland had a long tradition of constitutional legalism in defense of its alleged liberties. Most conspicuous in the Maryland tradition was Daniel Dulany, the elder, who in 1728 published *The Right of the Inhabitants of Maryland to the*

Benefit of English Laws. One of the extraordinary political commentaries of the early eighteenth century, this pamphlet exploits most of the arguments relative to colonial liberties found in treatises of the revolutionary era. Using classical writers, modern political theorists, and English jurists to bolster his case, the elder Dulany marshaled all his evidence to support the colonists' right to the enjoyment of the corpus of English law—both common and statuatory. Like his more famous son, Dulany's arguments smacked more of a lawyer's brief than a grand appeal to the populace. Yet, his pamphlet and the antiproprietary political agitation which brought it out mark an important milestone in the Chesapeake colony's drift from obedience to the restrictions of their charter. Nearly as significant were the "Remarks on the Maryland Government" appearing in the *American Magazine* in 1741. The anonymous author questioned the legitimacy of the Upper House of the General Assembly because the Councilors were not independent of the control of the Lord Proprietor and Governor as were the peers of England of the Crown. Citing such "Commonwealthmen" as Harrington and Trenchard, the author described "the despotic Nature of that Government" which resulted when "a Nobility assuming a distinct Legislative Power, should nevertheless be absolutely dependent on the Prince." Under such circumstances, he continued, "it cannot be supposed that the People could ever receive, in any one single Instance, the smallest Benefit from such an Institution." Such criticisms of colonial governance would continue and increase in the third quarter of the eighteenth century.[30]

Best known of the colony's constitutional whigs was the brilliant attorney, Daniel Dulany, the younger. His justly famous *Considerations on the Propriety of Imposing Taxes in the British Colonies for the Purpose of Raising a Revenue* (1765) became a classic argument against the Stamp Act. Obviously Dulany championed the colonial cause. He did so within the limitations of the law in which he was so well versed. His appeal was not to the natural law, but to the English constitution and the tradition of *stare decisis*. This meant that all common law decisions were perpetually valid and could not be changed to meet novel applications of them. Such a limited intellectual framework confined the area of action in which he felt the colonists could legitimately move. When the revolutionists' agitation went outside the law he had learned at the Inns of Court, Dulany failed to join the "out-of-door" politics of the period and found himself isolated from the rush to independence.[31]

Dulany's loyalty to the empire, however, was not due merely to dependence upon legalism. He continued to be a pragmatic politician who constantly sought compromise solutions to immediate problems. Strict legalism might lead to grievous losses to the empire he loved so well. Thus it was that in a letter to Lord Baltimore written after the Stamp Act crisis he warned the Crown or Parliament against efforts that might "induce the Colonies, to Coalesce in any Enterprise." Instead, all must be done to keep the American colonies as they then were: "Different in Religion and Polity, of dissimular Manners and Habitudes, all . . . clashing in Interests with one another, Disproportioned in Number of Inhabitants, and in Internal Strength, Jealous of, and dreading one another." His Majesty's government should not utilize its obviously legal power to make less republican the New England charters because such a utilization of power would cause a union of the diverse elements that currently existed. He concluded his letter, which was kept as a state paper by the Earl of Shelburne, Secretary of State for the Southern Department, by saying: "To talk now of the Ballance of Power in America, would expose one to Ridicule; but it may be hereafter a Consideration as Serious, and an Object as Important, as ever the Ballance of Power in Europe has been deemed to be." Accident, rather than any British design, "laid a Foundation for this Ballance in America, a little attention may secure it, and a little Reflection will discover, that whatever tends to a Union of the Colonies, will tend also to destroy that Foundation."[32] As a whig constitutionalist, Dulany found his opinions slipping behind the revolutionary tenor of provincial politics. As a pragmatic imperialist, his judicious insights into colonial control went unheeded at Whitehall.

From 1739 to the end of the colonial period, the House of Delegates and individual Marylanders conducted attacks on various features of the colony's charter. Their general tenor was to break down respect for the organic law of the colony and to make citizens seek outside the charter for redress of grievances. All of this political agitation was within the general pattern of constitutional whiggism of the period.

One such assault against the proprietary establishment came in

1753 when the Rev. Thomas Cradock preached to an Annapolis congregation consisting of Governor Sharpe and the provincial Anglican
clergy. Cradock was regularly the rector of St. Thomas Parish, Baltimore County, and a distinguished schoolmaster to the most affluent of
his fellow colonists; his doctrine was simply that public officials must
be held accountable for their conduct. He directed his fire primarily
against his fellow Anglican priests, many of whom he said were unworthy of their calling. He spoke of "persons of no Worth, no Learning, no Religion, [who] after attempting to live all the ways they can,
[and] find[ing] at last no other resource but the Church," secured
approval of the proprietor for cures in Maryland. They took these
benefices with large incomes, compared to those of England, and
amply repaid their parishioners "by living in a most scandalous and
dissolute manner." There must, he cried, be some remedy available
to colonists who supported the clergy by taxation from the oppression
imposed upon them by the Maryland charter, which gave Lord Baltimore the right of patrimony. Although he felt the solution lay in the
introduction of a bishop, his proposal was revolutionary; it cut at the
heart of proprietary power and, if carried to its logical conclusion,
affected those in civil offices as well.

For if the charter could be changed, and Baltimore's absolute power
over clerical appointments and tenure could be curtailed, so also might
the Lord Proprietor's control over civil officers be changed to provide
Marylanders with another source of succor from an inefficient, expensive, and incorrigible officialdom. After all, the colonists were heavily
burdened by taxes and fees to support the Maryland establishment
and they had no voice concerning the appointment or tenure of civil
or ecclesiastical officers.[33]

Ten years later, Dr. Richard Brooke, of a notable Prince George's
County family, published in the distinguished British journal,
Gentleman's Magazine, a series of "Queries" designed to bring into
question whether the constitution of Maryland was in accordance with
that of England and whether it deprived the colonists of their rights
as Englishmen. Doctor Brooke charged that the charter denied "the
equilibrium of an *English* constitution" by giving the proprietor control over the legislative, executive, and judicial branches of government. He spoke of Marylanders "being despoiled of their liberties"

and being denied, by their proprietor, the right to have an agent in London to represent their interests at court. They were descendants of Britons who, "by the noblest fortitude and perseverance, and at the expence of their blood" added to the crown's dominions a colony contributing great revenues and promoting the commercial and industrial activity of the Mother Country.[34]

Both Parson Cradock and Doctor Brooke brought into question the validity of the charter as it pertained to the rights of Englishmen. Here began one of the assaults on colonial government that characterized the Revolution in all British America. Marylanders questioned whether the document under which they were governed truly represented the ideals for which they felt their nation stood.

The influence of John Locke upon colonial thought was reflected in the writings of one "Fellow Planter" in the *Maryland Gazette.* This anonymous author directly opposed the concept of patriarchal origins of government utilized by Boucher, and claimed that there was once an equality of mankind in a state of nature and that societies were formed to protect "the Peaceable, Innocent, and Weak" from "the Strong, Rapacious, Crafty, and Violent." Although the "Fellow Planter" did not claim the right of resistance to tyranny, this right is implied in his statement *"That the Happiness and Safety of the People, is the true End of all Laws."*[35]

The "Fellow Planter's" appeal went beyond the legalism of a Dulany, a Cradock, or a Brooke. For him and a growing number of colonists, there was a higher law of public happiness against which all governments must be judged. "Fellow Planter" defined the "liberty" necessary to secure this happiness as requiring the people to be involved, either by themselves or through their representatives, in the making of the laws. Shortly after his 1753 letter to the *Gazette,* an increase of activities in the Lower House, leading to the assertion of its rights of parliamentary privilege, developed. Burgesses copied the House of Commons in points of organization, procedure, and privilege and demanded that these claims be accepted by the governor and Council. Governor Sharpe complained bitterly in 1758 about the tactics of the Lower House and its attempts to subvert the role of the upper chamber in the legislative process. Of all their demands, however, none was more significant than that of the right to determine membership in their body. When a dispute arose between former Speaker Philip Hammond of Anne Arundel and Delegate Samuel Wilson of Somerset, the chamber forced Wilson to leave because he would not personally apologize to Hammond. The joint stubbornness of the two protagonists kept Wilson from the House for three years, when the death of Hammond made a personal apology unnecessary. Between 1758 and 1760, a vigorous dispute arose over the seating of Dr. George Steuart as a delegate from the capital. This and similar actions by the Lower House culminated in its acquisition of total control over its membership.[36]

As the delegates asserted their power, so the electorate began to impose its will upon its representatives. Beginning with the conflicts over the Supply Bill and the Catholic question which raged during the last intercolonial war, several counties felt called upon to instruct their delegates on how to vote in forthcoming sessions of the Assembly. Undoubtedly many such instructions were arranged by the delegates themselves to reinforce the stand they were subsequently to take in the Assembly, a stand which might defy the wishes of both the Lord Proprietor and the Crown relative to the conduct of the war. One of the earliest such instructions was the petition of Prince George's County freeholders concerning the Catholic question. A year later in 1755, some leading Somerset County freeholders asserted the "Right which Constituents, under a British Government, claim of Instructing their Representatives." This tradition grew so strong that in 1776 Samuel Chase of Annapolis felt called, "in obedience as he conceived the instructions of Anne Arundel" freemen, to propose before the Maryland Convention changes in the credit system.[37]

To secure their happiness, the Maryland whigs sought to insure that local freeholders had a voice in the affairs of government directly affecting them. Such a desire brought into question the whole relationship of the colonies to the empire. Dulany's *Considerations* supported the colonial right of exemption from Parliamentary impositions on the grounds that there should be no taxation without representation. Squire Carroll "never understood the Lords & Commons of England Claimed any Dominion" over the colonies and held that the only difference between the colonial legislatures and Parliament was the "superior Power (understood as force) & opulence" of the latter. "Our Constitutionall dependence on the Crowne," he wrote in 1768, "is sufficiently & Effectually secured by its Appointment of Governors & all other Officers Civill & Military [and] by a Controul on the Laws passed by our Assemblies."[38]

Andrew Burnaby found many Chesapeake citizens considering "the colonies as independent states, not connected with Great Britain, otherwise than by having the same common King, and being bound to her by natural affection." This "natural affection" deteriorated when Charles Carroll of Carrollton expressed sentiments more radical than those of his father. He held in 1771 that the aristocratic government of Great Britain, like the Roman Senate, was incapable of governing an empire of the extent now controlled by the British crown.[39]

But the whiggish ideal did not require that all citizens participate in the governmental processes in order to secure their liberty. As Dulany's *Considerations* make apparent, suffrage was not a right of citizenship, but a privilege of ownership. William Paca, Carroll (barrister), and Chase all expressed similar sentiments. When, in 1787, Carroll of Carrollton looked back over the revolutionary era, he felt compelled to ask that the property requirement be tripled: "I would confine (in this State) the right of Suffrage as to the choice of Delegates, and of Electors of Senators, to persons possessed of 150 acres of Land in fee-simple." He did allow that in "Trading Towns" the "right of Suffrage should not be confined to Landed Property." Carroll reflected a prevailing opinion that the electorate should be limited to those citizens most likely to exercise "this important right most wisely."[40]

Similarly, officeholding was not a right of citizenship. The assemblyman should be one whose economic and social position automatically placed him in the role of political leadership. A fine illustration of gentry control of politics came in a letter of "An Elector of Anne Arundel County" to the *Gazette* just before the 1767 election. He recommended as the *"sound* Assembly-Man" one "able in Estate, able in Knowledge and Learning. By his Ability in the former, he at least is circumstanced to steer clear of all the dangerous Baits Corruption may lay to entrap him. By his Ability in the latter, to serve his Country, at all Times, with Effect, Repute, and Credit." "An Elector" concluded his statement by urging that a delegate "be '*a compleat*

Gentleman,' . . . A man of *Learning,* of *Honour,* of *strict Principle."* [41] Such candidates could obviously not come from all segments of the population.

The evidence indicates that the colony's politicians were men of neither mean abilities nor low estate. They were men who, with the exception of a few Tories among them, shared a common whiggish heritage. Marylanders elected "generally persons of the greatest consequence in their different counties: and many of them are perfectly acquainted with the political and commercial interests of their constituents." In the Assembly, one "heard subjects debated with great powers of eloquence, and force of reason; and the utmost regularity and propriety distinguish the whole of their proceedings."[42]

The colonial charter frustrated the complete development of the common whiggism of these politicians. That medieval document, based upon the long-extinct Durham palatinate, had little relevance to the political ideology of most of His Lordship's colonists. As a consequence, constant friction arose between the court party (which felt duty-bound to support the continuation of the charter and proprietary prerogative) and the country party (which used every incident to secure minor modifications of assembly privilege and power). The bitterness and length of many of these contests resulted in almost a reenactment of seventeenth-century English history. The proprietary opposition could find no compromise with a legal instrument which did not include any of the political principles they felt necessary for good government. At the same time, the proprietor felt that any concessions could result in the revocation or denudation of the charter and an end to the profitable proprietorship established by George Calvert. Maryland suffered from "division and disagreement at the center." The charter was on the far right of dominant political opinion Baltimore's privileges and colonial demands resulted from the lack of a central set of constitutional principles in which all political protagonists believed. Thus, although virtually all politicians were of the same class, they fought over minor issues, often to the discredit of both proprietary and representative government.[43]

None of their disagreements revolved around social change. The politicians of colonial Maryland were men of wealth, men of breeding, men of the established church, men who held common middle-class, whig, and mercantile attitudes, men who knew and respected each other despite occasional political differences. They governed, and expected to continue to govern, this Chesapeake province in its orderly conduct as a member of the British empire.

NOTES

1. Entry of May 19, 1744, "Journal of William Black, 1744," R. A. Brock, editor, *Pennsylvania Magazine of History and Biography,* I (1877), p. 127; H. Sharpe to C. Calvert, June 5, 1754, March 12, 1755, April 19, 1755, *Archives of Maryland,* VI, pp. 68, 183-184, 191; "State of the Province of Maryland in 1758," *Maryland Historical Magazine,* XXXIII (1938), p. 246.

2. C. Calvert to H. Sharpe, March 17, 1760, *Archives of Maryland,* IX, pp. 376-380.

3. H. Sharpe to C. Calvert, July 7, 1760, April 19, 1761; Sharpe to Calvert, March 12, 1755, *Archives of Maryland,* IX, pp. 426-431, 502; VI, quote 184.

4. H. Sharpe to C. Calvert, April 19, 1761, *Archives of Maryland,* IX, p. 502.

5. E. G. Bowie, *Across the Years in Prince George's County* (Richmond: Garrett and Massie, 1947); R.H. Spencer, "Hon. Nicholas Thomas," *Maryland Historical Magazine,* VI (1911), pp. 145-163.

6. See note to Table 8.

7. H. Sharpe to J. Sharpe, May 27, 1756, *Archives of Maryland,* VI, p. 425; P. H. Giddens, "The Public Career of Horatio Sharpe, Governor of Maryland, 1753-1769" (Ph.D. dissertation, University of Iowa, 1930), pp. 75–77, quote 112–113; J. P. Moore, "The Landed Gentry of Maryland: A Study of Their Political Influence on Colonial Society, 1770-1710" (M. A. thesis, University of Maryland, 1964), p. 17; R. G. Schonfeld and S. Wilson, "The Value of Personal Estates in Maryland," *Maryland Historical Magazine,* LVIII (1963), pp. 257-286; A. C. Land, "Economic Base and Social Structure: The Northern Chesapeake in the Eighteenth Century," *Journal of Economic History,* XXV (1965), pp. 639-654; A. C. Land, *The Dulanys of Maryland* (Baltimore: Maryland Historical Society, 1955); C. A. Barker, *The Background of the Revolution in Maryland* (New Haven: Yale University Press, 1940).

8. R. P. Davis, "Beginnings of Presbyterianism in Makemieland to 1788" (M. T. thesis, Union Theological Seminary, Richmond, Va., 1941), pp. 127-128, 172; *Archives of Maryland,* LII, pp. x-xi, xxx; T. J. Hall, *The Hall Family of West River and Kindred Families* (Denton, Md.: Rue Publishing Co., 1941), pp. 139-140; R. R. Beirne, "The Reverend Thomas Chase: Pugnacious Parson," *Maryland Historical Magazine,* LIX (1964), 1-14.

9. F. M. M. Beall, *Colonial Families of the United States* (Washington, D. C. Charles Potter & Co., 1929), *passim.* The actual identification of this Josias Beall is complicated by the fact that some 18 Bell, Beale, and Beall families settled in Maryland prior to 1700 and they repeatedly changed spellings of their names, and repeated the same first name numerous times amongst cousins. The appendage "Junior" did

not necessarily mean that the man's father had the same name; instead, it often meant that he was younger than another man of the same name in the same county; see also Bowie, *Across,* pp. 152-154, 536-538, for more on Beall.

10. "Minutes of the Third Haven or Tread Avon Friend's Meeting: Talbot County, Maryland," compl. A. W. Burns, 5 vols., typescript (Baltimore, 1940?), *passim.* The twenty landholders were compiled from names prominently mentioned in the Meeting's records 1753-1774.

11. D. M. Owings, *His Lordship's Patronage: Offices of Profit in Colonial Maryland* (Baltimore: Maryland Historical Society, 1953), *passim.*

12. J. High, "The Origins of Maryland's Middle Class in the Colonial Aristocratic Pattern," *Maryland Historical Magazine,* LVII (1962), pp. 334-345.

13. Barker, *Background,* pp. 174-175, quote 182.

14. G. T. Hollyday, "Biographical Memoir of James Hollyday," *Pennsylvania Magazine of History and Biography,* VII (1883), p. 438.

15. Land, *Dulanys;* M. McKenna, "Sotterley, St. Mary's County," *Maryland Historical Magazine,* XLVI (1951), pp. 80-182; H. Sharpe to C. Calvert, April 19, 1761, *Archives of Maryland,* IX, pp. 500-501.

16. O. Tilghman, "Lloyd Family," *Maryland Historical Magazine,* VIII (1913), pp. 85-88; C. Johnson, "Lloyd Family," *Maryland Historical Magazine,* VII (1912), pp. 420-430; E. Goldsborough, "The House of Goldsborough," 6 vols. (typescript, in Maryland Historical Society, 1932), IV, pp. 90-92; R. B. Harley, "Dr. Charles Carroll—Land Speculator, 1730-1755," *Maryland Historical Magazine,* XLVI (1951), pp. 93-107; W. S. Holt, "Charles Carroll, Barrister: The Man," *Maryland Historical Magazine,* XXXI (1936), pp. 112-126.

17. P. K. Guilday, *The Life and Times of John Carroll,* 2 vols., (New York: The Encyclopedia Press, 1922), I, genealogical chart between pp. 16 and 17; Giddens, "Governor Sharpe," p. 86.

18. Giddens, "Governor Sharpe," pp. 103-104.

19. Giddens, "Governor Sharpe," pp. 96-97; 113-114; H. Sharpe to W. Sharpe, July 8, 1760; H. Sharpe to Baltimore, June 11, 1767, *Archives of Maryland,* IX, p. 440, XIV, pp. 398-400; C. Carroll to Carrollton, April 12, 1771, "Extracts from the Carroll Papers," *Maryland Historical Magazine,* XIII (1918), pp. 175-176.

20. H. Sharpe to Baltimore, October 3, 1756, to C. Calvert, October 5, 1756, *Archives of Maryland,* VI, pp. 489, 491, give examples of various country party leaders.

21. *Archives of Maryland,* LVIII, xiv-xv; Carrollton to C. Carroll, September 30, 1774, "Extracts," p. 38.

22. Gilmor Papers, Maryland Historical Society, III, p. 23.

23. Barker, *Background,* p. 68.

24. J. Boucher to J. James, December 9, 1765, March 9, 1767, July 25, 1769, to W. Smith, May 4, 1775, "Letters of Rev. Jonathan Boucher," *Maryland Historical Magazine,* VII (1912), pp. 295, 340, VIII (1913), pp. 44-45, 240.

25. J. Boucher *A View of the Causes and Consequences of the American Revolution* (London: G. G. and J. Johnson, 1797), pp. 495-560. See also his sermons "On

Fundamental Principles," "On the Strife Between Abraham and Lot," "On the Character of Absalon," "On the Character of Ahitophel," and "The Dispute Between the Israelites and the Two Tribes and a Half, Respecting Their Settlement Beyond Jordan," pp. 194-492, for more of his political views. For discussions of Boucher's philosophy, see P. Evanson, "Jonathan Boucher: The Mind of an American Loyalist," *Maryland Historical Management,* LVIII (1963), pp. 123-136; J. L. Blau, "Jonathan Boucher, Tory," *History* (N.Y.) (May 1961), pp. 93-109; M.D. Clark, "Jonathan Boucher: The Mirror of Reaction," *Huntington Library Quarterly,* XXXIII (1969), pp. 19-32; V. L. Parrington, *Main Currents in American Thought,* I. *The Colonial Mind* (New York: Harvest Books, Harcourt, Brace and World, 1954), pp. 218-223; M. Savelle, *Seeds of Liberty: The Genesis of the American Mind* (New York: A. A. Knopf, 1948), pp. 301-305; A. Y. Zimmer and P. H. Kelly, "Jonathan Boucher: Constitutional Conservative," *Journal of American History,* LVII (1971-72), pp. 897-922.

26. Sermon "On Schisms and Sects," Boucher, *A View,* pp. 46-88.

27. J. Boucher to [W. Knox?], November 27, 1775, "Letters," *Maryland Historical Magazine,* VIII (1913), pp. 240-247; Boucher, *A View,* pp. xliii-xlv.

28. April 2, 1770, February 17, 1772, W. Eddis, *Letters from America* (London, 1792), pp. 51-54, 128; A. Burnaby, "Travels Through the Middle Settlements in North America in the Years 1759 and 1760," in J. Pinkerton, *A General Collection of the Best and Most Interesting Travels,* XIII (London: Longman, 1812), p. 715; Boucher to J. James, August 7, 1759, "Letters," *Maryland Historical Magazine,* VII (1912), pp. 4-5; Sharpe to C. Calvert, July 7, 1760, *Archives of Maryland,* IX, p. 430.

29. C. Calvert to H. Sharpe, March 17, 1760; Baltimore to Sharpe, February 7, 1765, February 16, 1767, *Archives of Maryland,* IX, pp. 375-387; XIV, pp. 194-195, 371.

30. Daniel Dulany, *The Right of the Inhabitants of Maryland to the Benefit of English Laws* (Annapolis: William Parks, 1728); "Remarks on the Maryland Government," *American Magazine,* I (1741), pp. 23-33, 35-47. See also Land, *Dulanys,* pp. 81-85; Barker, *Background,* pp. 163-168, 214-237.

31. The *Considerations* are conveniently reprinted in Bernard Bailyn, editor, *Pamphlets of the American Revolution, 1750-1776,* 4 vols. (Cambridge: Harvard University Press, 1965), I, pp. 599-658; for more on Dulany's political philosophy, see Land, *Dulanys,* pp. 263-270; E. S. Morgan & H. M. Morgan, *The Stamp Act Crisis: Prologue to Revolution* (Chapel Hill: University of North Carolina Press, 1953), chap. 6.

32. Extract of letter Dulany to Baltimore [1766?], Shelburne Papers, William L. Clements Library, Vol. 58, fol. 115-117.

33. "Thomas Cradock's Sermon on the Governance of Maryland's Established Church," D. C. Skaggs, editor, *William and Mary Quarterly,* Series 3, XXVII (1970), pp. 630-653. See also D. C. Skaggs, "Thomas Cradock and the Chesapeake Golden Age," *William and Mary Quarterly,* Series 3, XXX (1973), pp. 93-116.

34. R.[ichard] B.[rooke], "Queries relative to the Constitution of Maryland," *Gentlemen's Magazine,* XXXIII (1763), pp. 541-544.

35. *Maryland Gazette,* May 31, 1753.

36. H. Sharpe to W. Sharpe, January 1, 1758, to Baltimore, May 14, 1758, *Archives of Maryland*, IX, pp. 124-125, 177-178; LVI, pp. lii-lv, 108, 110-111; M. P. Clarke, "Parliamentary Privilege in the American Colonies," *Essays in Colonial History Presented to Charles McLean Andrews by His Students* (New Haven: Yale University Press, 1931), pp. 143-144; High, "A Facet of Sovereignty: The Proprietary Governor and the Maryland Charter," *Maryland Historical Magazine*, LV (1960), pp. 72-74; J. P. Greene, *The Quest for Power: The Lower Houses of Assembly in the Southern Royal Colonies, 1689-1776* (Chapel Hill: University of North Carolina Press, 1963), pp. 3-12.

37. *Maryland Gazette*, November 28, 1754, March 6, 1755; *American Archives*, P. Force, editor, 4th series, 6 vols. (Washington, D.C.: Clarke and Force, 1837-1846), VI, pp. 1501-1502; C. A. Barker, "The Revolutionary Impulse in Maryland," *Maryland Historical Magazine*, XXXVI (1941), p. 137.

38. C. Carroll to W. Graves, December 23, 1768, "Extracts," *Maryland Historical Magazine*, XII (1917), pp. 186-187; Dulany, *Considerations*, in Bailyn, editor, *Pamphlets*, I, pp. 633-634.

39. Burnaby, "Travels," pp. 715-716; Carrollton to E. Jenings, August 9, 1771, "A Lost Copy-Book of Charles Carroll of Carrollton," J. D. G. Paul, editor, *Maryland Historical Magazine*, XXXII (1937), p. 198.

40. Dulany, *Considerations*, in Bailyn, editor, *Pamphlets*, I, pp. 611-612; *Maryland Gazette*, August 22, 1776; "Charles Carroll's Plan of Government," P. A. Crowl, editor, *American Historical Review*, XLVI (1941), p. 593.

41. *Maryland Gazette*, December 3, 1767.

42. February 17, 1772, Eddis, *Letters*, p. 126.

43. Barker, *Background*, pp. 117, 214-237; C. A. Barker, "Property Rights in the Provincial System of Maryland: Proprietary Revenues," *Journal of Southern History*, II (1936), pp. 230-232.

Part

II

PROVINCIAL POLITICS

. . . could I be suffered to retire to my little farm and wear out the remainder of life in obscurity— in bewailing the miseries of my country which I can neither prevent nor remedy. But this I fear will not be permitted; . . . I think it probable that men who have shown a disposition to moderation and an aversion to changes will not remain unnoticed by those who shall ascend to the top of the machine.

James Hollyday, 1776

6

THE PROPRIETARY DEMISE, 1753–1774

During the two decades between the arrival of Governor Sharpe and the passage of the Coercive Acts, the relative effectiveness of the proprietary government in controlling Maryland politics declined. This development resulted in part from the common colonial reaction to royal and parliamentary attempts to more strongly control the North American colonies than had been done under the first two Hanoverian kings. Probably more important were three local issues that contributed to political discontent among His Lordship's subjects: (1) proprietary privilege versus colonial aspirations in economic, political, and social life; (2) the nature and extent of the system of taxation and fee collection; and (3) economic fluctuations in the tobacco economy. None of these issues involved any attempt to provide greater political equality or social opportunity to the masses. But they did bring about certain changes in the political processes, so that the imperial crises of the mid-1770s resulted in broader political participation by Marylanders.

The opening of what Lawrence Gipson called "The Great War for the British Empire" began one of the longest, bitterest political battles in Maryland history. Since it began shortly after Governor

Sharpe's arrival, the war brought to the new executive a lasting understanding of the political realities of the province. Military necessity, proprietary prerogative, and colonial liberties seemed in continual conflict. French retention of Fort Duquesne and Col. George Washington's defeat at Great Meadows made the enactment of a supply bill to support Maryland troops in the war a necessity. In 1754, the Assembly authorized a supply bill of £ 6,000, supported by a sinking fund based, in part, on increased taxes on ordinary licenses for taverns and places of lodging. Traditionally the power to grant ordinary licenses lay with the governor, and the revenues therefrom were part of the proprietor's private income. Both the governor and the Council assented to the use of this revenue to back the sinking fund. Lord Baltimore grudgingly approved. However, he prohibited any further concessions concerning the licenses in subsequent supply bills. The net result was, as the late Arthur Schlesinger wrote that "Maryland's official participation in the conflict may be characterized as a barren expanse of military inactivity, brightened here and there by the exploits of Lieutenant Governor Sharpe, performed on his own initiative, often at his own expense, and invariably in face of the opposition of the Assembly."[1]

The Maryland Assembly demonstrated a political immaturity during the war which left the impression of irresponsible and unenlightened leadership. The proprietor also relinquished any claim to responsible leadership by his demand that he retain the ordinary licenses as his private income, in spite of a threat to his domain and to his colonists. Even the younger Daniel Dulany, then out of either popular or proprietary office, complained in 1755 that any rise in the poll tax to support the war effort (which was advocated by His Lordship) would increase what was already "a grievous burthen." The whole issue of governmental irresponsibility brought Thomas Ringgold to conclude that it was "to the great shame of whoever is at fault." And Dulany said despairingly, "God knows when there will be an end to our disputes."[2]

In the midst of the rancor over the supply bill, Governor Sharpe decided to enlist every person he could to support the war effort. When a smallpox epidemic threatened an Assembly meeting in Annapolis, he called the legislature to Baltimore in April 1757. Then he requested the Rev. Thomas Cradock of nearby St. Thomas Parish to preach before the assemblymen in the hope that the popular clergyman might incline their hearts to back the imperial war effort. Using the "house divided" clause of Luke 11:17 as his text, Parson Cradock implored his listeners to forget their petty differences and join in a united effort. They must "all . . . join hands and hearts together to promote peace and unity, and to discountenance both by . . . words and actions all grumbling and uneasiness that may rise among" the colonists. "No argument but that of the common good and common safety should now . . . be listened unto," he pleaded. For "all, who bear the name of *Britons,*" must, the good parson concluded, throw off their "unseasonable disputes and quarrels" or leave themselves wide open for conquest by Roman Catholic tyrants.

It was all to little avail. Seven months support was given for a militia force on the frontier, but the country party subsequently refused further support for the war effort without some concessions from the proprietor. Baltimore refused to budge, and secured the support of His Majesty's attorney general Charles Pratt (later Lord Camden) in an opinion concerning the version of the supply bill offered by the Lower House.[3]

Governor Sharpe, knowing that many persons disliked the dereliction of duty embodied in the stand of the Lower House, took the issue to the people in the elections of 1758 and 1761. The governor's tactic was unsuccessful in the first election, and he found himself confronted with the same assemblymen who would deadlock the Assembly for another three years of the war. The election of 1761 improved the governor's position somewhat, but the court party was still a minority in the Lower House. To counter this enlarged opposition, the country party proposed an income tax levied on the large officeholders, professional persons, and merchants in the colony as well as new taxes on His Lordship's quitrents. These innovations were politically motivated, directed primarily against the proprietor and his favorites, with no expectation or desire that they become law or that they help to equalize wealth.

With the Peace of Paris in 1763, the supply bill no longer dominated the political scene. Nonetheless, it proved an important factor in later political developments. In order to retain political influence and to keep the political situation agitated, the gentry's delegates proposed radical taxing measures which, although designed primarily to hurt the proprietary faction, affected themselves adversely as well. Of equal importance was the mutual vindictiveness with which both the court and country parties attacked one another.[4] These attacks brought into disrepute the quality of gentry leadership, a factor tending to bring a decline in plebeian deference to their magistrates. Such developments had grave implications for the future of gentry domination of politics.

Governor Sharpe, who expected political tranquility in the colony once the French and Indian War ended, found instead mounting opposition. Both local discontent over the established church and universal colonial disgust over post-war imperial regulations passed by Parliament complicated the situation. Such dissatisfaction manifested itself in the elections of 1764, when many old and new foes of the proprietary government received Lower House seats. From this time forward, there was a steady decline in the number of proprietary delegates.[5]

Concurrently, the court party received two internal blows that compounded its problems. The first of these was the failure of Lord Baltimore and Secretary Calvert to oppose the Stamp Act. The law blatantly violated provisions in the Maryland charter denying the king or Parliament the right to levy taxes in the colony. Frederick Calvert's blunder in not blocking the application of the law to Maryland cost him and the court party dearly. Sharpe suggested that the Lord Proprietor's opposition to the hated Stamp Act might have been a brilliant coup uniting the colonists behind their proprietor.[6] Instead, his actions made it appear that he was concerned only with those charter provisions protecting his interests and income and not with the welfare of the colonists.

Hardly had news of the law been received in Maryland than Daniel Dulany delivered a second blow to the proprietary faction. He took the intellectual lead in the opposition to the Stamp Act. Other conservatives like Jonathan Boucher, Samuel Galloway, Edmund Key, Daniel of St. Thomas Jenifer, and Dr. George Steuart were willing to damn the Stamp Act and to expend "the last Drop of their blood before they would Consent to any such Slavery." The governor found himself almost alone in this crisis.[7]

Dulany's *Considerations* brought him fame and the title of the "Patriot Councillor," while at the same time dividing the leadership of the court party. He attacked the contention that taxation was a power Parliament enjoyed over the colonies. Taxation was held to be a function of the various colonial representative bodies wherein the electorate had a voice. He destroyed the argument of virtual representation saying that every inch of English soil had representation in Parliament, while not one inch of colonial soil was so represented. "The *Considerations,*" Lloyd Dulany proudly wrote his brother Walter, brought "Light where all was Darkness" among the citizens of Philadelphia.[8] Although its author remained outside the subsequent revolutionary movement, this pamphlet did much to break down the respect for order and stability that Daniel Dulany loved so well.

Considerations was part of the general response to what Marylanders thought was usurpation of authority. Before Parliament repealed the Stamp Act, several novel ingredients had been added to the Maryland political scene.

Foremost was the introduction of mob violence as a form of political pressure. On September 2, 1765, a mob of Annapolis rowdies, led by Samuel Chase and Matthias Hammond, gathered outside an uninhabited house recently leased by Zachariah Hood, stamp collector, pulled down the building, and forced Hood to resign his commission and leave the colony. Although Hood's lack of connections with the gentry undoubtedly contributed to his being so roughly treated, Governor Sharpe could not see how anyone could hold the office of stamp collector in the face of such widespread popular opposition to the act.[9]

This outbreak was shortly followed by another involving Matthias Hammond's cousin John Hammond and an officer of His Majesty's sloop *Hornet*. It would appear that as early as 1765 the Hammond family had garnered considerable support among the rowdiest elements of Annapolis.[10] Although the Hammonds were among the wealthiest of citizens in Anne Arundel County, their main political influence resulted from an ability to raise a mob on the slightest pretext. Their use of mass protest and violence or threats of force as a political instrument represented a radical departure from the past, when controversy had generally been conducted in a more genteel manner.

The result of such disturbances was that the Frederick County court remained open without the use of the hated stamps. Eventually the Sons of Liberty pressured the courts in Anne Arundel, Cecil, Queen Anne's, Somerset, and Worcester counties to open before word of repeal reached the colony. "The. Stamp Act," Carroll of Carrollton wrote Edmund Jenings in London, "continues to make as much noise as ever. The spirit of the people rather continues to increase than diminish."[11] Thus it was that all over the province mass action emerged as a force with which the established order had to contend.

Another novel ingredient was the emergence of extra-legal political organs to express discontent. Not only did the Assembly act against Parliament's stamp duties by supporting the Stamp Act Congress, but local protest groups such as the freemen, not freeholders, of Talbot County also declared that the principle of no taxation without representation was an inherent right of British subjects. Meeting at the courthouse, this group promised to risk "their lives and fortunes . . . by all lawful ways and means, to preserve and transmit to their posterity their rights and liberties." Here again was a form of political action deviating from the normal gentry control of politics. Moreover, the same men declared dissent from their views to be inimical to American rights and resolved to "detest, abhor, and hold in the utmost contempt" all persons connected with the stamp duties in any way. This proscription applied to any agent, "Stamp-pimp, informer or favorer of the said Act." Thus began one of the characteristic phenomena of the whole revolutionary movement— the demand for mass conformity to the radical line. To enforce such an aim required the services of the "inferior" elements of society. These *ad hoc* committees and their lower-class enforcers became an increasingly important factor on the revolutionary scene as time went on.[12]

Equally signficant was the introduction into Maryland politics of a new type of political figure, epitomized in the careers of Samuel Chase and the Hammonds. If Dulany's pamphlet supplied the rationale for the Stamp Act protest, their effective use of outdoor politics supplied the disrespect for authority necessary to discredit the whole basis of political sovereignty in the empire, the province, and the capital city.[13]

Because his father was an Anglican rector and because he had received a classical education from the Rev. Thomas Chase, Sam Chase had always been entitled to be designated a "gentleman." At the same time, he acquired patrician tastes when he had a plebeian income. Sam Chase never doubted that the few should rule the many (as long as he was one of the few), and he never deviated from his use of the many to support his rise to influence among the few. "Shackled to patrician ambitions, Chase bulled and bullied his way through life, channelling his physical vitality, his compulsion to act in endeavors more generally the province of the intellect. This was," Neil Strawser concluded, "essentially a rough, rugged, crude man, destined always to be a plebeian in the aristocratic social, economic and political worlds."[14]

Chase came to Annapolis to study law under John Hammond and John Hall in 1759. The association of Chase and Hall was to become an important factor in the politics of Annapolis and Anne Arundel County for many years. Chase soon entered the bar, married the beautiful but poor Anne Baldwin (an act not designed to insure success in a society where socially correct marriage was an asset of great financial and political importance), rode circuit with some of the Western Shore's best legal experts, and, in 1764, entered the political arena.[15]

For some time Dr. George Steuart, one of the proprietary leaders in the Lower House, held one of the two seats from Annapolis. With the backing of Carroll, barrister, Chase engaged in a bitter campaign to throw out the incumbent. He won easily. At the same time, Walter Dulany, who may have been a partner with Chase in the affair, kept the other seat. This began the rise of the middle class to power in the capital.[16]

Since, subsequent to this general election, Walter Dulany had accepted an appointive office, he had to run for his seat in a special election in 1765. Apparently any cooperation between Dulany and Chase had now disappeared. In his capacity as Mayor of Annapolis, Dulany presided at the Mayor's Court which judged the election. The mayor contested the qualifications of those voting against him and overruled all objections to the qualifications of those voting for him. The Lower House refused to seat the winner of this irregular election and ordered another election. This time Dulany apparently saw that his chances had dwindled to nothing; he therefore withdrew from the contest and Chase's law teacher, John Hall of the Vineyard, won without opposition.[17]

This was part of a general revolt of the tradesmen of the city against proprietary control. In the spring of 1765, two seats on the Common Council went to Isaac Harris, grocer, and John Campbell, tailor. The next year saw Jonas Green, printer, and William Roberts elevated to the Mayor's Court, while Samuel Chase and John Bullen were elected over conservative opposition to replace them on the Common Council. Thus, in three years, (1764-1766), Barrister Carroll, Chase, Hall, and a group of Annapolis tradesmen had taken control of the town government. It was now proved that in that part of the colony where the suffrage requirements were the lowest and getting to the polls the easiest, control of politics by the gentry could be modified.[18]

More obscure, but probably no less significant, was the rise to political influence of the two Hammond brothers. Sons of Philip and Rachel (Brice) Hammond, Matthias (1740-1786) and Rezin (1745-1809) Hammond were boys when their cantankerous father died in 1760. Philip Hammond was a long-time Anne Arundel County delegate and speaker of the House at the time of his death. He left a legacy of political influence, extensive landholdings, and coarse behavior that also characterized his sons. Although they had the land titles and the barrister credentials that would ordinarily entitle them to seats in the Assembly, competition from a large number of prominent men desiring the Anne Arundel and Annapolis seats—combined with their unpredictable personal temperaments—kept either of them from places of authority before 1773, when Matthias entered the House. There is some indication that they became closely associated with John Hall in the 1770s after Hall and Chase apparently clashed on several issues. The revolutionary movement pushed both to the fore, especially in the county assemblies, where their oratory and their friendship with the lower-class elements gave them influence not accorded them in the drawing rooms of the other gentry. It was they who attacked the ruling of the committee of observation in the *Peggy Stewart* affair, it was they who proved a thorn in the side of the gentry in the conventions of 1774-1776, and it was Rezin who was the only member of the county's delegation to the constitutional convention of 1776 who favored universal manhood suffrage. It was also Rezin who gathered about himself what his obituary called "a little warrior band," ready to do his bidding in whatever action he felt necessary to protect his "country's" interest. Charles Carroll of Carrollton proclaimed the Hammonds demagogues who "under the cloak of procuring" privileges for the populace introduced a levelling scheme by which they would profit. Carroll depicted these "selfish men" as leading the province toward "all the horrors of an ungovernable and revengeful democracy," which would be dyed in the blood of its "best citizens."[19]

The Hammonds were robust, virile, and crude, willing to enter the type of boxing matches and drinking bouts that would endear them to the masses. Although never allowed to share in the places of power in the convention's committees or on the Council of Safety, there can be little doubt that the Hammonds were important in the emerging revolutionary ferment despite the infrequent references to them in the extant epistles and documents of the periods. Theirs was the obscurity usually given to local political leaders who never sit in the official councils but whose actions nevertheless influence the course of events.

The emergence of these three men in Anne Arundel County was symptomatic of the emergence of their type elsewhere in the colony, especially on the Western Shore. In Baltimore County such men as Samuel Purviance, Jr., William Lux, Capt. Charles Ridgely, and Thomas Cockey Deye soon came to the fore. In Prince George's County, Walter Bowie's contentious personality began to make an impression. In general, however, political influence still rested with those controlling the drawing rooms of the major plantations and Annapolis townhouses.

Perhaps as significant as the emergence of these new political personalities was the notable change occurring in the motivation of the traditional country forces. Formerly, the court-country rivalry had been between the "ins" and the "outs." In 1756, so ardent a patriot as Stephen Bordley could be bought by proprietary forces with a few well-paying positions. A dozen years later this was not the case. Behind the governor's back, Lord Baltimore tried to carry into effect the proposals of Secretary Calvert that such positions be offered to country faction men to secure their loyalty to the government. Using John Morton Jordan as his agent, the proprietor offered Matthew Tilghman and his son-in-law Charles Carroll, barrister, influential public posts on His Lordship's Council. Their blunt refusal of the offer came as a slap in the face of Frederick Calvert. By declining these nominations, Tilghman and Carroll served notice that the country party represented more than envious longing for the fruits of patronage. Politics was no longer the "ins" against the "outs." Some members of the party were now willing to refuse any proprietary offers of lucrative posts in order to maintain a position of political independence from the proprietor. Such a refusal marks another step in the decline of the court party. Patronage was the principal device by which His Lordship had maintained support in Maryland. No man of the stature of Tilghman or Carroll subsequently accepted such appointments.[20]

Finally, during this period one begins to see a decline in the traditional deference shown the gentry by the rest of the freemen. A seemingly insignificant event in Trinity Parish, Charles County, illustrates this trend. For years the congregation had followed the English custom of recognizing social rank by reserving special pews for gentlemen and their families. When, in 1755, it was proposed to award pews by lot rather than by rank, the gentry protested, only to see themselves overruled at a mass meeting of the Protestant freeholders of the parish. In the years following the Great War for Empire, such disputes became more frequent in such widely scattered places as Chester Parish, Kent County, Prince George's Parish, Frederick County, St. Luke's Parish, Queen Anne's County, and elsewhere. As minor as these events may appear individually, they do indicate a slight shift in the established mode of conducting local affairs, and point to a possible change in the attitudes of the less affluent segment of society toward the gentry.[21]

Concurrent with this declining deference to one's social superiors within the colony was a declining respect toward things British. This was all part of what Prof. Edmund S. Morgan has called the "Puritan ethic," which caused many Americans to identify British society with vice and colonial society with virtue. As Trevor Colbourn aptly put it: "Virtue was considered as important to the body politic as virginity

to a young maiden. Americans were repeatedly told that they represented a last outpost of English freedom, that they were the last senti-
nels of English virtue." For Marylanders, expressions of these concepts came in reports like those of Charles Lath, who, after many
years as a merchant in the colony, returned to Scotland to find "the
present Race of Britons whose fathers nobly bled & died for Liberty, . . . so sunk & lost in Lusting Sloth & Effeminacy, as to be
ready to bow the neck to the yoke of slavery & bend the knee to
oppression and tyranny." Such reports must have compelled John
Beale Bordley (1727–1804) to tell his son, a student at Eton: "I
wish you may not be put off from your affection for your own country,
by growing prejudices, &c. You went away young; don't forget you
are a Buckskin; I hope you are an improved one; which is better
than to be a spoilt Englishman." In these small ways, the colonists'
decreasing respect for British life spread throughout Maryland.[22]

The Stamp Act crisis was the first of several incidents that would
wreck the court party. The use of mob violence, the transfer of political influence to extra-legal organization, the emergence of new political leaders, the reorientation of the country party, the decline in deference to established authority and tradition begun during the period
of reorganization of the empire: these constituted the opening shots
in a campaign that saw the final capitulation of the proprietary government. By the time of the Lower House elections of 1767, the court
party had lost all its support in the House of Delegates. The only
refuge of that faction lay in the Upper House, whose members were
appointed by the governor.[23]

In the midst of post-war disputes over imperial taxation and regulation came a series of problems concerning the Anglican Church. These
problems would also help to undermine proprietary support in the
colony. Although by its very establishment, the Church of England
appeared to be in an advantageous position, it was in considerable
trouble. There were at least four sources of conflict over the established church: (1) the lack of ecclesiastical or lay supervision of the
clergy; (2) the desire by local vestries to have some control over the
selection of rectors; (3) the rate of taxation necessary to support the
church; and (4) plural holding of rectorships by individual priests.[24]

The charter gave the Lord Proprietor the right to appoint the rectors but denied an effective power to discipline those unworthy of their calling. There were three solutions to the problem: (1) install a colonial bishop or suffragen bishop to supervise the priests; (2) institute a system of lay and clerical presbyteries in the province with disciplinary powers; (3) begin local congregational control of the church and its ministers. Only the first of these was within the tradition of the Church of England, but it was opposed by most colonists, who feared new encroachments upon their liberties. As a result, none of these plans reached fruition.[25]

Lord Baltimore compounded the problem by using the parish system as a reward for personal friendship rather than for religious piety. Despite the modern efforts of the Rev. Nelson W. Rightmyer to rehabilitate the reputations of these Anglican rectors, despite the fine work done by such priests as Jonathan Boucher, Thomas John Claggett, James Sterling, Thomas Bacon, Thomas Cradock, and David Love, and despite the fact that much criticism was often a conflict between "high church" and "low church" elements within Anglicanism, there was the ever-present accusation that a number of the clergy lacked the zeal, the ability, and the morals necessary for such a profession. The fact that the compulsory taxation which supported the church provided more than one benefice rivaling those of an English bishop did not help the reputation of the clergy in a land where so many lived in want.[26]

No man displayed a greater public disgust at the conduct of all too many Anglican clergymen than the Rev. Thomas Cradock. In 1753 he pleaded with the General Assembly to call for a bishop in the colony to discipline his fellow priests. The plea went unheeded because it offended too many interests—dissenting Protestants, proprietary perquisites, and widespread fears that the installation of an episcopacy would bring the corruption of privilege to the New World. In a series of "Maryland Eclogues in Imitation of Virgil's," which circulated privately, Cradock

> . . . found the Parsons here such Clods of Clay,
> . . . .
> [Who] resemble those at Home no more,
> Than Saints of Modern Days do Saints of yore. 11. 29, 33–34.

He found the name of Anglican clergyman "almost scandalous" in the province. Like the planters for whom they were to be examples, the clergy would

> . . . rant, drink, & smoke;
> Toast baudy Healths, or crack a smutty joak;
> . . . in Bumbo, or in Cyder swill.[27] 11. 86–88.

The conduct of all too many of the established clergy tended to bring not only their own profession, but also the entire proprietary establishment, into discredit.

Finding Cradock's plea for a bishop not an acceptable answer to their woes, laymen turned to other expedients. Vestrymen of Coventry Parish, Somerset and Worcester counties, led a spirited attack on the proprietor's right to appoint the rector of their parish. After the death of their disreputable parson, Nathaniel Whitaker, in 1766, the vestry petitioned Governor Sharpe to induct as priest of the parish the Rev. Thomas B. Chandler, a missionary of the Society for the Propagation of the Gospel. At the time a rector in Elizabeth, N. J., Chandler gave several sermons to a pleased congregation. But the governor jealously guarded the proprietary prerogative and sent the Rev. John Rosse to the parish. Rosse resigned his position in the face of concerted local opposition. Sharpe then sent the Rev. Philip Hughes.

Led by William Allen, Worcester County assemblyman, and other politicians who were its members, the vestry demanded the right to elect their rector since they, as the taxpayers, and not the proprietor, were the real patrons of the parish.[28] Supported by what Hughes described as "Swamp men and Shingle Makers, and the rest of their Banditti," the vestry terrorized the countryside and made it impossible for those favoring Hughes to express themselves, due to threats to their persons and property. Daniel Dulany wrote an opinion opposing the vestry's stand and advocating recourse "to legal compulsory Methods for the Punishment of Outrage." He said "that the Authority and Rights of his Lordship ought to be vigorously supported . . . [for] the Reins of Government are not to be surrendered into the Hands of any Vestry." Gov. Robert Eden inherited this three-year-old problem when he came to the colony. He appointed the Rev. Samuel Sloane to Coventry in 1769. Apparently taking a less dogmatic stand than Dulany had done, Eden received the approval of the vestry before acting, and Sloane met no opposition.[29]

High churchmanship is not a characteristic generally attributed to Maryland colonists. Yet this isolated parish on the banks of the Pocomoke asked to its pulpit America's most outspoken advocate of the episcopacy. The fact that the Rev. Dr. Chandler, author of *An Appeall to the Public in Behalf of the Church of England in America* (New York, 1767), even considered the offer demonstrates the economic inducements of Maryland's establishment to a New Englander living near his wife's relatives and his religious mentor, the Rev. Dr. Samuel Johnson of King's College. Impressed by the sobriety and piety of the Coventry laity, Chandler found his hope of becoming their rector frustrated by Governor Sharpe's insistence upon maintaining the proprietary prerogative.[30] While the vestry's request to name their rector smacks of Presbyterianism, their call to Chandler demonstrates hitherto unknown support of episcopalianism.

The Coventry Parish controversy represented a further deterioration in the traditional deference shown the proprietary will. Citizens now openly defied the desires of the proprietor, governor, and council. To insure the success of their task, the leadership turned to using lower class whites to terrorize those favoring the duly constituted authority. To some this incident signified the emergence of the "Swamp men and Shingle Makers" as a political force.

There are other reasons why the Coventry affair has a prominent place in the development of Maryland life and thought in the period. Probably none is more important than the fact that this event best represents, with its appeal to a higher law than the organic charter and statutes of the colony, the extent to which concepts of the Enlightenment had penetrated Maryland. Here, in an isolated corner of the province, far from the drawing rooms and libraries of the powerful gentry, came a cry for the social compact in behalf of local interest.[31]

This dramatic opposition in one of the outlying parishes reflected similar activities among the more affluent and influential parishioners of St. Anne's, Annapolis, in a dispute with their rector. In 1766, Frederick Calvert sent his close friend, the Rev. Bennet Allen, to the province, with instructions to Governor Sharpe that Allen be given one or two lucrative parishes. When St. Anne's did not provide the income that Allen thought he deserved, Sharpe gave him the adjoining vacancy in St. James Parish, Herring Creek. Pluralism, however, violated the 1702 establishing act unless it was approved by both vestries. Allen's incompetence attracted the attention of both court and country partisans. Led by such men as Walter Dulany, Brice Thomas Beale Worthington, and Thomas Johnson, Jr., the St. Anne's vestry refused to approve the dual rectorship. Worthington and Johnson, also delegates in the Lower House, and Dulany, a councilor, threatened to bring the whole issue before the Assembly. Governor Sharpe feared that this outright violation of existing law might be enough spark "to kindle a new Flame in the Country that will not be soon extinguish't." The death of Thomas Bacon allowed Sharpe to dispose of Allen by appointing him to Bacon's wealthy benefice. Although the vestry of All Saints', Frederick County, disapproved of Allen also, the recalcitrant parson broke into his new church, installed himself in the office, hired two curates to perform his duties, and retired to Philadelphia to live off the £ 1,300 sterling income provided by the taxes imposed on the hapless citizens of the frontier county.[32]

Combine the Coventry controversy and the Allen affair with the suspected, but unproved, murder of a slave by the Rev. Richard Brown of King & Queen Parish, St. Mary's County, and there was enough disturbance to unite the usually warring court and country factions behind a proposed sweeping reform of the whole establishment. Sponsored by three vestrymen already affected by these cases— William Allen of Coventry and Thomas Johnson and Walter Dulany of St. Anne's— and joined by such men as James Hollyday, Thomas Ringgold, Sr., Edward and Matthew Tilghman, Samuel Chase, William Paca, and Daniel Dulany, a supplementary act to the 1702 establishing act sailed through the 1768 Assembly. The bill, not approved until 1771 because the governor refused to sign such novel legislation until Lord Baltimore assented, established a commission consisting of the governor, three Anglican clergymen, and three Anglican laymen to investigate charges of ministerial irregularity made to the governor by the vestries. The board could admonish or suspend a curate, or totally deprive a guilty parson of his benefice.[33]

Of course the clergy knew what such a commission meant. It transformed their church from an "episcopal" to a "presbyterian" one.

Three priests—Thomas John Claggett, Henry Addison, and Hugh Neill— each wrote the Bishop of London urging that he oppose the creation of the commission form of church government. None of them doubted the necessity of a means of calling irregular clergymen to account; they only demanded what they thought was the true episcopal discipline of their faith. Because of ecclesiastical opposition to the proposed law in London, this commission never functioned in the province. Claggett lived to be consecrated the first Bishop of Maryland.[34]

The Coventry controversy, the Allen affair, and the proposed commission were attempts to cope with particular problems within the established church. By the 1770s, several members of the country party assaulted the legitimacy of the establishment itself. Their contention, that the 1702 law establishing the church was invalid, was legally untenable. Nevertheless, it became politically inexpedient for persons to remain on the vestries. Robert Tyler, assemblyman of Prince George's County, resigned his position on the Queen Anne's Parish vestry in 1772 on grounds that the law was "totally void." St. Paul's Parish faced a mass of resignations and refusals to serve during 1772–1773. These resignations included those of Richard Tilghman Earle, Queen Anne's County delegate and thrice-previously elected vestryman, James Earle and William Hemsley, former vestrymen, as well as Nathaniel Wright, Robert Browne, and John Kerr. Chase and Paca, among a number who were called "a few meddling, half-learned, popular lawyers of Maryland" by Boucher, challenged the "Tory priest" to a long, vigorous "paper war" in the *Maryland Gazette* over the whole question of the established church and the episcopate.[35]

Boucher, looking back at the pre-revolutionary agitation, noted that this anti-establishment activity of 1765–1775 was inextricably linked to the assault on all sources of legitimate authority in the colony. He wrote in 1797:

That the American opposition to the episcopacy was at all connected with that still more serious one so soon afterwards set up against civil government, was not indeed generally apparent at the time; but it is now indisputable, as it also is that the former contributed not a little to render the latter successful.[36]

There can be little doubt that the established church helped to bring into disrepute the whole proprietary establishment. Whatever the fine work done by most of the clergy, the actions of a significant minority, and the failure of Lord Baltimore to do anything about them, discredited all. The misconduct of all too many clergymen brought into disrespect all persons occupying positions of authority and prestige. If such attitudes were common towards the ecclesiastical officers, they could easily be transferred to the civil officers of His Lordship's government.

One important attack on civil authority was due to an indiscretion on the part of Governor Eden, which resulted in the final demise of the court party as a political force outside the Upper House. In 1770, the tobacco inspection act of 1763 came up for renewal. This law regulated the fees paid to civil and clerical officers, set the rates of commutation at which tobacco could be converted into currency, and established a system for tobacco inspection and grading. With the increase in population, the income from fees to various officers rose rapidly in the last decades of the proprietary period. The burgesses decided that the incomes of these officers were excessive. The councilors, who benefited most from these lucrative offices, took a stand designed to insure their income. When the 1770 legislative session ended, no action had been taken on the problem, and Governor Eden issued a proclamation continuing the old inspection law and fee rates. [37]

The proprietary faction's greed, foolishness, and insolence now became more evident than before. At one point, its members tried to bargain with the country faction by saying they would agree to a limit on the incomes of the more important offices of £ 600 sterling a year. [38]

Actually the Fee Proclamation caused little stir in the colony's political arena until after a 1771 session of the Assembly resulted in another stalemate. Seeing the hand of his arch-rival, Daniel Dulany, guiding the governor, Carroll of Carrollton announced: "War is now declared between Govern[men]t and the People, or rather between a few placemen, the real enemies to Govern[men]t, and all the inhabitants of this Province." Conflict over who was the heir to the colony after Frederick Calvert's death postponed any discussion on the issue during 1772, but with new elections due the following spring, debate over the Fee Proclamation emerged in the *Gazette*. [39]

Dulany provoked an attack upon his views when he defended the proclamation in the *Maryland Gazette,* January 7, 1773. Carroll of Carrollton, making what must have been the most important decision of his political career and one of the most momentous in the annals of American Catholicism, cast aside any inhibitions which the legal restrictions against political activity might have imposed on him and engaged in an assault upon the governor's action. The protagonists, using the pseudonyms of "Antilon" and "First Citizen," waged one of the longest and most popular public debates in colonial history. Enthusiasm was such that people crowded the Greens' small printing office each Thursday to buy the paper fresh off the press.

As "Antilon," Dulany had the entire British legal tradition on his side and used his arguments effectively. The "First Citizen," obviously more influenced by the rationalism of his education in France than by his instruction at London's Inns of Court, took a natural rights position. The acrid conflict worsened when Dulany revived latent anti-Catholicism by denouncing Carroll's opinions as "papistic." This personal abuse did not meet with the usual anti-Catholic response among the populace.[40]

Attorney General John Hammond now entered the fray in behalf of the governor. His learned comment claimed that the governor "was legally and constitutionally invested under the charter of our province, confirmed by act of assembly; with all the necessary prerogative" to issue the proclamation and "the duty of *his* station then required the exercise of" that power to protect the citizens from exorbitant demands by the officers. To this came the equally learned and painfully long reply of three of the province's most active patriots, Johnson, Chase, and Paca. Their five-and-a-half page essay constituted a powerful argument (probably of better legal validity than Carroll's "First Citizen" letters) against the proclamation.[41]

Following the suggestion of "A Voter" of Baltimore County, the 1773 Assembly agreed to an inspection law without any provision for the fee payment. The legislators agreed that inspection was necessary if the price of tobacco shipped from the colony was not to continue in a depressed state. Since the solution represented a major concession to the proprietary forces, it continued to foster resentment against the existing government.[42]

One of the most remarkable features of this affair was the fact that Dulany and Hammond wasted their considerable talents defending a position, no matter how legally valid, which had been previously conceded by the Board of Trade. The Board ruled in a similar dispute in North Carolina in 1761 that the "most reasonable, effectual and constitutional Method of settling Fees" was by statutory regulations, not by executive edict.[43] The archaic nature of the Maryland charter and the antiquated attitudes of its defenders were never more apparent than in the battle over the Fee Proclamation.

The results of the fee controversy were far-reaching. First and most important was the decline of Dulany's popularity, which had been greatly enhanced by his masterful treatise against the Stamp Act. As early as 1771, Carroll claimed that although Dulany's "retainers puff him off, & talk much of his vast influence, it is pretty well known to be greatly on the decline; the loss of his popularity chagrins him to the quick, & the improbability of regaining it adds to his mortification." His defense of the Fee Proclamation continued this decline until Carroll described him as one waiting to see which way the tide would turn and then swimming with the current, until the "union of all America has swallowed him up in the great vortex." Carroll elaborated his metaphor thus: ". . . he follows its motion, but not daring to be the first mover, nor possessing a temper sufficiently intrepid to guide its course; he is carried away with the Whirlwind, he does not ride on it, nor directs the storm."[44]

Dulany's departure from the center of the political stage left the court party without its most brilliant advocate. The former "patriot councillor's" ill-advised support of the proclamation placed him, in the minds of his countrymen, on the far right of the political spectrum. As the court faction left the scene, a host of country party leaders emerged to take their places. After 1773, all political battles were within the old country faction, which was torn between right and left wings—between the whigs and the democrats.

Leading the right wing of this new alignment was Charles Carroll of Carrollton. The arguments of the "First Citizen" brought him to the forefront of public attention. Parson Boucher, who tried valiantly to enlist the Roman Catholics in the loyalist cause with a sermon

"On the Toleration of Papists," conceded that Carroll's espousal of whiggism "seemed to settle the wavering disposition of the Catholics of Maryland." Between 1774 and the signing of the Declaration, Carroll became an active member of various revolutionary committees, a delegate to the Provincial Convention, a member of the Council of Safety, and finally a member of the Continental Congress. His risky decision to back the Revolution placed the fate of his religious group in the hands of a Protestant-dominated popular movement providing no guarantees of religious freedom. The move was one of the most significant developments on the road to minority rights, not only in Maryland, but in America generally.[45]

If in polite society Carroll assumed a leading role in the Revolution, other elements also came to the surface and presented their demands. The emergence of those previously denied a voice in the colony's affairs was one of the dominant features of Maryland politics in the last few years before war broke out. We have already noticed the use of mob action in the destruction of the stamp collector's house and in the Coventry affair. Each new imperial regulation was followed by more of this type of popular expression.

Passage of the Townshend Acts resulted in the formation of associations by the colonists designed to stop the importation of British goods until the acts were repealed. The committees set up to enforce this association had no legal power, of course, but their influence went far beyond that of any legal force on the continent. When accusations of violating the agreements were made against T. C. Williams & Co. of Annapolis, the proprietor claimed the censure cast on his company "was premature, and serves to cast public Odium particularly on us." It was the "public odium" that the merchants feared, for it could entail great financial loss to them.[46]

The climax of this type of opposition came in 1770 when the Annapolis committee turned back the brigantine *Good Intent,* containing £ 10,000 sterling in cargo consigned to James Dick and Anthony Stewart. Governor Eden admitted his inability to control the situation. His only excuse to the Board of Trade was that similar incidents were occurring in other provinces.[47]

The *Good Intent* affair was the highwater mark in the use of Daniel Dulany's tactic of non-importation to secure colonial liberties. The significance of the associations formed to enforce these agreements was that they required the cooperation of small merchants, mechanics, and farmers who had previously not held any important place on the political scene. Such men demanded action against any form of imperial regulation which threatened their livelihoods.

Concurrent with the Townshend Duties came a revision in the imperial customs service and a transfer of its legal enforcement to the admiralty courts. John Williams, Customs Inspector General for America, reported to his superiors in 1770 that the entire custom collecting system in Maryland needed reformation. Some of these alterations were necessary jurisdictional changes, such as providing a stricter delineation of district boundaries and the establishment of a Patapsco district centered in Baltimore to take care of the growing trade of that city. More important was the introduction of customs officials who owed their positions to royal, not proprietary, favor and whose obvious intent was to use the offices for their personal profit. The fact that jurisdiction in customs cases left the local courts for the stricter admiralty courts also incited local opposition to the new system.[48]

Upon assuming their new posts, the royal inspectors found strenuous disapproval of their presence. Samuel Purviance, Jr. (c. 1728– c. 1788), Baltimore merchant and leading patriot of the city, ordered the skipper of the sloop *Speedwell* to unload some of his cargo before Robert Moreton, Baltimore customs officer, inspected it. Apparently Purviance had secured Moreton's permission to do the unloading, although this technically violated the customs regulations. Moreton used his oral permission as a device to entrap the Baltimore merchant, because he subsequently went aboard, found that the captain had broken bulk before securing the necessary entry papers, and declared the remaining cargo forfeit, making the cargo and vessel subject to royal confiscation. This was a racketeering tactic similar to that employed by customs officials in Boston and Charleston against "patriotic" merchants John Hancock and Henry Laurens. But unlike Hancock and Laurens, who fought confiscation in the courts, Purviance took to the streets. After Moreton left the city for Annapolis in an effort to get some legal backing, on the night of April 30, 1773 "a great number of Merchants and Masters of Vessels . . . [t]heir faces being black'd and disguised in Sailors Jackets and Trousers," tarred and feathered two of the assistants of the customs inspector and broke into Moreton's home in a vain search for him. Mrs. Moreton wrote to her husband that he should stay away from the city because the mob was conspiring to murder him. Later, Moreton fled the province because the culprits offered £ 22 for his capture. Although George Steuart, Judge of the Court of the Admiralty in Maryland, found Purviance guilty of violating the law, Governor Eden was so disgusted at the collector's action that he refused to accept the third of the crown's seizure that was rightfully his. The other Marylanders involved in the case—judge, attorney general, and defense lawyers—refused to take the fees that the defendant rightfully owed them. The duplicity and avarice of His Majesty's revenue officer in this instance caused Eden to label Moreton's behavior "as being too much *Satan* like, in first giving leave to land, & afterward taking advantage of that step, of which he was the only cause, to the destruction of the Vessel to the owners."[49]

Thus, at the same time that respect for the proprietary system was disintegrating in Maryland, His Majesty's government had declined so much in public esteem that one of its officers could be publicly forced to leave the colony as a result of mob violence. And, although they obviously participated in the incident, the merchants and masters of Baltimore felt it necessary to defy law and order and to include lower-class elements in the decision-making process. This incident also points out the glaring inability of both the proprietary and the royal governments to support their officials at a time when the British government was attempting to become more strict in its regulation of the empire.

The extent of this weakness became apparent in Maryland when Parliament enacted the Coercive Acts to suppress Boston after its famous Tea Party. Frederick Green's *Gazette* continued to incite popular unrest over the problem by printing articles taken from Boston, Charleston, Philadelphia, and New York papers, showing their opposition to the various parliamentary infringements upon colonial rights and liberties. On May 25, 1774, the people of Annapolis gathered to pass a unanimous resolution to support the suffering citizens of Boston by joining in an intra- and inter-colonial system of associations designed to stop all exports to Great Britain, to halt any suits for debt by Britons against Marylanders, and to refuse trade with any colony not joining in this common effort. They appointed Hall, Johnson, Paca, Chase, Barrister Carroll, and Matthias Hammond as a local committee of correspondence and observation to coordinate efforts with the rest of the province. Similar associations were formed spontaneously throughout the province, such as the ones which met at Brascup's Tavern in Easton, Talbot County. Committees in that county consisted of such notables as Edward Lloyd IV, Robert Goldsborough IV, Jacob Hindman, Robert Lloyd Nicols, James Lloyd Chamberline, Matthew Tilghman, Pollard Edmundson, Nicholas Thomas, and the Rev. John Gordon.[50]

In the political vacuum left by the eclipse of proprietary authority and the failure of the royal government to assert itself in the midst of a rising colonial opposition to parliamentary control, Marylanders established a system of extra-legal county meetings, committees of observation and correspondence, provincial conventions, and a council of safety. Until the autumn of 1775, the revolutionary movement was in the hands of the conservatives. Men of property and propriety headed the committees and participated in the mob actions. Moderation reigned. A large number of Annapolitans, led by Lloyd Dulany and James Tilghman, could publicly protest a resolution calling for the end of suits in behalf of British creditors. Toleration of legitimate criticism of revolutionary trends continued to be public policy.[51]

The time for moderation quickly passed. To be effective, the American response had to be united. To bring about this unity required the use of coercion upon those not cooperating with the revolutionary movement. And to succeed, coercion necessitated the use of violence or threats of violence. The demise of the court party and the proprietary government left little to prevent the swing to the left. Radicalism became an increasingly important factor during the next two years.

NOTES

1. L. H. Gipson, *The British Empire Before the Revolution,* 15 vols., (New York: A. A. Knopf, 1936-1970), VI, pp. 30-32, P. H Giddens, "The French and Indian

War in Maryland," *Maryland Historical Magazine,* XXX (1935), pp. 281–310; *Archives of Maryland,* LII, pp. xi– xxii; J. V. L. McMahon, *An Historical View of the Government of Maryland* (Baltimore: Lucas & Deavor, 1831), pp. 296–393; A. M. Schlesinger, "Maryland's Share in the Last Intercolonial War," *Maryland Historical Magazine,* VII (1912), p. 120.

2. Schlesinger, "Maryland's Share," p. 123; *Archives of Maryland,* LII, pp. xxii–xxiii; W. S. Hanna, *Benjamin Franklin and Pennsylvania Politics* (Stanford, Calif.: Stanford University Press, 1964), pp. ix, 133; D. Dulany, "Maryland Gossip in 1755," *Pennsylvania Magazine of History and Biography,* III (1879), p. 148; T. Ringgold to J. Hollyday, September 27, 1755, G. T. Hollyday, "Biographical Memoir of James Hollyday," *Pennsylvania Magazine of History and Biography,* VII (1883), p. 431; D. Dulany, "Military and Political Affairs in the Middle Colonies in 1755," *Pennsylvania Magazine of History and Biography,* III (1879), p. 25; H. Sharpe to Gov. R. H. Morris of Pa., April 24, 1756, *Archives of Maryland,* VI, p. 391.

3. T. Cradock, Sermon on Patriotism, Luke 11:17, Maryland Diocesan Archives; C. A. Barker, *The Background of the Revolution in Maryland,* (New Haven: Yale University Press, 1940), pp. 241– 247; *Archives of Maryland,* LV, pp. xxiii–xxxii, 119–129. Exact proof that Cradock delivered the sermon before the General Assembly is not available. Since the session was in Baltimore, the *Maryland Gazette* carried little information about the event and the sermon would not have been delivered during an official session but rather during an unrecorded church service. He spoke of "chance" having brought him from "the narrow circle of his own Parish" and of the "late fatal event of the taking of Oswego" by the French which occurred August 13– 14, 1756. Cradock also wrote two versions of this sermon (the only such repetition in the entire Cradock collection in the Maryland Diocesan Archives), which may indicate preparation for possible publication. With few exceptions, all printed sermons in colonial Maryland were those preached before the General Assembly.

4. *Archives of Maryland,* LV, pp. xxvi–xxviii, 445–446, 455–456, 457–458; H. Sharpe to C. Calvert, August 28, 1756, to Baltimore, November 3, 1756, *Archives of Maryland,* IX, pp. 257, 295; Sharpe to Calvert, May 11, 1762, *Archives of Maryland,* XIV, pp. 52– 53, *Archives of Maryland,* LVI, pp. xiv–xv, xxxvii–xxxviii; LVIII, pp. x–xi, xv–xvi, 113–114; LIX, pp. 358, 364–368, 388–389, 397, 415–416, 456; McMahon, *Historical View,* pp. 308–312.

5. H. Sharpe to C. Calvert. December 15, 1764, *Archives of Maryland,* XIV, p. 186; LXIII, p. xi.

6. "Sharpe's Confidential Report on Maryland, 1765," A. C. Land, editor, *Maryland Historical Magazine,* XLIV (1949), pp. 127–128; C. Calvert to H. Sharpe, January 16, 1765, *Archives of Maryland,* XXI, pp. 558–559.

7. Dulany, "Maryland Gossip," p. 148; "Sharpe's Confidential Report," Land, editor, p. 126; H. Sharpe to C. Calvert, May 8, 1764, *Archives of Maryland,* XIV, p. 160; J. Boucher to J. James, December 9, 1765, "Letters of the Rev. Jonathan Boucher," *Maryland Historical Magazine,* VII (1912), p. 295; "Journal of a French Traveler in the Colonies, 1765," *American Historical Review,* XXVII (1921), pp. 71– 73; L. C. Wroth, *A History of Printing in Colonial Maryland, 1686-1776* (Baltimore:

The Typothetae, 1922), pp. 83–84; "Four Daniel of St. Thomas Jenifer Letters," S. S. Bradford, editor, *Maryland Historical Magazine,* LVI (1961), p. 294.

8. E. S. Morgan & H. M. Morgan, *The Stamp Act Crisis: Prologue to Revolution* (Chapel Hill: University of North Carolina Press, 1953), pp. 71–87; L. Dulany to [W. Dulany], March 20, 1768, Dulany Papers, Maryland Historical Society.

9. Sharpe to Baltimore, September 10. 1765, *Archives of Maryland,* XIV, pp. 223–224; "Sharpe's Confidential Report," pp. 126–127; Sharpe to Gage, September 6, 1765, Sharpe to Gage, September 23, 1765, *Archives of Maryland,* pp. 222, 228–229; Gage to Sharpe, September 16, 1765, Vol. 42, Gage Papers, William L. Clements Library. Note how this incident and the other innovations on the Maryland political scene after 1765 are similar to those observed by Morgan & Morgan, *Stamp Act,* chap. 16.

10. Sharpe to Gage, September 23, 1765, *Archives of Maryland,* XIV, pp. 226–227, 229.

11. Carrollton to Jenings, September 5, 1765, K. M. Rowland, *The Life of Charles Carroll of Carrollton, 1737–1832,* 2 vols., (New York: G. P. Putman's Sons, 1898), I, pp. 73–74; Sharpe to Baltimore, October 3, 1765, *Archives of Maryland,* XIV, p. 232; P. H. Giddens, "Maryland and the Stamp Act Controversy," *Maryland Historical Magazine,* XXVII (1952), pp. 79–98.

12. O. Tilghman, *History of Talbot County, Maryland: 1661–1861,* 2 vols., (Baltimore: Williams & Wilkins, 1915), II, pp. 44–45.

13. N. E. Strawser, "Samuel Chase and the Annapolis Paper War," *Maryland Historical Magazine,* LVII (1962), p. 178.

14. N. E. Strawser, "The Early Life of Samuel Chase" (M. A. thesis, George Washington University, 1958), pp. 5–7.

15. Strawser, "Early life," pp. 28–30, 41–51, 60–66.

16. H. W. Sellers, "Charles Willson Peale, Artist-Soldier," *Pennsylvania Magazine of History and Biography,* XXXVIII (1914), pp. 261–262; *Maryland Gazette,* November 29, 1764; *Archives of Maryland,* LIX, pp. xix.

17. *Archives of Maryland,* LIX, pp. xii, xix, lxiv–lxv, 73; Annapolis City Records, Maryland Hall of Records, III, pp. 60–67, 68.

18. *Maryland Gazette,* June 19, 1766; Strawser, "Samuel Chase," pp. 182–185, 192–193; F. F. Beirne, "Sam Chase, 'Disturber,' " *Maryland Historical Magazine,* LVII (1962), p. 89.

19. Strawser, "Early Life," pp. 250–256; *Maryland Gazette,* August 22, 1776, September 6, 1809; J. D. Warfield, *The Founders of Anne Arundel and Howard Counties, Maryland* (Baltimore: Kohn & Pollock, 1905), pp. 180–181; Carrollton to C. Carroll, August 20, 1716, Charles Carroll of Annapolis Papers, Maryland Historical Society; see also the account of the *Peggy Stewart* affair in chap. 7, pp. 143–145.

20. Sharpe to Baltimore, October 31, November 28, 1768, *Archives of Maryland,* XIV, pp. 550–551, 557; T. Ringgold to J. Hollyday, June 5, 1756, Hollyday, "Biographical Memoir," p. 438.

21. J. N. Barry, "Trinity Parish, Charles County," *Maryland Historical Magazine,* I (1906), p. 325; Vestry Proceedings, Prince George's Parish, Kent County, February

18, 1766; Vestry Proceedings, Prince George's Parish, Frederick County, August 4, September 1, 1772; Vestry Proceedings, St. Luke's Parish, Queen Anne's County, January 7 & 22, 1773, all at the Maryland Hall of Records. For a detailed discussion of the pew controversies, see G. E. Hartdagen, "The Anglican Vestry in Colonial Maryland" (Ph.D. dissertation, Northwestern University, 1965), pp. 105–114, and his "The Anglican Vestry in Colonial Maryland: A Study in Corporate Responsibility, *Historical Magazine of the Protestant Episcopal Church,* XL (1971), pp. 461–467.

22. Edmund S. Morgan, "The Puritan Ethnic and the American Revolution," *William and Mary Quarterly,* Series 3, XXIV (1967), pp. 3–43; H. Trevor Colbourn, *The Lamp of Experience: Whig History and the Intellectual Origins of the American Revolution* (Chapel Hill: University of North Carolina Press, 1965), p. 187; C. Lath to H. Hollyday, September 25, 1769, Maryland Colony & Revolutionary Papers, Duke University Library; E. B. Gibson, *Biographical Sketches of the Bordley Family of Maryland* (Philadelphia: Henry B. Ashmead, 1865), p. 86.

23. *Archives of Maryland,* LIX, pp. xix; LXI, pp. ix, xlii–xliii.

24. S. Ervin, "The Established Church of Colonial Maryland," *Historical Magazine of the Protestant Episcopal Church,* XXIV (1955), pp. 269–270: N. W. Rightmyer, "The Anglican Church in Maryland: Factors Contributory to the American Revolution," *Church History,* XIX (1950), pp. 197–198; N. W. Rightmyer, *Maryland's Established Church* (Baltimore: The Church Historical Society for the Diocese of Maryland, 1956), pp. 97–106.

25. Rightmyer, "Anglican Church," pp. 197–198; Ervin, "Established Church," pp. 269–270; W. S. Hudson, "The Quest for Freedom Within the Church in Colonial America," *Journal of Church and State,* III (1961), pp. 10–14; C. E. Jones, "Congregation, Magistrate, and King: A Puritan Pattern for the Church of England," *Journal of Church and State,* VI (1964), pp. 288–295; W. W. Sweet, "The Role of the Anglicans in the American Revolution," *Huntington Library Quarterly,* XI (1947), pp. 69–70; H. Hammersley to H. Sharpe, November 10, 1767, *Archives of Maryland,* XIV, p. 431; "Eighteenth Century Maryland as Portrayed in the 'Itinerant Observations' of Edward Kimber," *Maryland Historical Magazine,* LI (1956), pp. 323–324.

26. N. W. Rightmyer, "The Character of the Anglican Clergy of Colonial Maryland," *Maryland Historical Magazine,* XLIV (1949), pp. 229–250; J. Boucher to J. James, March 9, 1767, June 8, August 25, 1770, July 10, 1772, "Letters," *Maryland Historical Magazine,* VII (1912), p. 340, VIII (1913), pp. 169, 171, 176, 181; T. G. Claggett to W. Butler, July 1, 1768; G. B. Utley, *The Life and Times of Thomas John Claggett* (Chicago: R. R. Donnelley & Sons, 1913), p. 20.

27. "Thomas Cradock's Sermon on the Governance of Maryland's Established Church," D. C. Skaggs, editor, *William and Mary Quarterly,* Series 3, XXVII (1970), pp. 631–653; [T. Cradock], "Maryland Eclogues in Imitation of Virgil's, by Jonathan Spritly, Esqr., Formerly a Worthy Member of the Assembly, Revis'd & Corrected by his Friend Sly Boots," Ecloga No. 1, Cradock Papers, Maryland Historical Society; D. C. Skaggs, "Thomas Cradock and the Chesapeake Golden Age," *William and Mary Quarterly,* Series 3, XXX (1973), pp. 93–116. See Dr. Alexander Hamilton. *History of*

the Tuesday Club (Evergreen House, Johns Hopkins University, Baltimore), February 20, 1753, November 5, 1754.

28. *Archives of Maryland,* XXXII, pp. 222–224; Rightmyer, *Maryland's,* pp. 97–100.

29. *Archives of Maryland,* XXXII, pp. 223–224; Vestry of Coventry Parish to H. Sharpe, January ?, 1767, *Archives of Maryland,* XIV, pp. 363–369; Rightmyer, *Maryland's,* p. 100; see also *Archives of Maryland,* LXI, pp. lxii, 513–517; LXII, pp. 463–466

30. Chandler to Bishop Richard Terrick, October 21, 1767, Fulham Papers, Lambeth Palace Library, American Colonial Section, Library of Congress, VI, pp. 164–167; C. Bridenbaugh, *Mitre and Sceptre: Trans-atlantic Faiths, Ideas, Personalities, and Politics, 1689–1772* (New York: Oxford University Press, 1962), pp. 204–206, 289–307.

31. C. A. Barker, "Maryland Before the Revolution: Society and Thought," *American Historical Review,* XLVI (1940), pp. 16–17

32. Rightmyer, *Maryland's,* pp. 101–104; J. Boucher to J. James, June 8, 1770, "Letters," p. 169; A. W. Werline, *Problems of Church and State in Maryland During the Seventeenth and Eighteenth Centuries* (South Lancaster, Mass.: The College Press, 1948), pp. 93–97; H. Sharpe to H. Hamersley, November 27, 1767 to Baltimore, February 9, May 15, & 27, 1768, *Archives of Maryland,* XIV, pp. 460–461, 465, 494, 497; A. Clem, "The Vestries and Local Government in Colonial Maryland," *Historical Magazine of the Protestant Episcopal Church,* XXXI (1962), pp. 227–229; J. Fischer, "Bennett Allen, Fighting Parson," *Maryland Historical Magazine,* XXXVIII (1943), pp. 299–322, XXXIX (1944), pp. 49–72.

33. *Archives of Maryland,* LXIII, pp. xxxiii–xxxiv, 290–293; LXI, pp. lxix–lxxi, 304–305, 315, 319, 361, 383, 400, 405, 406, 412, 420; Rightmyer, *Maryland's,* pp. 104–108.

34. H. Neill to Bishop of London, September 20, 1768, T. J. Claggett to same, September 20, 1769, H. Addison to same. October 24, 1769, *Historical Collections Relating to the American Colonial Church,* W. S. Perry, editor, 4 vols. (Hartford: Privately Printed, 1870–1878), IV, pp. 337–341; see also C. Bridenbaugh, *Mitre and Sceptre,* pp. 315–316.

35. Vestry Proceedings, Queen Anne's Parish, Prince George's County, November 17, 1772, Maryland Hall of Records, pp. 333, 341; Vestry Proceedings, St. Paul's Parish, Queen Anne's County, 1772–1773, Maryland Hall of Records, pp. 101–103, 107, 110–113, for samples of the Boucher, Chase, Paca quarrel, see *Maryland Gazette,* December 31, 1772, January 14, February 4, April 1 & 29, May 6, 1773; for other arguments, see *Maryland Journal,* August 20, November 6, 1773; J. Boucher, *A View of the Causes and Consequences of the American Revolution* (London: G. G. & J. Robinson, 1797), pp. 89–150, quote 223n.

36. Boucher, *A View,* p. 150.

37. Rightmyer, "Anglican Church," pp. 196–197; C. A. Barker, *Background of the Revolution,* pp. 344–348; Boucher, *A View,* pp. 202–240.

38. C. Carroll to Carrollton, November 2, 1770, "Extracts from the Carroll Papers," *Maryland Historical Magazine,* XIII (1918), pp. 69- 70.

39. Carrollton to Carroll, bar., December 3, 1771, "Lost Copy-Book of Charles Carroll of Carrollton," J. D. G. Paul, editor, *Maryland Historical Magazine,* XXXII (1937), p. 210.

40. Dulany's articles appeared in the *Maryland Gazette,* January 7, February 18, April 8, June 3, 1773, and Carroll's on February 4, March 11, May 6, July 1, 1773; Barker, *Background,* pp. 351-354; B. C. Steiner, *Life and Administration of Sir Robert Eden* (Johns Hopkins University Studies, Series XVI, Baltimore, 1908), pp. 64- 68; T. Ringgold to S. Galloway, March 15, 1773, Galloway, Maxcy, Markoe Papers, Library of Congress, XII; C. Carroll to Carrollton, March 17, 1773, "Extracts," p. 368; A. C. Land, *The Dulanys of Maryland* (Baltimore: Maryland Historical Society, 1955), pp. 301- 307.

41. Hammond, *Maryland Gazette,* July 29, 1773; Chase, Johnson, Paca, *Maryland Gazette,* September 9, 1773.

42. *Maryland Journal,* August 20, 1773; *Archives of Maryland,* LXIV, pp. xv-xviii, 151-192.

43. J. P. Greene, *The Quest for Power* (Chapel Hill: University of North Carolina Press, 1963), pp. 148, 167-168; McMahon, *Historical View,* pp. 380-396.

44. Carrollton to C. Carroll, bar., August 9, 1771, "Lost Copy-Book," Paul, editor, p. 200; Carrollton to C. Carroll, October 27, 1774, "Extracts," p. 40.

45. Boucher, *A View,* pp. 241-293, quote 242; C. Carroll to Carrollton, March 17, 1773, "Extracts," pp. 368-369; *Maryland Gazette,* May 27, June 17, 1773; Rowland, *Life,* I, pp. 132-135, 178, 180, 186, 197.

46. McMahon, *Historical View,* pp. 375-378; *Archives of Maryland,* LXII, pp. xi-xii, 457-462; *Maryland Gazette,* June 7, 1770.

47. R. Eden to Ld. Hillsborough, August 7, 1770, "Aspinwall Papers," *Collections of the Massachusetts Historical Society,* 4th Series, Vols. IX-X, (Boston, 1871), X, pp. 624- 625; Land, *Dulanys,* pp. 287-288; Barker, *Background,* pp. 324-325.

48. "Papers Relating to the Officers of the Customs in North America," *Maryland Historical Magazine,* XXVII (1932), pp. 231- 239; October 19, 1769, W. Eddis, *Letters from America* (London: The Author, 1792), pp. 25- 26.

49. *Archives of Maryland,* LXIII, pp. 425- 436; O. M. Dickerson, *The Navigation Acts and the American Revolution* (Philadelphia: University of Pennsylvania Press, 1951), pp. 208-256.

50. *Maryland Gazette,* January 6 & 13, April 7, May 5 & 26, 1774; Tilghman, *History,* II, pp. 54, 65-67; *Maryland Journal,* November 16, 1774.

51. *Maryland Gazette,* June 2, 1774.

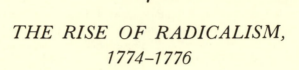

Chapter

7

THE RISE OF RADICALISM,
1774-1776

The demise of the court party occurred when other factors seriously affected the maintenance of political stability and harmony in the province. The passage of the Coercive Acts prompted many Americans to urge a united continent-wide effort to secure their objectives. Their response was a rigorously enforced non-importation agreement. Commercial life on the Chesapeake dwindled. In fact, the depression following the non-importation agreements only acerbated an already declining economy following the boom of 1768—1771. Economic stagnation and depression made men more desperate for an answer to their troubles, and their attempts at a solution often took the form of violent action. All of this jeopardized the status of the traditional laadership, whose defense of colonial liberties contrasted with the desire of others for a more drastic alteration of society. The designs of this latter group influenced the rise of a more radical political environment in Maryland than had existed previously.

A major international credit crisis began in 1772 and hit the Maryland commodity markets by the fall of that year. By mid-1773, the effects were felt by the great domestic mercantile houses. Charles Ridgely (1733—1790) of Baltimore and Stephen West (1726—1790) of the Woodyard were among the more prominent Maryland merchants who were confronted with lawsuits attempting to settle their obligations to English creditors. The credit crisis radicalized many such normally rational and dispassionate men. Both Ridgely and West later became members of the more ardent faction within the revolutionary movement, men who wanted more than mere redress of grievances with the British and the maintenance of the traditional society.[1]

The depression affected more than a few merchants; the general populace felt it acutely. The Rev. David Love wrote ex-Governor Sharpe that if the economic stagnation occasioned by the boycott continued, "this country will be distressed beyond conception." Baltimore's wheat prices, which had been at seven shillings, three pence per bushel in 1773, had fallen to three shillings, six pence, by the fall of 1775. The price of corn, selling for five shillings per bushel in 1772, dropped to three shillings in 1776. Tobacco fell from 24 shillings per hundredweight in 1769 to 13 shillings, six pence in 1774.

The "fatal effects" of this disaster came in the form of continuing mob action. "The farmers," Sharpe learned from Parson Love, "begin to complain, & threaten to mob the merchants." Governor Eden told the Board of Trade that "An Assembly of rash people soon becomes a lawless and ungovernable Mob; which, grown desperate from Necessity, arising from total Neglect of their peaceable Trades & Occupations, and kept constantly heated by the incendiary Harangues of their Demagogues, are a formidable Enemy to encounter with words only, founded on Reason & Arguments of Moderation."[2]

"Amor Patriae" wrote one such incendiary harangue for the *Journal*'s readers. He warned that if "our suffering brothers at Boston should, through a shamefull pusillanimity on the part of the other colonies, be reduced to a servile submission to taxation, the rod of oppression will be exercised over us All, we must ALL FALL, ALL share in one common ruin!" We must, he continued, "Forbid it, Maryland! Forbid it, America's better genius! Persevere, my brethren, in the virtuous struggle, and consider with the brave Spartan of old, that the good of your country is the first human duty, and that death should be despised when it comes in opposition."[3]

The tenuous ties that held the empire together were slowly being broken. In Talbot County, a group of "gentlemen" gathered at Easton to proclaim the right of resistance to tyranny. The end of government was the preservation of the rights of Englishmen and the maintenance of the right to hold private property. When these rights "are invaded—when the mode prescribed by the laws for the punishment of offences, and obtaining justice, is disregarded and spurned—when, without being heard in their defence, force is employed, the severest penalties are inflicted;" then "the people" (note the clear appeal to mass participation politics) "have a right not only to complain, but likewise to exert their utmost endeavors to prevent the effect of such measures, as may be adopted by a weak or corrupt ministry to destroy their liberties, deprive them of their property, and rob them of their dearest birthright as Britons." Probably resulting from the leadership of Matthew Tilghman, this resolution helped cast the Maryland die for independence. When men acknowledge the right of revolution instead of Boucher's passive obedience, the other side must have sufficient power to suppress organized resistance to the established forms of government. Great Britain never had the force or the desire to suppress such resistance. Although Maryland was the next-to-last colony to join the independence movement, she made her real choice not in June 1776, but at the Talbot County courthouse two years earlier.[4]

Marylanders took up these cries for action in a series of aggressive moves in the second half of 1774. During August, Georgetowners forced the ship *Mary and Jane* to leave the Frederick County port without unloading any of its cargo of tea and other commodities. In late November, John Parks, a merchant of that city, burned his tea stock on the street upon the insistence of the local committee. Some yet unsatisfied elements of the community violated the directives of the committee of observation and broke the doors and windows of Parks' establishment before leaving him alone. This popular disobedience of a ruling by a gentry-controlled committee followed on the heels of an even more dramatic incident in Annapolis.

A visitor in London when he heard of the Maryland non-importation agreements, Thomas Charles Williams bought 17 chests of tea and shipped them aboard the brigantine *Peggy Stewart* to his Annapolis mercantile house. The vessel, owned by James Dick and his son-in-law Anthony Stewart, arrived at the Maryland capital in mid-October. Already under suspicion for his conduct in the *Good Intent* affair of 1770, the imprudent Stewart paid the duty on the tea and expected to unload the ship, when the local committee of observation met to take action on the matter. The committee decided that the tea should be brought ashore and burned. Committeeman Matthias Hammond, who with his brother Rezin was one of the most radical leaders of Anne Arundel County, objected to the proposal and asked for a general meeting of citizens to decide what should be done. Apparently Carroll, barrister, and most other committeemen felt they could carry any popular meeting; hence, they consented to the proposal.[5]

Since the provincial court was in session in the capital at the time, however, several men from the Western Shore went home and gathered followings to bring to the meeting. Such non-Annapolis groups as those headed by Rezin Hammond, Dr. Ephraim Howard, Dr. Alexander Warfield of Anne Arundel County, Walter Bowie of Prince George's County, Charles Ridgely, Baltimore County assemblyman, and Mordecai Gist and John Deavor of Baltimore Town constituted an important and volatile segment of the resulting assembly. At the meeting of October 19, 1774, Matthias Hammond made a particularly inflammatory speech condemning the committee's decision. When Carroll, the chairman, asked for the sense of the assembled persons, a large majority approved the committee's proposal to burn the tea. The dissident elements, led by Doctor Warfield, Charles Ridgely, and Rezin Hammond, demanded the burning of the tea on the vessel, so that the hated leaf would not contaminate Maryland's shores. While they may have constituted only a fourth of the assemblage, their threats against Stewart's store and home, where his wife lay pending childbirth, forced the ship's owner to agree to the burning and to accept a loss of £ 1,896. Stewart, along with James and Joseph Williams, partners in T. C. Williams and Company, boarded the vessel "with her sails and colours flying, and voluntarily set fire to the tea, and in a few hours, the whole, together with the vessel, was consumed in the presence of a great number of spectators."[6]

When Thomas C. Williams returned to the colony, the committee forced him to admit that he acted "with the design to avail himself of an advantage from an expected scarcity of" tea and that his activities "supported the assumed power of parliament to tax America, and endangered the rights and liberties of America." He expressed his "sincere" regret for the incident and promised to contribute to the fund for the relief of Boston. The same committee had previously forced Stewart to sell 24 pipes of Madeira wine, the profits from which sale he "gave" to the same fund.[7]

Probably no incident in the whole of revolutionary history illustrates the radical trend in American politics as clearly as the burning of the *Peggy Stewart*. Minority action triumphed. What had been enough to incite Parliament to impose the Coercive Acts on Boston no longer sufficed in Maryland. The opinions of such notable and prominent citizens as Charles Carroll, barrister, fell before those of a few demagogues. "In a word," wrote Arthur Schlesinger in his appraisal of the event, "Annapolis had out-Bostoned Boston."[8]

The Piscataway factor, Alexander Hamilton, forecast class warfare if the non-importation agreements lasted much longer. He wrote his Glasgow employer that should the restrictions of "imports & exports be strictly adhered to, the poor people and all those who would not lay in more Goods than would answer their present Necessitys will be in the Utmost Distress, and will I am affraid be exceedingly riotous against the better sort of people who have fully supplyed themselves for a Length of time."[9]

John Galloway, son of the squire of Tulip Hill, told a friend of the effect the burning had upon Maryland's conservatives: "I think Sir I went to Annapolis yesterday to see my liberty destroyed which was done when fire was put to the brig. . . . If this be Liberty, If this is Justice, they certainly must have found a new code of Laws . . . but they must be different from any others ever was penned by man or ever appeared heretofore on the face of this Earth." A "Gentleman at Bladensburgh" wrote his brother in Glasgow on November 1st: "Since the burning of the ship at Annapolis, the common sort seem to think they may now commit any outrage they please." He recounted an incident at Georgetown where the Committee of Observation forced a merchant to lower his prices because they felt he expected excessive profits. Finally he asked rhetorically: "What do you think of this land of Liberty, when a man's property is at the mercy of any one that will lead a mob!"[10]

The plight of the law-abiding citizens of Maryland was never more poignantly expressed than in a letter by one "Americanus" —probably Thomas C. Williams— to the British *Public Ledger,* which was reprinted in the *Maryland Gazette,* April 13, 1775.

"Americanus" pointed out that the governor was without any police force and was, therefore, "unable to cope with, or curb the fury of an exasperated people, there are no military in the province." While Governor Eden found words insufficient to stop demagogues and mobs, his confidant, Eddis, continued to counsel moderation: "It is high time some methods were adopted to conciliate these growing differences. The colonies are daily gaining incredible strength. They *know,* they *feel,* their importance; and *persuasion,* not *force,* must retain them in obedience." This judicious advice went unheeded.[11]

The winter of 1774–1775 was critical to the rise of radicalism. The two wings of the country party, the whigs and the democrats, resorted increasingly to mass meetings and extra-legal government as devices to force conformity to their ideas. The old court party made its last defense, usually on the grounds of loyalty to the Crown and of defending the British tradition of political liberalism. Their futile effort came principally in the form of appeals in the local press. They saw that the mass meetings and extra-legal organizations were forcing a conformity to the revolutionary line and were denying the right of dissent.

One such meeting of Anne Arundel citizens resolved on January 16, 1775 that anyone not giving active support to the patriot cause "is and ought to be esteemed, *an enemy to America.*" The issue of guilt by lack of association brought an immediate response from those who condemned the action as an attack upon the colony's traditional concept of minority rights and freedom of opinion. "A Friend of Liberty and Moderation"— a pseudonym for William Eddis— wrote to the *Gazette* questioning whether an assembly of 250 persons "can, with propriety, be called a *full meeting of the inhabitants of Anne-Arundel county.* " He further asked whether such a group had the right to assume power contrary to the sentiments of the gentry-dominated committee of observation, whether the resolution had not really been agreed to late in the day after many of the rural residents had left for their homes, whether the resolution had not been presented without the knowledge of those who left or who might have come had they realized such a proposal might be made, and whether this attempt to single out citizens for public censure was warranted by any edict of the Continental Congress.[12]

At the same time an unsigned letter championed minority rights, asking: "Is it consistent with liberty— the distinguishing characteristic of British subjects! to condemn, with a partial fury, those who dissent from any popular opinion— can it consist with freedom, to point them out as victims of vengence, to the hazard of the public peace, the distress of worthy families, and the destruction of private property?"[13]

A conservative calling himself "The Citizen," and a radical under the name "An American," argued with particular vigor over the issue of what to do about citizens who refused to give active support to the revolutionary cause. The Baltimore committee of observation, with Ridgely presiding, called William Edmiston, an Anglican rector, before it to answer charges that he favored the Quebec Act and called militiamen traitors to the king. The Reverend Mr. Edmiston acknowledged that he had made the statements, but claimed he was a sincere lover of Maryland liberties and that his only hope was that peace would be restored between the Mother County and the colonies. Events in Baltimore became so inflamed that many "moderate people" found themselves "threatened with expulsion, loss of life &c. for not acceding to what we deam treason and rebellion." This report by James Christie, Jr., a merchant, claimed: "We have some violent fanatical spirits among us, who do everything in their power to run things to the utmost extremity."[14]

For all practical purposes, the proprietary government existed only insofar as the Maryland Convention, an extra-legal assembly of delegates chosen at annual popular elections in each county, would allow it to function. The convention felt increasingly compelled to demand conformity to the patriotic ideology. In mid-February they sent copies of an "Association of Freemen of Maryland" to the local committees for signature by the citizens of each county. This document, pledging support to the revolutionary cause, required any non-associator to disarm himself or to be disarmed, to post bond that he would not betray secrets "to the enemy," and to "behave himself peaceably and quietly in the present unhappy contest between Great-Britain and the colonies." Those not signing or posting bond were to be imprisoned. The local committees also received the right to grant passes to non-associators desiring to leave the province. The estate of anyone leaving was liable to tax for the burden Maryland incurred in the defense of American liberty. Again the radicals won, and a Baltimore committee shortly thereafter censured James Dalgleish "as an Enemy to the Liberties of Americans."[15]

As spring came to the Chesapeake, violence or threats of violence increased. British ships in particular encountered local opposition. In March Talbot Countians turned away the ship *Baltimore,* belonging to the Glasgow firm of Spiers, French & Co., and in June the *Johnston,* owned by Gildart, Gawith & Co. of Liverpool.[16]

Another example of the rise of radicalism occurred in Kent County. Presumably the British revenue acts regulated not only intercolonial commerce by sea, but also commerce by land. For years there had been no resident customs collector on the Sassafras River, and local merchants regularly shipped goods between this upper Eastern Shore area and points in Delaware and southeastern Pennsylvania. As part of the reform of the customs collection system, the commissioners appointed Robert Stratford Byrne riding surveyor of Bohemia and Sassafras, stationed in Cecil County. Although his salary was only £ 50 sterling a year, he expected to make over £ 500 from fees, fines, and seizures. With few entrances and clearances by sea in the area, he turned to collecting from teamsters bringing goods overland. When he found two wagons loaded with freight bound from Duck Creek on the Delaware to Chestertown, Maryland, Byrne arrested the drivers and confiscated their goods on the grounds that they did not have the proper entry papers, bills of lading, and bonds. When the wagoners stopped their teams for a rest at a local mill, a mob gathered, robbed Byrne, beat him, and dragged him over the countryside. Finally, after about three hours of such punishment, the leaders, described as "Men of Property," told him to quit the province and never to accept such a position again. They warned that Lord North could expect similar treatment were he to fall into their grasp. Oliver Dickerson described this little-known event in rural Maryland as "almost as significant as the destruction of the tea at Boston."[17]

As word of continued military activity in Massachusetts reached the Cheaspeake, Marylanders found themselves being dragged into war. Carroll of Carrollton thought armed conflict inevitable as early as September 1774. But many citizens, like the mother of William Duke, a Methodist circuit rider, felt saddened with "apprehensions of great Destress and Calamitys like to be occasioned by the expected War between England and America." Still, war seemed the only answer when men like George Plater III received communications from London telling how the Prime Minister proposed to occupy principal American ports, burn towns to ashes, and stop all trade between the colonies and the outside world. "America," Plater learned, "must be prepared for the worst."[18]

Another ship of Gildart, Gawith and Company encountered the full wrath of the most radical elements of society. The *Totness,* bound for Baltimore, ran aground in July 1775 near the mouth of West River, a few miles south of Annapolis. The ship's master assured a local committee of observation that he had no contraband aboard. The committee accepted his statement and ordered that he be allowed to proceed to his port. Since the tide did not rise enough, however, the vessel remained aground for several days. When the associators learned, probably through some too-talkative sailors at a local tavern, that there were proscribed goods in the cargo, an armed group of young men boarded the *Totness,* forcibly disembarked the master and crew, and burned the vessel.[19]

This event was the most flagrant action against private property in the whole history of Maryland's revolutionary movement—probably in the whole of English America. Organized and armed by the militia system then in effect, incensed by the low prices for farm produce, angered by the duplicity of the ship's captain, and aroused by the military maneuvers of General Thomas Gage in Massachusetts against fellow colonists, these young men defied the authority of their elders and destroyed private property. They did not use even the subterfuge of the *Peggy Stewart* affair where Anthony Stewart "voluntarily" set fire to his ship. A hapless and helpless governor could do nothing to bring the culprits to pay for their crime, and no other authority was capable of meting out justice.

According to Eddis, this "second burnt-offering to liberty" and other "instances of popular fury" were "heartily condemned by very many, even of the patriotic party."[20]

Slowly but surely, the Revolution slipped from the hands of the gentry. They still controlled a majority of the convention's delegates, but balloting for the convention was on an easier suffrage requirement than had existed under the proprietary government, and some of the more radical leaders entered the convention. Persons made prominent by the *Peggy Stewart* affair, like Rezin and Matthias Hammond, Dr. Ephraim Howard, Walter Bowie, and Charles Ridgely, appeared in the summer 1775 session.[21]

During the summer of 1775, the Baltimore committee began a series of actions against activities of those suspected of pro-British leanings. One of the first to feel their wrath was Scottish-born James Christie, Jr., a local merchant. The committee intercepted Christie's letter of February 22 to his cousin Lt. Col. Gabriel Christie, commander of His Majesty's forces in Antigua, in which the merchant recommended the stationing of troops in the colony to insure its loyalty. The committee found Christie guilty of unamerican crimes "of so dangerous and atrocious a nature" that they stationed a guard with him in his house, forced him to pay for the guard's keep, and hauled him before the Convention for further discipline. The Convention fined him £ 500 sterling and banished him from the colony.[22]

An intercepted letter from George Munro, clerk at the Bladensburg store of Richard Henderson, revealed similar sentiments. Munro, also a Scot, fled in fear of a tar and feathering by a local mob which refused to await a decision by the Prince George's committee.[23]

The radicals did not limit themselves to attacks on British interests. In Charles County in September 1775, a group of friends and relatives broke into the jail and freed a prisoner held for non-payment of a large domestic debt. This mob defied the will of the local committee of observation and of the convention. A similar riot occurred in Baltimore County, where "some disorderly people" freed another debtor. Only the intervention of two Continental Army companies restored order and returned the prisoner to the sheriff. At the same time, disappointed farmers threatened to mob merchants who were paying low prices for farm commodities. In such conditions Hamilton wrote his Glasgow employer that there was little reason to expect payment of debts, since such incidents forced the convention to take a more radical position and suspend all obligations to British creditors.[24]

The *Totness* arson, the rise of radical elements to the control of the committees of observation and correspondence, and the decline of gentry dominance in the political affairs of Baltimore, caused Governor Eden to lament to Lord Dartmouth: "All power is getting fast into the Hands of the very lowest of the People. Those who first encouraged the Opposition to Government, and set these on this licentious Behaviour, will probably be amongst the first to repent thereof."

"Government is now almost totally annihilated," lamented William Eddis, "and power transferred to the multitude." This leading aide to the governor found freedom of speech curtailed, letters intercepted, and confidences betrayed. By mid-1775, the proprietary official succinctly summarized the situation: "Every measure evidently tends to the most fatal extremities: the sword is drawn and, without some providential change of measures, the blood of thousands will be shed in this unnatural contest."[25]

A second "Association of the Freemen of Maryland, July 26, 1775" gave the best evidence of this shift to the left. The February association was no longer stringent enough. The July Association pledged military and financial support against the British forces in America and called for forty companies of militia to back the common quest of security "for the lives, liberties and properties of the subjects in the united colonies." Patriots insisted that everyone sign the document. Hamilton reported that the "most unexceptionable Conduct will not screen any man, the cry is now if they will not fight for us, they are against us." Pressure on aliens like Hamilton, a Scot, and other outspoken men like the Rev. Jonathan Boucher and Lloyd Dulany increased.[26]

The despair of Maryland's moderate patriots became more and more apparent. Thomas Johnson (who was shortly to be named the first governor of the State of Maryland) wrote Gen. Horatio Gates that all he had wished was the establishment of American liberties and the continuation of the imperial union. The first, however, came before the second. The crown's rejection of the remonstrances sent by the continentals brought anguish to men of Johnson's temperament. Their only recourse appeared to be a "break from a [heretofore] reasonable and beneficial connexion with the Mother Country." Johnson looked in vain for a way out of the dilemma.[27]

In contrast with Lord Dunmore of Virginia, Governor Eden tried to chart a course through the political storm by preserving a nominal "hold on the Helm of Government." His hope was expressed in these words: ". . .that I might steer, as long as possible, clear of those Shoals, which all here must sooner or later, I fear, get shipwreck'd upon."[28]

Governor Eden steered this course until April 1776, when troops under Gen. Charles Lee intercepted a letter of his recommending that a British regiment be sent to Maryland to insure the colony's allegiance to the crown. Instead of sending the documents incriminating the governor to the Council of Safety (a committee appointed by the convention to govern the province when the convention was not in session), headed by conservative Daniel of St. Thomas Jenifer, General Lee forwarded them to Samuel Purviance, Jr., radical chairman of the Baltimore committee of observation. When Purviance tried to seize Eden and hold him as a hostage, the Council of Safety let the governor escape aboard a British man-of-war then in the Chesapeake. Lee, Purviance, and many Continental Congressmen (except the Maryland delegates) wanted Eden as a hostage, and they raged against the council's decision. The defense of Maryland's position was probably the first instance of state's rights arguments being used in the yet-to-be-formed nation.[29]

Purviance charged that the Council, controlled by Jenifer, a former proprietary councilor, endeavored "to wreck their Vengence on" him because he was "too Zealous & forward in the present Struggle, a Crime of which too many amongst us are very clear." This was but one of a series of incidents in the mounting criticism of the Council of Safety and its members.[30]

None of these critics equalled the insight expressed in a January 1776 letter of merchant-planter Stephen West of the Woodyard, Prince George's County:

Pray Answer me what Governing Power here will have authority to stop the Invaders? Are we to be Governed by a Council of Safety who will never meet— or if they do— do nothing, if we are to Judge by what has Past. Upon the appointment of this Council our safety depends. . . . I am much afraid that our Province will be found very weak, especially in Council, & Consequently in all. Can the present Proprietary government exist and we defend ourselves effectually? The Powerful People of this Province love Ease and are not fond of Change, especially those that are uncertain and tend with danger. Who are willing and Able to turn out E_____ [Eden] & who will support them in it? These are difficult Questions. I fear no Council of Safety can be found to do it and Consequently we shall have no Council of Safety at all.[31]

West's criticism of the "Powerful People" in the province and their control of the revolutionary movement reflected the growing disenchantment with the way of the gentry leaders. The *Peggy Stewart* burning, the Byrne affair, and the *Totness* arson are but dramatic illustrations of increasing popular disillusionment with genteel politics of the Tilghmans and the Carrolls. More important was the threat that such episodes had upon the maintenance of the deferential society. The democrats needed an instrument to express their discontent with the existing order. This they would find in the emerging militia system.

NOTES

1. Johnson to Wallace, Davidson & Johnson, August 9, 1773, Wallace, Davidson & Johnson Letterbook, Maryland Hall of Records, Copy of interrogation by the General Court of the Western Shore in George Stack *vs.* Hannah West, executrix of Stephen West, and other documents in Oden Papers, Maryland Historical Society. On the credit crisis see Ronald Hoffman, "Economics, Politics and the Revolution in Maryland" (Ph. D. dissertation, University of Wisconsin, 1969), pp. 163–181; R. B. Sheridan, "The British Credit Crisis of 1772 and the American Colonies," *Journal of Economic History*, XX (1960), pp. 161–182.

2. D. Love to H. Sharpe, January 29, September 15, 1775, "Letters of the Rev. David Love to Horatio Sharpe, 1774–1779," J. H. High, editor, *Historical Magazine of the Protestant Episcopal Church*, XIX (1950), pp. 365–366; see Table 9 in D. C. Skaggs, "Democracy in Colonial Maryland, 1753–1776" (Ph. D. dissertation, Georgetown University, 1965), p. 131, for wheat and corn prices. For tobacco prices, see Inventories, Baltimore County, Liber K, folio 354, Liber L, folio 224, Maryland Hall of Records. R. Eden to Ld. Dartmouth, August 27, 1775, "Correspondence of Governor Eden," *Maryland Historical Magazine*, II (1907), p. 12.

3. *Maryland Journal*, June 4, 1774.

4. *Maryland Gazette*, June 2, 1774.

5. *Maryland Gazette*, August 11 & 18, December 22, 1774; B. C. Steiner, *Western Maryland in the Revolution* (Johns Hopkins University Studies, Series XX, Baltimore, 1902), pp. 9–10.

6. *Maryland Gazette*, October 20, 1774; A. Hamilton to J. Brown & Co., October 31, 1774, "The Letterbooks of Alexander Hamilton, Piscataway Factor," R. K. MacMaster and D. C. Skaggs, editors, *Maryland Historical Magazine*, LXI (1966), pp.

318-319; Fisher Transcripts, Maryland Historical Society, XI, pp. 4-6; October 26, 1774, W. Eddis, *Letters from America* (London: The Author, 1792), pp. 171-184; "Account of the Destruction of the Brig 'Peggy Stewart,' at Annapolis, 1774," *Pennsylvania Magazine of History and Biography,* XXV (1901), pp. 248-253.

7. *Maryland Gazette,* December 15, 1774, January 12, 1775.

8. A. M. Schlesinger, *The Colonial Merchants and the American Revolution, 1763-1776* (New York: Facsimile Library, 1939), pp. 388-392, quote 392.

9. A. Hamilton to J. Brown & Co., October 31, 1774, "Letterbooks," MacMaster and Skaggs, editors, p. 319.

10. "Account of 'Peggy Stewart'," pp. 249-251.

11. *Maryland Gazette,* April 13, 1775; R. Eden to Ld. Dartmouth, August 27, 1775, "Correspondence of Eden," p. 12; October 26, 1774, Eddis, *Letters,* p. 169. For more on Eddis and his unique place in Maryland history, see G. H. Williams, "William Eddis: What the Sources Say," *Maryland Historical Magazine,* LX (1965), pp. 121-131.

12. *Maryland Gazette,* January 19, 1775.

13. Ibid. For similar sentiments, see J. Boucher, *Reminiscences of an American Loyalist,* 1738-1789, J. Boucher, editor (Boston: Houghton Mifflin, 1925), pp. 128-130.

14. *Maryland Gazette,* January 26, February 2, 1775; *Maryland Journal,* January 23, 1775.

15. *Maryland Gazette,* February 23, 1775; *Maryland Journal,* May 10, 1775.

16. O. Tilghman, *History of Talbot County, Maryland: 1661-1861,* 2 vols. (Baltimore: Williams & Wilkins, 1915), II, pp. 67-70.

17. Fisher Transcripts, *Maryland Historical Society,* VI, pp. 1-7, 16-17; O.M. Dickerson, *The Navigation Acts and the American Revolution* (Philadelphia: University of Pennsylvania Press, 1951), pp. 251-254.

18. E. Merrit, "The Lexington Alarm, April 19, 1775: Messages Sent to the Southward After the Battle," *Maryland Historical Magazine,* XLI (1946), pp. 89-114; *Maryland Gazette,* May 18, July 6, 1775; Carrollton to C. Carroll, September 12, 1774, "Extracts," *Maryland Historical Magazine,* XVI (1921), p. 35; May 5, 1775, William Duke Journal, Maryland Diocesan Archives;——to G. Plater, July 6, 1775, Ethan Allen Collection, Maryland Diocesan Archives.

19. R. Eden to B. Calvert, J. Ridout, W. Eddis, August 12, 1775, Calvert, Ridout, Eddis to Eden, August 18, 1775, Eden to Ld. Dartmouth, "Correspondence of Eden," pp. 6-7, 97; *Maryland Gazette,* July 20, 1775.

20. Eddis, *Letters,* pp. 217-218.

21. *Archives of Maryland,* XI, pp. 3-67; *Maryland Gazette,* December 29, 1774.

22. Christie, *Case; Archives of Maryland,* XI, pp. 9, 11, 12, 13, 44-48, 51, 52.

23. Henderson's petition, August 4, 1775, *Archives of Maryland,* XI, pp. 39, 49-51.

24. A. Hamilton to J. Brown & Co., September 18, October 10, 1775, "Letterbooks," MacMaster and Skaggs, editors, pp. 162-163; *Archives of Maryland,* XI, p. 33; D. Love to H. Sharpe, September 15, 1775, "Letters," High, editor, p. 366.

25. R. Eden to Ld. Dartmouth, October 1, 1775, "Correspondence of Eden," p. 101; July 25, 1775, Eddis, *Letters,* pp. 215–216.

26. *Maryland Gazette,* August 24, 1775; A. Hamilton to J. Brown & Co., August 2, 20, & 29, September 8, 1775, "Letterbooks," MacMaster and Skaggs, editors, pp. 148–156; see Boucher's sermons on "The Dispute Between the Israelites and the Two Tribes and a Half, Respecting Their Settlement Beyond Jordan" and "On Civil Liberty; Passive Obedience, and Non-Resistance" in J. Boucher *A View of the Causes and Consequences of the American Revolution* (London: G. G. & J. Robinson, 1797), pp. 450–560; *Naval Documents of the American Revolution,* W. B. Clark, editor, 3 vols. to date (Washington, D. C.: Government Printing Office, 1964–1968), I, p. 1245, II, p. 65.

27. T. Johnson, Jr., to H. Gates, August 18, 1775, *Letters of Members of the Continental Congress,* E. C. Burnett, editor (Washington, D. C.: Carnegie Institution, 1921), I, p. 190.

28. R. Eden to Ld. Dartmouth, August 27, September 9, 1775, "Correspondence of Eden," quote 11, p. 98.

29. Steiner, *Life,* pp. 105–134; see various epistles by T. Johnson, T. Stone, R. Alexander, R. H. Lee in *Letters,* Burnett, editor, I, pp. 425–429, 431–432, 440,"General Samuel Smith to Thomas W. Griffith," *Maryland Historical Magazine,* V (1910), pp. 151–152; C. Lee to D. Jenifer, May 6, 1776, Brown Books, VIII, 1, Maryland Hall of Records.

30. S. Purviance, Jr., to C. Lee, May 2, 1776, Purviance-Courtney Papers, Duke University Library.

31. S. West to——, January 10, 1776, Gilmor Papers, Maryland Historical Society, III, p. 72.

8

EMERGENCE OF THE MILITIA, 1775–1776

In order to successfully protect themselves from alleged encroachments of British tyranny upon American liberties, Maryland politicians found it necessary to form, train, and equip a military force. The emergence of this force, originally designed to provide armed opposition to parliamentary and royal oppression, resulted in the creation of a potent political instrument. During 1775–1776, the traditional whiggish leadership of the colony became hard-pressed to contain the militia within the limits of the political opposition they intended to exert.

When, for the third time since the previous June, the Convention convened in Annapolis in early December 1774, one of its most important concerns involved the establishment of a militia. Ever since the end of the last imperial war with France in 1763, the militia structure of the colony had deteriorated. The loyalty of many of its officers to the revolutionary cause could not be trusted. The *Peggy Stewart* affair may have caused many of the more conservative elements of society to hope that a properly led military force might curb such rowdyism in the future. Since Annapolis had "out-Bostoned Boston," fear may also have arisen that the affair might incite a second set of Coercive Acts designed to do to Maryland what had been done to Massachusetts Bay after the Boston Tea Party.

Whatever the reasons, the December convention created a rudimentary military force. It resolved: "That a well regulated militia, composed of the gentlemen, freeholders, and other freemen, is the natural strength and the only stable security of a free government." In language typical of the eighteenth-century English commonwealthmen, the resolution noted "that such militia will relieve our mother country from any expence in our protection and defence, will obviate the pretence of a necessity for taxing us on that account, and render it unnecessary to keep any standing army (ever dangerous to liberty) in this province." The Convention called upon all of the specified inhabitants aged sixteen to fifty to form themselves into companies of sixty-eight men and to elect their officers and noncommissioned officers. The Convention instructed the companies to "use their utmost endeavours to make themselves masters of the military exercise" and to "be in readiness to act on any emergency."[1]

Of particular note in this decision was the Convention's whiggish division of society into gentlemen, freeholders, and other freemen. The concept of graduations of citizenship and honor typified the ordered society envisioned by most of the gentry. Remarkable in this document was the requirement that officers should be elected. Hitherto, the appointment of officers had lain in the hands of the governor. Probably believing that the lesser freeholders and other freemen would elect only gentlemen to such positions, the Convention unwittingly opened a Pandora's box leading eventually to democratization of the militia. This first preparedness call contained many inadequacies. There was no hierarchy of officers above the rank of captain. There was no provision for placing the newly-created force under the command of either the Convention, Council of Safety, or the Committees of Observation. The lack of any enforcement powers to effect the universal conscription called for in the resolution, and the lack of any centralized control of the militia companies, resulted in the establishment of only a few companies in the hands of the most ardent revolutionary zealots. The lack of an adequate supply system insured that the militia would not be an effective fighting force.

Recruiting for the new militia companies began immediately after the Convention recessed on December 12. In less than a month, Anne

Arundel countians formed two companies in Annapolis, another in Severn Hundred, and a fourth in Elkridge Hundred. The *Maryland Gazette*'s editor noted with satisfaction that the companies were "composed of all ranks of men in this city [Annapolis], gentlemen of the first fortunes are common soldiers; this example, it is not doubted, will be followed by every town and county in this province."[2]

The support of such units required funds. Without any legitimate source of taxation for their support, the militiamen turned to coercion and virtual extortion. At a meeting of 250 inhabitants held in Annapolis on January 19, 1775, and presided over by Charles Carroll, barrister, a resolution was passed proscribing any person not contributing "to the purchase of arms and ammunition" as *"an enemy to America."* Such persons were to have their names published in the *Gazette*.

This decision brought outraged protest from dissenters to the revolutionary line who insisted that the proscription was neither democratically arrived at nor "consistent with liberty — the distinguishing characteristic of British subjects! to condemn, with a partial fury, those who dissent from any popular opinion" and not consistent "with freedom, to point them out as victims of vengeance, to the hazard of the public peace, the distress of worthy families, and the destruction of private property." The policy of coercion continued to be hotly debated in the public press, so much so that the publishers could not print letters from all those wishing to comment; handbills appeared signed by protagonists on both sides.[3]

Following the engagements at Lexington and Concord, a definite increase in military activities occurred in Maryland. Philip Vickers Fithian noted that Georgetown in Kent County was "warmed with the Martial Spirit." At Greenberry Point, just outside Annapolis, David Kerr noted in a business letter that there was little of substance to write about, "only Warlike preparations; which I think will be very necessary."

To meet the needs created by the beginnings of hostilities, the military system would have to be more rigidly organized, and funds for its support more vigorously solicited, if Marylanders were to back the New Englanders in their hour of need. Thus the Convention that met in late July and early August 1775 created an even more massive armed force in its Association of the Freemen of Maryland. The Association called again for every able-bodied freeman to enroll himself in a militia company. Each county Committee of Observation received authorization to form its companies into battalions of approximately eight companies each. For the first time, artillery companies could be formed. While company officers continued to be elected, the Convention reserved the right to commission the battalion or field-grade officers.

The members of the Convention also realized that the militia system was incapable of quick reaction to the threats imposed by Lord Dunmore's naval and military force that was operating from the mouth of the Chesapeake. In addition to reorganizing the militia, the Convention authorized the creation of 40 companies of minutemen. The 29 Western Shore companies constituted three battalions, while the 11 companies on the Eastern Shore were left in an independent status subject to the control of the Convention or the Council of Safety. As with the militia, the enlisted men chose their own lieutenants and their captain, but the Convention or the Council of Safety issued commissions to the field-grade officers. The Convention ordered the minutemen to be equipped from "the public arms" possessed by Colonels Joshua Beall of Prince George's County, Henry Hooper of Dorchester County, Edward Lloyd of Talbot County, and Richard Lloyd of Kent County.[5]

The Association of the Freemen of Maryland recognized that in a society influx, the distinction among gentlemen, freeholders, and other freemen was hardly tenable. The distinctions of class broke down in a quest to determine allegiance. Polarization of Maryland politics between patriots and loyalists continued apace during the summer and fall of 1775.

This was the summer of the *Totness* burning, the expulsion of Customs Collector Byrne, and the banishment of James Christie. The impact of the Association upon those who hoped to remain neutral caused them either to flee, to turn loyalist, or to withdraw. In order to protect the interests of his Scottish employers, Alexander Hamilton induced two of his assistants to join the militia. He hoped thereby to keep an agent in Maryland to insure that someone would be able to continue the collection of debts due to James Brown and Company of Glasgow. Marylanders would have little of this devious tactic. One of his subfactors fled rather than fight against George III's troops; the other died before he had an opportunity to protect Brown's property from confiscation. In Charles County, where extensive debts were owed to English and Scottish merchants, citizens resolved on September 12, 1775 to establish a committee for licensing suits in order to protect debtors from expropriation of their property into the grasping hands of the foreign factors.[6]

As the number of options open to Marylanders narrowed to a choice between signing the Association or declaring loyalty to the Crown, many chose the latter course. This was especially true on the lower Eastern Shore where proximity to Lord Dunmore's stronghold at Norfolk provided a refuge and a possible source of military support. The Worcester County Committee had particular trouble with men like Abraham Gibbs, who publicly stated that "in the Case the Ministerial Troops are sent over here to lay their hands upon the Congress," he "would be one of the first Men who wou'd Join them." A graver threat came from William Barclay Townsend, who, with his son Levin Townsend and Isaac Costin, attempted to get Worcester countians to join Dunmore at Norfolk and to outfit a tender that would attempt to seize prizes and the Worcester Committee.[7]

Lord Dunmore's threat to the exposed Maryland shoreline necessitated a more concerned and concerted effort for defense. A Convention meeting in December 1775–January 1776 again reorganized the colony's defenses. The constant reorganization in the past year constituted the best witness that the military posture of the colony remained weak. First, the Convention disbanded the minutemen. Then it ordered that a force of regular Maryland troops, consisting of a battalion of infantry, seven independent infantry companies, two companies of artillery, and one company of marines "be immediately raised, and paid and supported at the expense of this province, for the defense of the liberties thereof."

The Convention ordered the battalion, consisting of eight regular infantry companies and one light infantry company, to divide its men between Annapolis and Baltimore. Each of these ports also received a company of artillery. Another directive stationed five of the independent companies on the Eastern Shore, with one each in Worcester, Somerset, Talbot, and Dorchester counties and the remaining company to be divided between Kent and Queen Anne's counties. Of the two Western Shore independent companies, one stationed itself in St. Mary's County and the other billeted half its troops in Charles and half in Calvert counties. The regular troops were a small force, consisting of fewer than 2,000 officers and men. Still, the battalion under the command of Col. William Smallwood would eventually win renown as the famous Maryland Line, one of Washington's best fighting units in the Continental Army. The opponents of the stationing of British Army troops in America had now created their own standing army.

Although the Convention's record supplies only a skeleton outline of what happened in its deliberations, it is evident that the body decided to take control over the commissioning of all the regular officers. No provision was made for the enlisted men to choose their commanders, even at the company level. From Colonel Smallwood to the lowest third lieutenant, the Convention decreed its right to name each officer. It is entirely probable that most of these commissions went to officers of the minutemen companies. It was now firmly established that the Convention had control over the commissioning and command of this small regular army.[8]

The militia still constituted the main fighting force for the province. Even though in some counties there were "not any battalions formed" as late as January 1776, the Convention decided to place its principal reliance on this poorly equipped, ill-trained, and slowly mobilized force. On January 4, it resolved to create five militia brigades, one each in five districts into which the province was divided. A brigade, which supervised the activities of eight battalions, was commanded by a brigadier general, assisted by an adjutant and a quartermaster. As would be expected, the Convention again reserved its right to name these officers.[9]

Once Dunmore left the Bay area, the regular battalion became part of the Continental Army and came under the command of General Washington. Smallwood's men joined the commander-in-chief in New York, leaving Maryland's defense in the militia's hands. It had been assumed that the militia units would remain in the province. The expected British counter-attack after the withdrawal from Boston made it imperative, however, that the colonies cooperate in the utilization of their forces. On June 3, 1776, the Continental Congress requested that Pennsylvania, Delaware, and Maryland create a common "flying camp" of militia for duty until December 5. Even before declaring independence, the Maryland Convention, on June 25, raised a 3,405-man brigade of militia under the command of Thomas Johnson. This brigade constituted a secondary force, supplementing its regular troops, for the common defense.[10]

In the year-and-a-half after initially creating the militia in late 1774, Maryland raised three types of forces— the Continental Army regulars, the flying camp militia, and the local militia. By the time the Declaration of Independence had been signed, the total mobilization was for more than 18,700 officers and enlisted men. Of this number, 1,700 were officers. Although not all these obligations were met, such a requisition constituted a major drain upon the resources of the new state.

The effect of such a demand, combined with the necessity of organizing and manning the new state and continental governments, placed a severe strain upon the sources of leadership within the gentry class, which traditionally ran the province. In colonial Maryland, public offices went to the upper quarter of landowners (owning over 500 acres) or their brothers, cousins, and in-laws. This group could no longer provide the experience, expertise, and numbers necessary to fill such a large manpower demand. In addition, many gentlemen were reluctant to risk their lives, honor, and fortune by taking up arms or offices against the King. Consequently, this manpower vacuum had to be largely filled by persons whose social and economic status traditionally would have prohibited them from offices of public profit and responsibility. The large number of new civil and military offices created a situation in which a new group could move into the officer corps.

An analysis of the landholdings of Maryland militia officers suggests that a significant number of heretofore socially deprived persons took advantage of the situation. A list of 403 names of those commissioned from Baltimore, Harford, Prince George's, Queen Anne's and Talbot counties provides a good cross-section of the officer corps. The largest number of commissions went to men representing either the lower half of the landholders (approximately 200 acres or less), or those who apparently owned no land at all. Combining the positively and marginally identified categories shown in Table 9 together, only 12.9 percent of all officers owned over 1,000 acres, 18.9 percent owned between 500 and 999 acres, 24.9 percent owned 200 to 499 acres, 13.4 percent owned 100 to 199 acres, and 10.0 percent owned one to 99 acres. Some 19.9 percent remain unidentified. The younger sons

TABLE 9

LANDHOLDINGS OF MILITIA OFFICERS COMMISSIONED IN 1776[1]

	Field Grade Officers											
	Positively Identified Individuals					Marginally Identified Individuals					Uniden-tified Individ-uals	Totals
County	over 1000 acres	999-500 acres	499-200 acres	199-100 acres	99-1 acres	over 1000 acres	999-500 acres	499-200 acres	199-100 acres	99-1 acres		
Baltimore	3	3	3	3	0	0	3	0	0	0	0	15
Harford	2	2	2	0	0	1	0	0	0	0	0	7
Prince George's	4	2	0	0	0	4	2	0	0	0	1	13
Queen Anne's	3	2	1	2	0	0	0	0	0	0	1	9
Talbot	1	0	1	0	0	1	1	0	0	0	1	5
Total	13	9	7	5	0	6	6	0	0	0	3	49
% of Total	26.5	18.4	14.3	10.2	0	12.2	12.2	0	0	0	6.1	100.0

	Captains											
	Positively Identified Individuals					Marginally Identified Individuals					Uniden-tified Individ-uals	Totals
County	over 1000 acres	999-500 acres	499-200 acres	199-100 acres	99-1 acres	over 1000 acres	999-500 acres	499-200 acres	199-100 acres	99-1 acres		
Baltimore	2	5	9	3	2	3	3	4	2	5	7	45
Harford	1	3	3	1	3	3	1	2	2	0	3	22
Prince George's	2	3	5	2	2	0	6	5	1	0	0	26
Queen Anne's	3	0	2	1	2	1	1	2	1	0	3	16
Talbot	0	0	5	1	0	3	2	4	0	2	2	19
Total	8	11	24	8	9	10	13	17	6	7	15	128
% of Total	6.3	8.6	18.8	6.3	7.0	7.8	10.2	13.3	4.7	5.5	11.7	100.0

TABLE 9 - Continued

LANDHOLDINGS OF MILITIA OFFICERS COMMISSIONED IN 1776[1]

Lieutenants

	Positively Identified Individuals					Marginally Identified Individuals					Unidentified Individuals	Totals
County	over 1000 acres	999-500 acres	499-200 acres	199-100 acres	99-1 acres	over 1000 acres	999-500 acres	499-200 acres	199-100 acres	99-1 acres		
Baltimore	1	5	6	3	3	5	8	8	11	7	40	97
Harford	0	3	2	3	3	5	1	9	5	3	8	42
Prince George's	1	1	1	0	3	1	9	11	2	1	5	35
Queen Anne's	0	1	2	3	2	2	6	5	4	1	4	30
Talbot	0	0	3	3	1	0	3	5	1	0	5	21
Total	2	10	14	12	12	13	27	38	23	12	62	225
% of Total	0.9	4.4	6.2	5.3	5.3	5.8	12.0	16.9	10.2	5.3	27.6	100.0

[1]Names of the 402 officers are found in *Archives of Maryland*, XI, XII, XVIII, and the Proceedings of the Conventions of December 1775, May 1776, and June 1776. Only those officers whose county of residence could be specifically identified have been included. This list has been compared with the landholders found in the quitrent Debt Books for the four counties (Harford being part of Baltimore County) in 1771 (1769 in the case of Queen Anne's County where later records are not extant), Maryland Hall of Records.

of the large property holders should appear in the marginally identified lists. Thus, for the first time in Maryland history, large numbers of persons from outside the gentry class moved into positions of local leadership. They accomplished this through what was probably the most democratic electoral procedure in the colony's history— universal suffrage to all militiamen.

As can be seen by Table 9, the figures for particular grades indicate that, especially in the lieutenancies and slightly less in the captaincies, the tendency toward an open admission policy in militia rank was evident. In the two counties bordering Pennsylvania (Baltimore and Harford) there was less respect for the gentry than in those counties farther south. More than a third of the lieutenants appointed in these two counties cannot be identified as either landholders or members of landholding families just five years before the commissions were issued. Only 23 percent of the lieutenants from the five counties were in the group holding more than 500 acres. On the other hand, 70 percent of the field grade officers owned over 500 acres. Thus, in those ranks whose commission depended upon convention approval, gentlemen received most of the rewards of office.

Despite this, men without the usual gentry credentials commanded and staffed the battalions. The most important of these included the officers who usurped control of a Queen Anne's County battalion. Their situation is discussed in detail below. Also commanding battalions were Maj. Thomas Jones of the Baltimore Town battalion, owner of 122 acres, and Maj. Joshua Stevenson of the Upper Gunpowder battalion, who owned but 100 acres. Another such appointment was that of Christopher Birckhead as colonel of the 4th militia battalion stationed in Talbot County. This merchant apparently owned no land in his own name in 1771, but enjoyed the confidence of a county gentry that dominated its militia officerships in a manner unparalleled in the other four counties. Birckhead's marriages into the prominent Harrison and Trippe families no doubt had served him well. [11]

Besides these statistical data, evidence that militia officerships constituted an avenue for social mobility comes from contemporaries. The militia call of December 1774 directed that the company officers be elected, but the Council of Safety assumed the right to issue commissions in such companies where vacancies occurred after the original election. Usually this meant the other officers would all be promoted one level, but there were exceptions. The enlisted men tended to possessively guard their prerogative. Similarly, gentlemen tended to desire the captaincies to be held by persons with genteel credentials.

For instance, when the council appointed George Wailes to a vacant captaincy in a Somerset County company, so much discontent arose "among the whole of the company" that Captain Wailes resigned his commission and the company chose its own officers by ballot. Capt Andrew Beall of Prince George's County expected promotion to a battalion staff vacancy but objected to the elevation of William Hamilton, his first lieutenant, as his successor as company commander. Beall explained to the council: "Mr. Hamilton is a poor man and . . cannot make the appearance that an officer ought to make, is a person of no Education, neither is he qualified in any respect whatever to keep company with the other Gentlemen Officers . . . ." In neighboring Charles County there was a similar case. The committee of observation sought to overturn a company's vote for officers deemed not to have the proper gentlemanly credentials. Instead, the committee wanted and secured the council's approval of a more acceptable roster of officers.[12]

Even men already chosen were threatened with the loss of their status by disgruntled enlisted personnel. In the fall of 1776, a majority of Capt. Richard Chew's company in Anne Arundel County petitioned the council for a new election in order to replace their captain and ensign for political reasons. At a time when local militiamen were petitioning the constitutional convention for universal manhood suffrage, Captain Chew supposedly remarked "that no poor man was entitled to vote, and those that would insist upon voting, if he had his way should be put to death." To this his brother, Ensign Samuel Chew, replied, ". . . a poor man was not born to freedom, but to be a drudge on earth."[13]

Such statements by members of one of the first families of Maryland indicate just how far the revolutionary nature of the ferment unleashed by the War for Independence had gone. Nowhere is the decline of traditional deference to authority more apparent than in this petition by forty militiamen (fifteen of whom could not sign their own names) against two members of the prominent Chew family.

The revolutionary ferment brought with it opportunities for advancement not only to the less affluent, but also to ethnic and religious minorities that had previously been victims of discrimination. In July 1776, Baltimore County raised two German companies. Of the eight officers appointed, not one was listed as a landholder in 1771. Whether Lt. Christian Myers was a member of the family of that name which possessed very modest holdings is unknown. No one of the Graybill (Grayble), Lhora, Shugart, Keeports, Gerrock, Ritter, or Lindenberger families (to whom the other commissions were given) owned land in the county five years earlier.[14]

For the Roman Catholics, advancement into the officer corps contrasted strongly with the prohibition against their service in the colonial militia. Col. Jeremiah Jordan, Maj. Ignatius Fenwick, Jr., and Maj. Samuel Abell became the most prominent of this group as officers in the St. Mary's County battalions.[15]

The heady effect of the sudden influx of political democracy involved in the election of company-grade officers spilled over into demands by the enlisted men and subalterns for a voice in the selection of battalion officers. Of constant concern to the provincial convention and the Council of Safety was the growing demand for the democratization of the entire officer selection process. A new democratic ethic increasingly came to dominate political thought. It was part of a "contagion of Liberty" in revolutionary America, as Bernard Bailyn calls it, which led to a breakdown in the bonds of respect for authority, status, and stability in society. Conventional thinkers of both whig and tory persuasion felt the very sinews that kept society from disintegrating into anarchy were being destroyed by the rhetoric of revolution, which preached disobedience to authority and favored equality among men.[16]

The controversies over the appointment of battalion officers dramatized this incipient democracy. When the December 1775 Convention named 50 of its 80 members to field grade and general officer positions, the outcry against such political and class partisanship was immediate and loud. Henry Ridgely of upper Anne Arundel County protested the appointment of Thomas Dorsey as colonel of a battalion, despite the fact that Dorsey allegedly "most shamefully and cowardly quitted his post" during the French and Indian War. Many militiamen felt that not only company grade but also field grade officers should be elected. Echoing this belief were the contributions of "An American" to the *Maryland Journal*. The author, who may have been Rezin Hammond, a democratically-oriented leader from Anne Arundel County, decried the Convention's bargaining for votes to secure the colonelcies and brigadierships for its members because it smacked of a "monopoly in trade or power [that] will not be tolerated in a free government." "Merit," he continued, "should be the only recommendation to office." And so from the militia came one of the first cries against the system of special privilege that had heretofore characterized both proprietary and country politics in Maryland.[17]

A number of instances of similar attitudes emerged at various places in the province. After attending a meeting of the Soldier's Delight battalion of which he had been named a major only a few weeks before, Dr. John Cradock of Baltimore County resigned his commission because "the Battalion declare, that they will be commanded only by officers recommended by themselves." Problems of a similar nature led to confusion in leadership in the two Prince George's County battalions, and no officers with gentlemanly credentials and popular approbation could be found for the Kent County battalion.[18]

By far the most dramatic assault against legislative supremacy and social deference occurred in Queen Anne's County. In January, the convention appointed Thomas Wright to the colonelcy and members of the prominent Tilghman and Hemsley families to staff positions in the 20th battalion in the lower portion of the county. Perhaps some of the agitation that apparently convulsed the Kent County militia spilled over into Queen Anne's. Whatever the reason, both the Council of Safety and the May convention had to intervene in arguments over Wright's methods of operation.[19]

In June, Capt. James Bordley and Lt. James Kent led a majority of one company which "regardless of the resolutions and appointments of the convention and the Council of Safety have refused to acknowledge the field officers of" the 20th Battalion "appointed by the Convention or to Act under them and have nominated[,] acted under and appointed other field officers in their stead." The company "refused to acknowledge and act under" two other company officers "appointed by the Council of Safety but have also nominated and act under others, appointed by themselves." According to one observer, Captain Bordley and Lieutenant Kent "openly and avowedly countenance[d] the irregular proceedings . . . by refusing to acknowledge the officers appointed by the Convention and Council of Safety and acknowledging and acting with those appointed by the people." Such a feeling was common throughout the battalion. It was inflamed by the agitations of Turbutt Wright (one of the county's delegates to the convention), Captain Bordley, and Captain James O'Bryan. These three acted in concert at a meeting of the battalion held in mid-September. Delegate Wright (a cousin of the despised colonel) "publickly advised the people not to meet in Battalion under any appointment but their own." Despite Colonel Wright's protests, the assemblage chose O'Bryan as its new colonel, Bordley as lieutenant colonel, and two other captains, John Dames and George Hanse, as majors for the battalion. In effect, the *vox populi* discharged the four officers appointed by the convention.

The most extraordinary fact about this election was that neither O'Bryan nor Hanse could justly claim to be gentlemen under the usual definition of the term. Bordley owned 1,125 acres of land in 1769 (the last year such records are available); Dames owned 649 acres; O'Bryan owned but 185 acres; and no record that Hanse owned any property in the county is extant. Virtually all of the colonels appointed from the counties surveyed in this study owned more than 1,000 acres of land. After this election no other county except Queen Anne's had two field grade officers from the lower end of the socio-economic scale (as represented by landownership).

The modification of traditional deference to the gentry, and the democratization of officeholding resulting from the agitation in the militia ranks, represents one of the more revolutionary aspects of Maryland's road to independence. Colonel Wright expressed the dismay of the tradition-minded when he wrote to the Council of Safety concerning his battalion's usurpation of the right to name field officers: "The people have been induced to believe they ought not to submit to any appointments, but those made by themselves."[20] The democratic voice of Maryland was heard despite accepted standards of order and status in society.

Such demands caused Michael Earle of Chestertown to write with alarm and exasperation to protest what such activities portended:

If the attempts respecting your Militia field off [ice]rs are not discontinued. & the promotions of them handled with some Degree of Roughness & that roughness administered in such manner & with a tenderness too *as* to show the people at large, their common Interest made it needful, & that they are reprehended from mere motives of the public good, & to keep up some order & good Government among them, all those Evils must everafter [follow] & will inevitably lead to Anarchy & Confusion.[21]

The reactions of men like Colonel Wright and Michael Earle may overstate what was actually occurring. Even the statistical evidence presented in Table 9 has a number of limitations. The fact that the landholding records predate those concerned with officerships by from five to seven years means that considerable change could have ensued in the interval. Also, young males may have been placed in lower landownership than social categories due to the fact that their fathers kept title to most of their lands until death. Yet, most of the younger sons of the landholders should have emerged in the marginally identified category. The unknown category of officers may have included many members of landholding families who were recent migrants to the colony. This may have particularly affected conclusions relative to Baltimore and Harford counties, where emigration from Pennsylvania was particularly large. However, since landholding was becoming less common throughout the colony, one could expect that such migrants were more likely to be engaged in tenant farming than freeholding.

While landownership was the principal yardstick by which a person's wealth and status was measured on the colonial Chesapeake, it was not the sole determinant. The case of Colonel Birckhead of Talbot County indicates that a propitious marriage provided access into the plantation drawing rooms that superseded any land titles. The Buchanans of Baltimore Town invested more in ships and mercantile goods than in land, yet Andrew Buchanan became a brigadier general and William Buchanan a militia colonel. Surely the lists contain a number of names of merchants, artisans, doctors, and lawyers who enjoyed social prestige beyond that expected on the bases of real property ownership.

There also emerges the question of whether what occurred represented anything more than a normal change for the typical American. At least one scholar believes that the rise of social opportunity that greeted the revolutionary generation was due to factors other than the political ferment of the times. P. M. G. Harris, in a provocative analysis of the social origins of American leaders through three centuries, describes a fluctuation of opportunity that happens on a regular cyclical basis, regardless of the exterior political and economic conditions. This normal occurrence was reinforced by peculiar demographic factors which provided unusual opportunities for upward mobility for persons born during periods of low birth rates and immigration. The normal 22-year cycle Harris describes, and the modest population growth occurring in the decade 1745–55, combined with the chances for advancement offered by the necessary expansion of the civil and military service, meant that men born 20 to 30 years before the Declaration were confronted with extraordinary opportunities for mobility. Harris found that men born in ordinary homes in 1746 had a much better opportunity for high public office than men similarly born in 1761.[22] It is apparent that Harris' national sample describes a situation of mobility that is applicable to Maryland.

How long would the militia act as such an upward mobility force? Would the new officers seize the opportunities that were theirs and achieve something beyond the tinsel of honor their commissions represented? If they did so, would they use their newly-won status to produce a new elite which might be as limiting as the old? All these are questions beyond the scope of this inquiry, but questions worthy of studious investigation. The point is that the opportunity existed in the mid-1770s and many felt some significant social upheaval was in the making.

In creating the revolutionary militia establishment, the conventions and the Council of Safety allowed a degree of democratization in officeholding unknown in the colonial period. Into the newly established military officerships came many men whose economic, ethnic, or religious status would previously have disqualified them from officeholding. These men were not members of a colonial lumpenproletariate, but mostly members of middle level farmer, artisan, merchant class who could, by their personal magnetism, inspire the loyalty of their subordinates. Many were scions of the great families of the upper Chesapeake; their positions became contingent as much on their personalities as on their social status. The required elections at the company level and the quest for elections at the field grade level indicate that even those officers representing the traditional leadership had either to accommodate themselves to the new democratic ideology or face stiff opposition from the ranks. The expansion of opportunity created by the new nation and its demand for public servants, especially in the military, opened the door to many men of modest social status. The risks were extraordinary, but for those willing to take them, the rewards might mean a transformation of social status. The military provided more than individual social mobility. It constituted an instrument which could require the democratization of Maryland politics in a manner similar to the democratization of military affairs. Hence, the militia became a potent force by the summer of 1776.

NOTES

1. *Proceedings of the Conventions of the Province of Maryland, Held at the City of Annapolis, on the twenty-second day of June, 1774; on the twenty-first day of November, 1774; on the eighth day of December, 1774; on the twenty-fourth day of April, 1775; and on the twenty-sixth day of July, 1775* (Annapolis: Frederick Green[1775]), p. 7.

2. *Maryland Gazette,* December 22, 1774, January 5, 12, 1775.

3. *Maryland Gazette,* January 19, 26, February 2, 1775.

4. *Philip Vickers Fithian: Journal,* 1775-1776, May 11, 1775, R. G. Albion and L. Dodson, editors (Princeton: Princeton University Press, 1934); D. Kerr to W. Love, May 27, 1775, John Leeds Bozman Papers, Library of Congress, I, f. 69.

5. *Proceedings of the Conventions of . . .* [1774-75], pp. 14-18, 25.

6. A. Hamilton to J. Brown & Co., August 29, October 10, 1775, "The Letterbooks of Alexander Hamilton, Piscataway Factor," R. K. MacMaster and D. C. Skaggs, editors, *Maryland Historical Magazine,* LXII (1967), pp. 152, 163; *Maryland Gazette,* October 19, 1775; G. Washington to L. Washington, August 20, 1775, *The Writings of George Washington,* J. C. Fitzpatrick, editor, 39 vols. (Washington D.C.: Government Printing Office, 1931-1944), III, pp. 432, 434.

7. Exec. Papers, Box I, f. 13, Maryland Hall of Records; *Archives of Maryland,* XII, pp. 369-383.

8. *Proceedings of the Convention of the Province of Maryland, Held at the City of Annapolis, on Thursday the seventh of December, 1775* (Annapolis; Frederick Green, [1776]), pp. 24-26, 29-31, 42-43, 46.

9. *Proceedings of the Convention of . . . December, 1775,* pp. 31-32.

10. *Proceedings of the Convention of the Province of Maryland, Held at the City of Annapolis, on Friday the twenty-first of June, 1776* (Annapolis: Frederick Green, [1776]), pp. 5, 8, 20-21.

11. For sources, see note for Table 9. The rankings have been grouped into three categories—positively identified, marginally identified, and unidentified. In the first category, the names of an officer and of a county landholder are the same. While such identification is not perfect, it would appear to be reasonably accurate and does weigh the figures in favor of landholding. In the marginally identified group are the persons whose own names do not appear in the debt books, but whose family surname does. The average of the family holdings is used to categorize an individual. Again, such a scale tends to weigh the statistics in favor of the landholders. Finally, the last category includes all those whose surnames do not appear on the debt books as landholders. However, since the landholding records are from 1771 (or 1769 in the case of Queen Anne's· County), they may have been landholders by 1775-1776. It is assumed that the error factor involved here is compensated in major part by the overweight given landholders in the other two categories.

12. G. Dashiell and W. Horsey to Council, February 10, 1776. Report of Charles County Committee, February 26, 1776, Josias Ray *et al.,* to Council, April 10, 1776. A. Beall to Council, April 18, 1776, *Archives of Maryland,* XI, pp. 151-152, 186-187, 206, 324-326, 350-351. After discussing the genteel backgrounds of a few field

grade officers, Cecil County's historian remarked: "Little is known of the other officers of the battalions." G. Johnston, *A History of Cecil County* (Elkton, Md.: The Author, 1881), p. 326.

13. Petition of Chew's Company, October 5, 1776, *Archives of Maryland,* XII, pp. 322–323.

14. *Archives of Maryland,* XII, pp. 27, 32; Debt Book, Baltimore Co., 1771, Hall of Records; D. Cunz, *The Maryland Germans: A History* (Princeton: Princeton University Press, 1948), pp. 133–135.

15. *Proceedings of the Convention . . . of December, 1775,* pp. 33–39; C: H. Metzger, *Catholics in the American Revolution: A Study in Religious Climate* (Chicago: Loyola University Press, 1962), pp. 187–207.

16. B. Bailyn, *The Ideological Origins of the American Revolution* (Cambridge: Harvard University Press, 1967), pp. 273–319; G. S. Wood, "Rhetoric and Reality in the American Revolution," XXIII (1966), pp. 25–32; J. Boucher, *A View of the Causes and Consequences of the American Revolution . . .* (London: G. G. & J. Robinson, 1797), pp. 495–560.

17. H. Ridgeley to the Convention, May 20, 1776, T. Dorsey to Council May 26, 1776, *Archives of Maryland,* XI, pp. 432–433, 446–447; *Maryland Journal,* July 3, 1776.

18. R. Tyler to Council, November 10, 1775, A. Beall to same, February 29, 1776, J. Beall to same, March 6, 1776, Tyler to J. Hall, March 7, 1776, John Cradock to Council, July 1, 1776, *Archives of Maryland,* XI, pp. 92, 195–196, 205, 210, 539; Joseph Sim to Council, September 23, 1776, ibid., XII, 296; *Proceedings of the Convention . . . of May, 1776,* pp. 3, 10, 23, 24; *Proceedings of the Convention . . . of June, 1776,* p. 32.

19. Council to T. Wright, March 18, 1776, *Maryland Archives,* XI, p. 260; *Proceedings of the Convention . . . of May, 1776,* pp. 18, 29.

20. T. Betton's Petition to Convention, ca. June 13, 1776, *Archives of Maryland,* XI, pp. 487–488; T. Wright to Council, September 20, 1776, XII, pp. 287–289; Debt Book, Queen Anne's Co., 1769, Maryland Hall of Records.

21. M. Earle to T. Ringgold, Jr., May 8, 1776, Henry Hollyday Papers, Maryland Historical Society.

22. P. M. G. Harris, "The Social Origins of American Leaders: The Demographic Foundations," *Perspectives in American History,* III (1969), pp. 163–164, 185, 199–212, 220–248. For a summary on the declining Maryland growth rate beginning in the 1740s, see A. E. Karinen, "Numerical and Distributional Aspects of Maryland Population, 1631–1840, " (Ph. D. dissertation, University of Maryland, 1958), pp. 139–140. The even lower socioeconomic origins of the revolutionary enlisted man, as compared with the officer corps, is documented in E. C. Papenfuse and G. E. Stiverson, "General Smallwood's Recruits: The Peacetime Career of the Revolutionary War Private," *William and Mary Quarterly,* Series 3, XXX (1973), pp. 117–132.

9

INDEPENDENCE AND THE
CONSTITUTION OF 1776

The road to Yorktown was paved with stones marking the end of careers of Maryland gentlemen who failed to modify their views in the face of rapidly changing conditions. Those who successfully marched down that road found themselves traveling what was often a very narrow path between thickets of traditional political, economic, and social control by the gentry on the one hand and, on the other, a swamp filled with demands that the War for Independence be accompanied by a social revolution. One of the most torturous segments of that road involved traversing that portion concerned with the decision for political independence and the quest for a new fundamental law for His Lordship's former province, now a self-proclaimed state.

The drift toward independence marked the final dividing line among the members of the gentry leadership—what Stephen West called the "Powerful People" of the province. They made their decisions from the summer of 1775 to the summer of 1776. By that time there was no turning back. The Rubicon had been crossed; their ultimate fate now rested upon the test of arms.

Some outspoken court party conservatives like Lloyd Dulany, Henry Addison, and Jonathan Boucher felt called to leave their fortunes to save their lives and honor by fleeing to England. Some like Daniel Dulany and Dr. John Stevenson, withdrew into their private shells and refrained from political participation. A very few, like William Eddis and James Tilghman, held on to their offices until the tide of revolution swept them out. Still others, like Daniel of St. Thomas Jenifer and William Bordley, members of His Lordship's Council, joined the Council of Safety "for the sake of being instrumental in preventing Disorder, & Violence."

For the old country party conservatives, the choice was a particularly difficult one. Led by Edward Lloyd IV, Robert Goldsborough III, and Charles Carroll of Carrollton, they wanted to retain all the old privileges, but without the odious restrictions of proprietary control. As late as mid-June 1776, the convention was under their direction and still unwilling to vote for independence.

The moderate country party leaders—Samuel Chase, William Paca, Thomas Johnson, Matthew Tilghman, and Charles Carroll, barrister—allied themselves with their conservative counterparts. During 1776, however, their base for political control dwindled as radicals took over the committees (once a source of moderation–witness the committee decisions in the *Peggy Stewart* and *Totness* affairs). Convention members found themselves in a position of being unable to oppose the often violent activities of the committees against non-associators because of the threat opposition posed to their political standing.[1]

Criticism of the committees and the convention system of government had to be made, not on the grounds that it was disloyal, but that it violated the very principles of government that the colonies pretended to be interested in preserving. Writing under the name of "A Friend of Amity," Eddis attacked the committee system as unconstitutional, since it violated the principle of separation of powers. The committees assumed the roles of the executive, legislative, and judicial branches of government in opposition to the principles of Montesquieu. Eddis struck at the "vindictive, arbitrary system, which under the fallacious pretense of supporting the interests of constitutional freedom, exerts a tyrannical authority."[2]

Similarly, young Benjamin Galloway, completing his studies in London and wanting to return to America with his law books, found Samuel Chase blocking the importation of the tomes as a violation of the association. Enraged at this affront to his dignity by a man he considered of mean station, Galloway wrote: "What a scandalous Thing is it, that such a Fellow should have it in his power to govern a whole province whose existence as a Man of Importance in the Political World depends upon his keeping up the Ball of Confusion."[3]

Chase was hardly the wild-eyed radical Galloway thought him to be, and he was losing his grip in the control of the revolutionary movement. Moderates of Chase's stripe and many conservatives grew to feel that they could continue to exercise political control only if they had a constitutional mandate under which to govern. Government by county meeting and militia assembly had to be stopped. The end of the proprietary government left the gentry without an anchor to hold the ship of state against the tide of radicalism which threatened to sweep it onto the shoals of anarchy. The solution seemed to be independence and a new state constitution drawn along conservative lines. Favoring this position were men like Carroll of Carrollton, Matthew Tilghman, Paca, Chase, and Johnson, who urged the convention to favor independence.[4]

But it was not without misgivings that the decision for separation was reached. Thomas Stone wrote: "The die is cast, the fatal stab is given to any future connection between this country and Britain, except with relation of conqueror and vanquished which I can't think of without horror and indignation." Stone felt that there had been a rush to independence led by "the rash and precipitated councils of a few men" just when, in his opinion, the restoration of American rights by Britain was at hand.

Col. Benjamin Rumsey described how he and his fellow councilors proceeded with an olive branch in one hand and a sword in the other. "We have taken Care . . . to guard so as not to fall into Independence, yet that the way should be prepared for it in Case of an absolute Necessity." While "making all the preparations in their power to defend their Country and arming all" the patriotic citizens of the province, the Council of Safety was "Strongly inclined to a Reconciliation on constitutional Terms."

"Thus Alas! are we proceeding by degrees to that crisis we so much deprecate," wrote James Hollyday a month before the convention agreed to follow the congressional lead and to declare for independence. No matter how much a man like Hollyday wanted to retire from the public scene, he knew that men like himself who had "shown a disposition to moderation and an aversion to changes will not remain unnoticed by those who shall ascend to the top of the machine." Despite their reluctance to support separation, the one thing the moderate revolutionaries did not want was a reduction in their privileged position in society.[5]

Dissension in the ranks of the gentry over the move toward final separation was common. In the May meeting of the convention, a "small Fracas" arose between Col. Richard Lloyd, who urged independence, and Robert Goldsborough III, who opposed. According to one viewer, Colonel Lloyd "pulled Mr. Goldsborough by the Nose" in his campaign for a change in the status of Maryland. After long and conspicuous association with the Revolutionary leaders, Continental Congressman Robert Alexander withdrew from the Council of Safety and retreated to his Cecil County birthplace.[6]

While many of the traditional leadership group felt that the convention was moving too fast, the emerging radical elements in society demanded that the convention be replaced because of its obvious conservatism. None was more vigorous in these feelings than "An American," who found it incompatible with the principles of the "justly celebrated Montesquieu" to allow all powers of government to be reposed in one body. He made vigorous demands for rotation in office, moderate salaries for officers, separation of power between the various branches of government, and the apportionment of the legislature according to population. He made specific citations to "the ingenious and learned Dr. [Richard] Price," a liberal dissenting London minister, who wrote several pamphlets on government and in behalf of the American Revolution. "An American," obviously widely read and highly literate, opened the attack on the gentry's attempt to utilize governmental change in order to maintain the status quo.[7]

That such was the intention of the more conservative elements of society is without question. Michael Earle of Chestertown wrote delegate Thomas Ringgold, Jr., that the attempts by lower-class individuals to usurp control over the naming of militia field-grade officers must be discontinued, even if this meant handling the promoters of such disturbances "with some Degree of Roughness." Acknowledging the role that public opinion must play in such action, he said that this "roughness" must be "administered in such manner & with a tenderness" but must also "show the people at large, [that] their common Interest made if needfull, & that they are reprehended from mere motives of the public good." All this would be done to maintain "order & good Government" and to prevent those evils which otherwise "will inevitably lead to Anarchy & Confusion."[8]

Thus, by June 1776, the radicals and the moderates desired a severance of the last ties with the British crown. In the convention, however, a conservative faction under the capable direction of James Tilghman of Queen Anne's County kept the province within the empire. This was done despite the efforts of what Eddis called a group of "violent and inflammatory men" who were "industriously straining every nerve, to excite general confusion, and plunge us fatally deep in schemes of independence."[9]

Congress was not going to wait much longer for a dilatory Maryland to make up its mind. By June 14, 1776, an exasperated John Adams wrote Samuel Chase condemning the failure of his colony to join the others in resolving for independence. Chase was told to come to Philadelphia by the end of June, bringing with him "the voice of Maryland in favor of independence and a foreign alliance." Adams noted: "Maryland now stands alone. I presume she will soon join company; if not, she must be left alone."[10]

Following Adams' urging, Congressmen Chase, Paca, and Matthew Tilghman returned to the province seeking a resolution for independence. They entered a debate that had been raging in the local press for several months. Various letters signed "Cato" (William Smith), "A Common Man," "The Forrester" (James Cannon), and "Cassandra" (Thomas Paine) appeared in the *Maryland Gazette,* attacking or championing the independence proposals. Finally, the old revolutionary gambit of attacking as disloyal all who would not join them was used. In May, the *Journal* printed an article signed "Hector," charging that most of those objecting to independence were Tories in disguise who "have changed their ground but not their principles." Such men used this new tactic as a cover for their true leanings, which were, of course, inimical to American liberties.[11]

In order to make the hesitant convention vote for independence, the leadership had to force action through the use of a device which it was reluctant to see employed. "The vox populi must in great measure influence your determination" for independence or not, wrote Congressman Thomas Stone. The drift towards democracy had gone so far that Stone felt that whatever the decision "it will be wise and prudent to have the concurrence of the people." With the urging of various continental congressmen, the pushing of some militia units, and the cooperation of gentry and radical leaders, various county meetings resolved to instruct their delegations to vote for independence. A convention session was called for June 21 to decide the issue. A prompt decision was necessary, as the Continental Congress was ready to announce its decision to sever connections with the British government.[12]

In all the earlier conventions, voting was by county, and a majority of a county's five delegates decided the way the county would vote. This meant that each shore had equal representation and that a minority of delegates could thwart the will of the majority. All the advantage lay with the Eastern Shore, where loyalist sentiment was strongest. The key vote in the Maryland Convention came on June 24, when a resolution changing the method of voting from a majority of counties to a majority of delegates was passed. The vote was seven counties affirmative, four negative, three divided, and two not voting. The division showed that all those counties opposed or divided were on the Eastern Shore. All the Western Shore delegates and seven of the twenty-seven Eastern Shore delegates favored the resolution. The way was now paved for a majority vote favoring independence. Four days later, Maryland joined the Union.[13]

All factions of the old country party were now ready to make their stands in the state constitutional convention. The conservatives and moderates wanted to stop the drift to the left by writing a document designed to retain the customary gentry privileges. The democrats desired to secure the few concessions already received and hoped to increase their relative influence.

Prior to independence, government by convention wrought several changes in the electoral process in Maryland. The old religious and immigrant restrictions fell away. A resolution of the convention on August 14, 1775, required a voter to be 21 years old, a freeholder or freeman with an estate of £ 40 sterling, or otherwise be qualified under provincial law to vote for burgesses. This last provision meant Annapolitans retained their old liberal voting laws for convention elections. The elimination of the old 50-acre freehold clause was the most novel innovation of the convention. This allowed any freeholder, regardless of the size of his holding, to vote. Another change was the division of Frederick County into three districts and four polling places. Annapolis lost its right to send a delegation to the convention, a right it had in the Lower House.[14]

After resolving for independence, the June Convention called elections for a Constitutional Convention. It made a few changes from the earlier requirements: freeholders must have 50 acres or a visible estate of £ 40 sterling; each county and the three districts of Frederick County sent four delegates; Annapolis and Baltimore sent two apiece. Voting in Annapolis was by the provincial system, but Baltimorians had to possess the same financial status as the county residents. A resident requirement of one year was imposed on all voters. Disqualified from the franchise were soldiers on active duty and persons published by the Committees of Observation as enemies of American liberties. Militia units were prohibited from mustering on election day.[15] Each election district in Frederick County represented a decision to divide that region into three counties.

The elections of early August almost proved a disaster for the conservatives. Public demonstrations against the duly constituted election judges took place in Kent, Prince George's, Queen Anne's, Worcester, and the lower district of Frederick counties. Johnson, Chase, and Paca, whom Carroll of Carrollton called "the Most Sensible part" of the revolutionary leadership in 1774, found themselves on the far right at these elections. All along the Western Shore, oldline country party leaders like Thomas Stone (who would sign the Declaration of Independence), Thomas Contee, Robert Tyler, Josias Beall, Walter Tolley, Jr., and John Moale lost their seats.[16]

In Baltimore County, one observer stated that the candidates offered were either "not so clever" or else those who were "clever . . . [would] not be elected." In surveying an election that sent Charles Ridgely, Thomas Cockey Deye, John Stevenson, and Peter Shepherd to the Convention, John McClure wrote Maj. Mordecai Gist: "Pray where is the difference between being disqualified or having a vote when these men are to represent you?" Eden's prediction that "those who first encouraged the Opposition . . . will probably be amongst the first to repent thereof" was, it seemed, about to bear its bitter fruit. Looking over the election results, an alarmed Council of Safety despaired that "there is a very great change in the members in all counties, according to the intelligence we have."[17]

At the Prince George's County polling place, the assembled freemen agreed that "every taxpayer bearing arms, being an inhabitant of the county, had an undoubted right to vote for representatives at this time of public calamity." They threw out the convention-appointed election judges, selected new ones, and chose as delegates Walter Bowie, Thomas Sim Lee, Luke Marbury, and Osborn Sprigg. Similar incidents occurred in lower Frederick, Worcester, and Queen Anne's counties. A takeover in Kent County was prevented by the judges, who closed the polls when "a number of people not qualified to vote" tried to force the judges to accept their ballots. These same Kent County persons petitioned the constitutional convention to change the electoral qualifications so that "every associator resident in the county one year, and 21 years of age, might be enabled to vote."[18]

The best documented of the disturbances at the polling places occurred in Annapolis. Despite the Convention's prohibition against the assembling of militia on election day, there were in the city members of the "flying camp" companies en route to that installation in New Jersey. After a few voters had made their choices known, a man stepped forward to vote and Capt. Thomas Watkins objected to his voting on the grounds that he did not possess the necessary property qualifications. At this point, a number of persons, presumably militia men, threatened Watkins' life and demanded that all persons bearing arms in behalf of liberty be allowed to vote. The election judges refused to violate their instructions, and cool heads urged the men to march out of the city and discuss the matter. This being done, several men spoke to the gathering on "Gallows Hill." Apparently Thomas Harwood and James Disney, Jr., explained the convention rule that voters must have either 50 acres of land or property worth £40. To this, one enlisted wag remarked that his whole company was not worth £40. Some speakers urged the men to lay down their arms and go home, but others told them to lay down their arms and go to the polling place and vote. There is conflicting testimony as to whether Matthias Hammond was in the latter group. There is no doubt that both Harwood and Matthias Hammond urged the election of Rezin Hammond to the constitutional convention on the grounds that he would most accurately reflect their rights and interests. Although this large body of armed men could have forced the issue, they did not, and the election "was carried on with great Strictness." [19]

The results of these Anne Arundel County elections sent tremors through the whig camp. Thomas Johnson, Jr., William Paca, and Charles Carroll of Carrollton lost their seats. Samuel Chase barely escaped defeat. In their places went capable and whiggish Charles Carroll, barrister, relatively unimportant Brice T. B. Worthington, and democratic-leaning Rezin Hammond. It took considerable maneuvering by the "Powerful People" to have Paca and Carroll of Carrollton elected from Annapolis and Johnson chosen from remote Caroline County, where he had no property. [20]

The impression created by these disturbances, generated for the most part by militiamen, was that a significant demand was developing for granting the suffrage to all those willing to support the independence movement. All these urgings for universal manhood suffrage received eloquent backing in an essay appearing in the *Gazette* the day after the constitutional convention opened. "Watchman," which may have been a pseudonym for one of the Hammonds, wrote protesting a resolution by the convention calling for elections using the same property requirements for voting as had been used under the proprietary government. In what must have been one of the finest essays ever to appear in the paper, "Watchman" argued that the convention resolution calling for a new government formed "by the authority of the people" excluded with such suffrage restrictions half the freemen from "the enjoyment of their inherent right of free suffrage." Continuing his attack, he held the "ultimate end of all freedom" to be "the enjoyment of the right of free suffrage. A constitution formed without this important right of free voting being preserved to the people would be despotic, and the people meer *[sic]* beasts of burden." Any government founded, as the new Maryland constitution was supposed to be, in truth, justice, and reason ought to include this principle.

Every poor man has a life, a personal liberty, and a right to his earnings; and is in danger of being injured by government in a variety of ways; therefore it is necessary that these people should enjoy the right of voting for representatives, to be the protectors of their lives, personal liberty, and their little property which, though small, is yet, upon the whole, a very great object to them.

Each Citizen of a state, "Watchman" felt, *"who lends his aid to the support of it, has an equal claim to all the privileges, liberties and immunities with every[one] of his fellow countrymen."* In a final plea for political equality and an end to social privilege, he concluded:

Let, therefore, all hateful distinctions cease, and elections, where made open, and by the free suffrage of the people, stand good and valid. The voice of the people should be heard with a solemn attention, and duly regarded. And let a government be established, where equal liberty can be enjoyed, the interest of the people promoted, and the cause of America maintained.[21]

The idea of universal manhood suffrage excited immediate enthusiasm in Anne Arundel County. Backing "Watchman," some 885 freemen, the largest number ever to endorse a proposition in the county's history, instructed their delegates, Carroll, barrister, Worthington, Chase, and Hammond, to support universal suffrage for all native Marylanders. Rezin Hammond favored the proposal, but Carroll, Worthington, and Chase resigned their seats rather than favor measures which were, "in their opinion, incompatible with good government and the public peace and happiness." The ensuing election, lasting four days, ended with Worthington and Chase re-elected, but Carroll replaced by John Hall of the Vineyard.[22]

When the Constitutional Convention assembled on August 14, 1776, it turned a deaf ear to these appeals for wider suffrage. It proceeded to call on "all friends to America" to support the Kent County judges in properly carrying out their functions. The vote was 49 to 10 favoring this resolution. The names of those in opposition constituted a radical segment that was to be heard throughout the convention's deliberations. The Baltimore County delegation was the key to this bloc. It was joined on this ballot by William Fitzhugh of Calvert

County, Walter Bowie and Osborn Sprigg of Prince George's, Elisha Williams of lower Frederick, Rezin Hammond of Anne Arundel, and John Archer of Harford. Subsequently the convention invalidated the returns from Prince George's in a 54–1 vote. Hammond was the lone dissenter. Returns from Queen Anne's, Worcester, and lower Frederick were similarly treated when it was found that ineligible persons had cast ballots. The required by-elections in these counties resulted in few changes from the original choices.[23]

While the controversy over electoral requirements raged, various citizens began to look forward to the other aspects of the new state government. Meeting on June 27, 1776, representatives of Anne Arundel County's militia battalions demanded a radical reform of government. They instructed their delegates to the convention to back the following features for a new state constitution:

1. A two house legislature annually elected by the people;

2. An executive department consisting of seven men annually chosen by joint ballot of the legislature;

3. A state judiciary and other offices annually chosen by joint ballot of the legislature;

4. A county government of justices, sheriffs, clerks, and surveyors annually chosen by the people;

5. A militia system with popularly elected officers;

6. A prohibition of plural officeholding, either civil or military, by legislators, councilors, or congressmen;

7. A guarantee of the preservation of the rights of trial by jury and of *habeas corpus;* and

8. A reform of the taxation system by creating a new fee schedule, abolishing the poll tax, and placing the burden of taxation on real estate.[24]

These Anne Arundel County resolves represented the most significant development in colonial Maryland's political thought and pointed to several radical departures from the proprietary system: (1) the supremacy of a popularly-elected legislature over a plural executive, (2) the decentralization of administration and the emergence of county governments, (3) a lessening of the tight gentry control of appointive offices, and (4) the end of the oppressive fees and poll tax on all citizens and the concentration of the burden of taxation upon those most capable of bearing it, i.e., the large landholders. These proposals (see Appendix II) were reindorsed by the 885 freemen who met in August. [25]

Further radicalism appeared when the author of a published letter on "The interest of America" demanded a completely new form of government. He accused those who wished to continue the older forms of engaging in self-interest, of trying "to retain or obtain places of profit or honour." He demanded a unicameral legislature, charging that bicameralism caused "perpetual contention and waste of time." He also desired an end to hereditary or life tenured offices and rotation in officeholding. [26]

Some of these changes were not new. There had long been discon-tent over the poll tax and the fee system. Since the French and Indian War, the Lower House had attempted to assert its supremacy over the Upper House. Possessors of proprietary patronage elicited, at the least, envy—at the most, resentment. [27] Yet these demands for political reform represented the strongest opposition to gentry control to appear in the era. The Revolution had spawned a radical element unknown in earlier years.

It is quite obvious that the ideas in Dr. Price's pamphlet containing *Observations on Civil Liberty and the Justice and Policy of the War with America* (London and Philadelphia, 1776), the principle of polit-ical equality expressed in Paine's *Common Sense,* and the infiltration into Maryland of the democratic liberalism of the Pennsylvania consti-tutional convention, all provided ammunition for the more democratic-minded delegates to the August convention. [28] Into that body they brought these Anne Arundel militia resolves for consideration.

This assemblage was considerably different in composition from the last Lower House which met in Annapolis in 1774. Of the 76 mem-bers, 50 had never served in the provincial assembly. All four delegates from Prince George's, Charles, upper Frederick, middle Frederick, Harford, and Somerset counties were new. Three new members joined the lower Frederick, Caroline, Cecil, and Worcester county delega-tions.

Forty-four of the delegates are classified as planters, i.e., listed in the latest debt book of their counties as holding over 400 acres. Twelve of them owned less than 400 acres and are classified as farmers. There were 13 lawyers, 14 merchants, six physicians, six manufacturers (mostly owners of ironworks), four millers, one dentist, and one clerk. (The excessive number listed here is due to the fact that several of the delegates were engaged in at least two occupations.) Of interest are the large numbers of farmers, physicians, and manufacturers in this assembly.

Many of these were men who had never shared political power previously. All the physicians—John Archer, Smith Bishop, Adam Fischer, John Love, John Parnham, and Henry Schnebely—sat for the first time in a legislative body. Only Dr. Thomas Sprigg Wootton, a dentist, had previous service. Among the farmers were Joseph Gilpin, who held 294 acres in 1766, and David Shriver with 300 acres in 1771. The farmers usually stood in the middle half of the landholders. Such men hardly compared in holdings with manufacturers like Samuel Beall of Hagerstown, whose holdings included more than 3,000 acres used to supply charcoal for his ironworks, or Samuel Hughs, who was a partner in an equally large enterprise. These men rose to new importance because their manufactories were important instruments in the creation of the revolutionary arsenal.

New ethnic groups also gained representation in this assembly. Schnebely, Shriver, and Stull represented German interests which had previously been denied a voice in the Lower House. Carroll of Carrollton, Ignatius Fenwick, Jeremiah Jordan, and possibly Benjamin Hall were Catholics. There can be little doubt that this assembly contained a younger, more diverse, and more representative group of Marylanders than the Lower House had ever contained (see Appendix III).[29]

Particularly obscure were the delegations from the southern Eastern Shore. Of the twelve delegates from Worcester, Dorchester, and Somerset counties, only four had Lower House service. That no one in the Somerset delegation had had previous legislative experience probably indicated the lack of real commitment to the revolutionary movement in that area. Col. Thomas Ennalls found people on the lower Shore "very lukewarm" in their opposition to the British. The bay coast from Hooper Island to Pocomoke Sound was subject to the depredations of Lord Dunmore's fleet, which had been operating in the Chesapeake. The constant threat of British attack, if one supported the revolution, or the hope of British protection, if one opposed the revolutionaries, undoubtedly had much to do with the feelings of the people.

But there was more to it than this. The southern Eastern Shore had long been a center of Presbyterianism in Maryland, and it appears that there was a deep enmity between the Anglican and Presbyterian congregations. The Anglicans tended to be loyalists. Led by the Rev. John Scott of Stepney Parish, Somerset County, the Rev. John Bowie of Worcester Parish, Worcester County, and Dr. Andrew Francis Cheney, the Anglicans kept this area a hotbed of discontent for several years against what Eddis called "the vindictive Republican Spirit of their Presbyterian Neighbours."[30] While working for a government outside His Majesty's Realm, the lower Shore delegates were quite conservative.

From an analysis of the voting in the Constitutional Convention, two factions become apparent. The first contained that small group of men who supported what will be called a "democratic" line. The second, much larger and more influential, traditionally followed what will be called a "whiggish" philosophy.

Most of the "democrats" came from the northern and western portions of the Western Shore. The core of their strength lay in Baltimore and Harford counties, where Thomas Cockey Deye, a great planter; Capt. Charles Ridgely, a wealthy planter, manufacturer and merchant; Peter Shepherd, a farmer; John Stevenson, a small planter; Jacob Bond, a small planter; and Dr. John Love represented the populace. Others among the top leaders of this group were Rezin Hammond of Anne Arundel County, great planter, lawyer, and militia colonel; John Mackall of St. Leonard's and Col. William Fitzhugh of Rousby Hall, both great planters representing Calvert County; Walter Bowie, Prince George's County merchant; and Elisha Williams, a farmer in Montgomery County (formerly the lower district of Frederick County). These men were not united on all issues—in fact, on many they were sorely divided—but they consistently represented the group most likely to vote against the majority, especially against the majority of those in the second faction.

Several obvious facts are important about this group of democrats. Although several were wealthy, only Capt. Ridgely, Col. Hammond and Col. Fitzhugh could be said to come from important families, and Fitzhugh's family was famous in Virginia, not Maryland. Only Hammond's wealth came through a long landed gentry tradition, while the Ridgely fortune was founded on mercantile and shipping enterprise and Fitzhugh's on his wife's inheritance. None of these men appear to have had the usual genteel credentials of a classical education, and only Ridgely appears to have had associations outside the colony. Of this group, only Deye, Fitzhugh, and Ridgely had previous legislative experience in the Lower House. They were, on the whole, men brought forward by the dislocation of traditionalism embodied in the revolutionary movement. None of these men ever shared in the seats of power before the Revolution (although Fitzhugh did for a short time sit on His Lordship's Council), and they are seldom, if ever, mentioned in the same context as the more prominent leaders of the Maryland independence effort. Yet their voting records indicate a definite democratic pattern. They favored land taxes, not poll taxes; wider suffrage, not restricted franchise requirements; elected local officials, not those appointed by the state governor; and majority rule, not elitism.

The members of this faction were quite similar to a group described by Jackson T. Main in the Confederation period in Maryland. "Side A," as Professor Main calls this group, "was based primarily on the counties of the northern Chesapeake Bay and the western part of the state. These sections were more recently settled, had accumulated less wealth and far fewer slaves, contained principally men engaged in diversified, often self-sufficient agriculture, and had fewer great plantations." In fact, many of the same men turn up in Main's statistics reported for the 1776 Convention. On this side in both 1776 and the 1780s were Love, Ridgely, Stevenson, Deye, and Hammond.[31] It becomes apparent that the origins of the political alignments found in the Confederation period of Maryland history go at least as far back as the Constitutional Convention of 1776.

On the other side was the group best described as the "whigs." Among the leaders of this faction were Charles Carroll of Carrollton, a very wealthy Catholic planter and iron manufacturer representing Annapolis; Richard Barnes, a large planter and son of a prominent St. Mary's County merchant; George Plater III, a great planter and former councilor also from St. Mary's; Samuel Chase, a prominent lawyer and land speculator from Anne Arundel County; his cousin, Jeremiah T. Chase, a Baltimore Town attorney; Thomas Johnson, a large planter with holdings in Frederick and Anne Arundel counties, but who this time represented Caroline; John Smith, a wealthy Baltimore Town merchant; Gustavus Scott, a Virginia-born, Scottish-educated, attorney from Somerset County (also George Scott from the same county, but about whom little is known); William Horsey, a miller and planter of Somerset; and Thomas Smyth, a merchant-planter from Chestertown, Kent County. Giving strong support to this group were men like Col. Ignatius Fenwick, Jr., of St. Mary's County, a great Catholic planter; Christopher Edelen of Frederick County, a merchant; John Dent of Charles County, a large planter and a future general in the militia; and Richard Mason, a Caroline County farmer.

Only Mason gave this group representation among the middle ranking farmers of the state; most of the group came from families with a long tradition of great landholding. The Carrolls, Platers, Dents, and Fenwicks were especially prominent in this respect. Richard Barnes' mercantile background was in many ways quite similar to that of Charles Ridgely, except that the latter came from an area with a booming economic growth. Thomas Johnson was a self-made man, risen from obscurity to importance through land speculation on the frontier and his legal practice; Sam Chase was trying to follow his example, but was doing it much less successfully. Men like Carroll, Plater, Barnes, Chase, and Gustavus Scott had classical educations; some of them were educated in Europe. This group had rather intimate associations with the outside world through the normal commercial and intellectual ties that permeated the Chesapeake tidewater. Many of these men were prominent in the revolutionary movement from the beginning. Plater had sat on the Council of Safety. Samuel Chase and Johnson previously had played leading roles in the Lower House, and virtually all of these men had held seats in the earlier conventions. Although their voting patterns were not fully consistent, they did demonstrate a definite whiggish pattern characteristic of a majority of the Convention. They generally favored a restrictive suffrage system, appointed local officials, indirect election of senators and the governor, and civil liberties which restricted majority rule. All the Roman Catholics of the convention voted with this bloc.

This group was much like that denominated "Side B" by Professor

Main, which "drew almost its entire strength from the eastern shore and the counties of the lower Chesapeake-Potomac." Professor Main elaborates: "These were the oldest, most thickly settled parts of the state, were or had been the wealthiest; still contained practically all of the slaves, and were characterized by tobacco plantations. The representatives of Annapolis and Baltimore town strongly supported that party." Many of the members of this Convention faction turn up on the same side during the Confederation period. Chase, Johnson, and Gustavus Scott continued the group's voting pattern in later years, as did such followers of the whigs in the 1776 Convention as Peter Chaille and James Lloyd Chamberlaine.[32]

To many of the old leadership group, the Constitutional Convention portended dire consequences. Carroll of Carrollton was particularly alarmed at "the desperate designs of the Hammonds," which threatened, he felt, to involve the state "in all the horrors of an ungovernable and revengeful democracy." Colonel Fitzhugh, who was "united with [Rezin] Hammond, Cockey Deye, and such men," was felt to have been a traitor to his class, bent upon playing a weak, outrageous, and wicked part in the writing of the new fundamental law. Carroll urged the "gentlemen who really mean well to their country and sincerely wish it prosperity" to unite, or government would fall into the hands of such "selfish men" as Hammond, Fitzhugh, and Deye. Under such nefarious leadership, all power would be thrown "into the hands of the very lowest of people." Now was the time for "the honest part of the community" to work together for the establishment of "a very good government in this state."[33]

A great fear that the rabble would take over and establish a democratic state caused Carroll and others associated with the old style of politics to stifle most threats to their established political position within the Constitutional Convention. With Matthew Tilghman in the chair as the convention's president, the whigs took immediate control of the meeting. Not a single member of the democratic faction sat on the important committee which drafted the Declaration of Rights and the Constitution of Maryland. Nothing indicates the power of the whig group more clearly than the membership of this committee—Tilghman, Carroll of Carrollton, Johnson, Plater, Paca,

Sam Chase, Robert Goldsborough, Robert T. Hooe, and, for a brief period, Carroll, barrister. Not a single one of these men represented the northern or western portions of the state. Since all of this committee's work and all of the deliberations in the committee of the whole were carried on in secret, unrecorded sessions, much of the maneuvering that went on is unknown to us today. Of seventeen committees organized by the Convention, containing a total of seventy-eight seats, the ten most conservative whigs mentioned held twenty-four seats while the ten most liberal democrats held only six seats. Moreover, men closely aligned with the whig group held many other seats. Paca held five, and four seats each went to Charles Grahame, Robert T. Hooe, and Brice T. B. Worthington, who tended to vote with the conservative whigs.[34]

The drafting committee paid little attention to the criticisms of the old order embodied in the letters of "An American," the "Watchman," the anonymous letter on "The interest of America," and the Anne Arundel County militiamen. Instead they turned to the more conservative political philosophy embodied in John Adams' *Thoughts on Government* (1776), and to their own whiggism as expressed by men like Carroll of Carrollton.[35]

Following the example previously set by the Virginia convention, the committee first submitted a draft of a Declaration of Rights. After announcing belief in a compact theory of government, transferring the liberties of English common law to Maryland, and proclaiming a right of revolution, the Declaration limited suffrage to those "having property in, a common interest with, and an attachment to, the community." Next the document contained a clause on the separation of powers. (The particular meaning of this clause in the context of the constitution will be discussed later; suffice it for now to say that the meaning in 1776 was obviously not the same as we would give the idea of separation of powers today.) There then followed a series of clauses delineating civil liberties which we now recognize as part of the United States Constitution or its first eight amendments. Some additional rights were also announced. Clause 13 terminated the much-hated poll tax and imposed taxes in accordance with one's "actual worth in real or personal property." Another (Clause 30) allowed for the impeachment of judicial officers "for misbehavior on conviction in a court of law." Clauses 31 and 32 demanded rotation in office and an end to plural officeholding. Clauses 33 through 36 disestablished the Church of England; limited gifts to religious denominations, modified the religious qualifications for officeholding to all professing "a belief in the christian religion," and allowed an affirmation to replace the usual oaths for Quakers, Mennonites and others. One final clause (39) found monopolies to be "odious, contrary to the spirit of a free government, and the principles of commerce, and ought not to be suffered."

On the Convention floor, the democrats tried desperately to change several clauses of the Declaration. With Colonel Fitzhugh in the lead, this faction asked the delegates to strike out the clause continuing the British common law in the new state, to disallow the provision for fines and fees to be imposed to require that convicted justices be removed by the governor upon request of the legislature instead of merely allowing it, and to allow per diem rather than annual salaries for judges. They failed in every attempt.

After the committee of the whole finished its draft of the Constitution and Form of Government for Maryland, the convention turned to final deliberations on the document. The constitution allowed for legislative dominance of the state when it created a bicameral General Assembly which chose the governor. The type of separation of powers the Maryland founders envisioned was to prevent persons from holding offices in several branches of government rather than to give off-setting powers to each branch. Completely independent executive and judicial departments were not considered at all. What the constitution in word and fact did was to forbid men from holding posts in the legislative, executive, and judicial branches, as His Lordship's Councilors had done under the proprietary government.

The legislative branch consisted of a House of Delegates and a Senate. Unique among Revolutionary era constitutions was the provision requiring the election of Senators by electors chosen by the people. There would thus, be a screening process to insure that the senators would represent the propertied classes. The electoral college was an innovation, supposedly conceived by Carroll of Carrollton. There were two other restraints upon popular control of the legislature. First, the Constitution continued the old requirement of a 50-acre freehold for voting or the possession of a visible estate of £ 30 *current money*. While continuing the old stake-in-society concept, the new visible estate provision did provide for a reduction of more than 50 percent in the property requirement from the earlier £ 40 *sterling* clause. More important in many respects was the introduction of property requirements for all officeholders. Delegates to the new General Assembly were required to have estates worth at least £ 500 current money and senators, twice that amount. Assuming the data on personal estates in Baltimore and Talbot counties illustrated in chapter three are valid, this meant that at most only a fifth of the freemen could serve in the House and only a tenth could serve in the Senate.

There was some democratization of the government other than the lowering of the visible estate requirement. There were no religious, racial, or national origin restrictions on voting. The House was somewhat more equitably apportioned, with the introduction of the new western counties of Washington and Montgomery and the allowance of two delegates from Baltimore Town (see Table 2). Still, there was no provision for reapportionment when population movements would necessitate such a change. This meant that Maryland, like most states, would spend nearly two hundred years quarreling over legislative apportionment.

While the House of Delegates was annually elected, the Senate was chosen every five years. The electors, two from each county, chose fifteen senators—six from the Eastern and nine from the Western Shore. Electors must be qualified in the same manner as delegates.

Elected annually by the two houses of the General Assembly, the governor had to be twenty-five years old, a five-year resident, and have a £ 5,000 estate, of which £ 1,000 worth must be in freehold. The qualifications for this office were so strict that probably only two percent of the citizens were eligible. The governor could serve only three consecutive terms before being ineligible for reelection for four years. The General Assembly also chose a council which met senatorial property qualifications. Its powers were such that the state virtually had a plural executive. The governor and council appointed all civil officers of both state and county governments: judges, justices, surveyors, and clerks. From this would ensue a centralization of authority in the capital instead of a diffusion of authority among elected county officials. The local autonomy desired by the Anne Arundel militia received little hearing in the convention. The only elected local official was the sheriff. He was chosen triennially by the electorate and had to have a £ 1,000 visible estate. After serving one term, a sheriff was ineligible to hold the office for four years. Ironically, with the disestablishment of the Church of England and the creation of property restrictions for officeholders, the middling farmer had no governmental post such as vestryman to aspire to. As far as officeholding went, the Maryland Constitution of 1776 was far more restrictive and less democratic than the proprietary charter.

The democratic faction realized this and set out to amend the document on the floor of the convention. Turbutt Wright joined them in proposing that the visible estate qualification be lowered to five pounds current money. When this went down to defeat (20 to 34), William Bayly wanted to amend the suffrage requirement to allow voting by all taxpayers. This lost 24 to 29. In behalf of his constituents, Jeremiah T. Chase proposed a sliding apportionment scale for Baltimore Town, so that its representation might increase should the town's population eventually exceed that of the most populous county. He was joined by most of the democrats in this unsuccessful effort at reform. They failed to prevent the inclusion of a £ 1,000 property requirement for sheriffs. Fitzhugh could get only fifteen delegates to join his futile attempt to allow the assembly the right to regulate lawyer's fees. There were other, equally significant, failures.

Victories for the democrats are hard to find in the convention's proceedings. Even the provision for election of the sheriff was offset by the provision that the governor was to appoint that officer from the two top vote-getters. The democrats did stop Sam Chase's attempt to make the shrievalty appointive rather than elective. Chase could secure votes only from Barnes, Carroll of Carrollton, Fenwick, Johnson, Benjamin Hall, Luke Marbury, Gustavus Scott, and Thomas Smyth for this motion.

The broadening of the suffrage franchise did little to change the situation from that of the colonial period. Philip A. Crowl estimates that in 1790 only about 55 percent of the white male freemen could vote. The removal of racial (for only a brief period), religious, and national origin restrictions did help to broaden the electorate and include members who might express opinions different from the traditional electorate on various issues. This provision was probably the most democratic feature of the entire document. The reapportionment of the legislature was also a major improvement over the colonial apportionment, but there was no guarantee of continued political change due to demographic changes.[36]

The whig constitution was in most respects an enlarged copy of the Virginia constitution adopted just before the Maryland convention met. The Maryland document was more fully developed as far as explicit description of offices, departments, and distribution of powers was concerned than the rather hastily drawn Virginia constitution. The Annapolis convention's inclusion of the electoral college constituted a distinct difference. The Virginia constitution also did not perpetuate gentry control through property requirements for officeholding. But the mode of electing the governor, the lack of real separation of power and checks and balances, and the domination of the legislative branch of government over the other two were similar in both documents. The Virginia gentry did retain greater control over the shrievalty than the Marylanders.[37]

The whig victory involved an almost complete rejection of the liberalism of the Pennsylvania constitution being adopted at the same time, the proposals of the Anne Arundel militia, and the ideas in the letters of "An American," "Watchman," and others. The militia's idea of a plural executive was virtually adopted, but its intention to give the executive branch decreased influence was partially lost when the constitution gave the governor and council extensive appointive powers. One house of the legislature was to be elected annually by the voters, but the other was chosen by an indirect ballot designed to preserve gentry influence. Except for the shrievalty, the idea of popularly elected county officials was defeated. Of course, "Watchman's" hope of universal manhood suffrage was left behind. Plural officeholding was not totally eliminated, since county justices could also be delegates. One did not ever have to receive approval of the electorate to become a senator, councilor, judge, or governor in Maryland. Restrictive property requirements meant that only a few could hope for elective office. This was hardly a democracy. As Elisha P. Douglass concluded: "The people of Maryland . . . could look forward to honest, efficient, and equitable government in their condition of independence, but not to popular rule."[38]

Triumphant though they were, the whigs were a bit apprehensive about their victory. When the new government was formed in early 1777, Daniel of St. Thomas Jenifer wrote his senatorial colleagues of certain insuperable obstacles to the successful maintenance of the new government. Foreseeing many of the problems of the coming decades, Jenifer observed:

In attempting to excell, there have been so many gradations and Exclusions that there will not be men enough found of sufficient abilities to turn the machine with that velocity which the present exigencys [sic] of our affairs require. Besides the Senate does not appear to me to be a Child of the people at Large, and therefore will not be Supported by them longer than there Subsists the most perfect Union between the different Legislative branches. How long that may be, you, who know mankind full well as I do, may easily determine . . . The two houses are composed of 89 members, 8 of whom have it in their power to counteract 81. Will they submit?[39]

In the face of what they felt to be a concerted attack against their position, Maryland's gentry stood resolute. In so doing, they did not merely survive the ordeal, they completely prevailed. Yet, there were misgivings about the almost total victory. Had they gone too far? How long could they continue to carry the burden they had assumed? Was the fact that the 1776 constitution maintained the status quo merely a Pyrrhic victory? In these questions and those of Jenifer lie the political history of the new state for the next seventy-five years, during which this constitution with amendments was the supreme law of the state.

NOTES

1. R. Eden to Ld. Dartmouth, August 27, 1775, "Correspondence of Governor Eden," *Maryland Historical Magazine,* II (1907), p. 11; 1776, W. Eddis, *Letters from America* (London: The Author, 1792), pp. 305–306. See also A. A. Allan, "Patriots and Loyalists: The Choice of Political Allegiances by the Members of Maryland's Proprietary Elite," *Journal of Southern History,* XXXVIII (1972), pp. 283–292.

2. March 13, 1775, Eddis, *Letters,* p. 199; *Maryland Gazette,* February 16, 1775.

3. B. Galloway to T. Ringgold, Jr., May 7, 1775, Galloway, Maxcy, Markoe Papers, Library of Congress, XIV.

4. See letters by M. Tilghman, T. Stone, J. Rogers in *Letters of Members of the Continental Congress,* E. C. Burnett, editor, 8 vols. (Washington D C., 1921), I, pp. 485, 492–493.

5. Letters of T. Stone to [J. Hollyday?], May 20, 1776, and Hollyday to Stone, May 26, 1776, in H. E. Klingelhofer, "The Cautious Revolution: Maryland and the Movement Toward Independence, 1774–1776," *Maryland Historical Magazine,* LX (1965), pp. 286, 288–289; B. Rumsey to W. Rumsey, June 3, 1776, " 'A jurisdiction Competent to the Occasion': A Benjamin Rumsey Letter, June, 1776," J. F. Vivian and J. H. Vivian, editors, *Maryland Historical Magazine,* LXVII (1972), p. 150.

6. Benjamin Rumsey to Benedict Edward Hall, May 20, 1776, Klingelhofer, "The Cautious Revolution," p. 302; J. B. Johnson, *Robert Alexander, Maryland Loyalist* (New York: G. P. Putnam's Sons, 1942), pp. 38–106. Another insight into the way the movement toward independence divided the Maryland gentry is in H. Hollyday to J. Hollyday, July 14, 1775, Henry Hollyday Papers, Maryland Historical Society.

7 *Maryland Gazette,* June 27, July 4 & 18, 1776 *Maryland Journal,* July 3, 1776.

8. M. Earle to T. Ringgold, May 8, 1776, Henry Hollyway Papers, Maryland Historical Society.

9. June 11, 1776, Eddis, *Letters,* p. 306.

10. J. Adams to S. Chase, June 14, 1776, *Letters,* Burnett, editor, I, pp. 491–492. See similar sentiments in Madison to his father, June?, 1776, in *The Papers of James Madison,* W. T. Hutchinson and W. M. E. Rachal, editors, 7 vols. to date (Chicago: University of Chicago Press, 1962—), I, p. 182.

11. *Maryland Gazette,* March 14–May 9, 1776; *Maryland Journal,* May 1, 1776.

12. T. Stone to J. Hollyday], May 20, 1776, in Klingelhofer, "Cautious Revolution," p. 286; *Maryland Gazette,* June 27, July 4, July 18, 1776; *Maryland Journal,* July 10, 1776; *Archives of Maryland,* XI, p. 490.

13. *Proceedings of the Convention of the Province of Maryland, Held at the City of Annapolis, on Thursday the seventh of December, 1775* (Annapolis: Frederick Green, [1776]), p. 3; *Proceedings of the Convention of the Province of Maryland, Held at the City of Annapolis, on Friday the twenty-first of June, 1776* (Annapolis: Frederick Green, [1776]), p. 3.

14 *Archives of Maryland,* XI, pp. 27–28.

15 *Proceedings of the Convention of . . . June, 1776,* pp. 16–17.

16. C. Carroll to Carrollton April 15, 1774, "Extracts," *Maryland Historical Magazine,* XVI (1921), p. 29.

17. J. McClure to M. Gist, August 1776, Gist Papers, Maryland Historical Society; R. Eden to Ld. Dartmouth, October 1, 1775, "Correspondence of Eden," p. 101; *Archives of Maryland,* XI, pp. 163, 186, 191, 234.

18. *Archives of Maryland,* XII, p. 212; *Proceedings of the Convention of the Province of Maryland, Held at the City of Annapolis, on Wednesday the fourteenth day of August, 1776* (Annapolis: Frederick Green, [1776]), pp. 2–6.

19. Depositions of J. Disney, S. Godman, J. Sellman, T. H. Howard, J. Burgess, and T. Harwood, August 27, 1776, Red Books, XI, pp. 8, 9, 10, 11, 127, Maryland Hall of Records.

20. E. S. Delaplaine, "The Life of Thomas Johnson," *Maryland Historical Magazine,* XVIII (1922), pp. 192-195.

21. *Maryland Gazette,* August 15, 1776. Italics mine

22. *Maryland Gazette,* August 22, September 12, 1776; see Appendix II *Proceedings of the Convention of . . . August, 1776,* pp. 12, 23. Of course, the property restrictions for voting were imposed in this by-election, thereby depriving many of those favoring a widened suffrage of the right to express their opinion. Carroll, barrister, subsequently was elected to replace the deceased Thomas Ringgold of Kent County but did not return to the Convention before it adjourned.

23. *Proceedings of the Convention of . . . August, 1776,* pp. 3-6.

24. *Maryland Gazette,* July 18, 1776; reprinted in Appendix II.

25. *Maryland Gazette,* August 22, 1776; reprinted in Appendix II.

26. *Maryland Gazette,* August 22, 1776.

27. *Archives of Maryland,* L, xxviii; C. A. Barker, *The Background of the Revolution in Maryland* (New Haven: Yale University Press, 1940), p. 117; "Eighteenth Century Maryland As Portrayed in the 'Itenerant Observations' of Edward Kimber," *Maryland Historical Magazine,* LI (1956), p. 323.

28. E. P. Douglas, *Rebels and Democrats: The Struggle for Equal Political Rights and Majority Rule During the American Revolution* (Chapel Hill: University of North Carolina Press, 1955), pp. 10-32, 263-286. For Price's influence on the Founding Fathers, see C. B. Cone, *Torchbearer of Freedom: The Influence of Richard Price on Eighteenth Century Thought* (Lexington: University of Kentucky Press, 1952).

29. For an analysis of these delegates, see Appendix III. Most of the Catholics are listed in C. H. Metzger, *Catholics and the American Revolution* (Chicago: Loyola University Press, 1962), pp. 117-207. Thomas Sim Lee became a Catholic many years later.

30. *Archives of Maryland,* XI, pp. 93, 118, 328-329, 542-543; XVI, p. 504; W. Eddis to R. Eden, July 23, 1777, Public Record Office Transcripts, CO 5/722, 10-11, Library of Congress; Bowie, "John Bowie," *Maryland Historical Magazine,* XXXVIII (1943), pp. 141-160; N. W. Rightmyer, *Maryland's Established Church* (Baltimore: 1956), p. 117.

31. J. T. Main, "Political Parties in Revolutionary Maryland, 1780-1787," *Maryland Historical Magazine,* LXII (1967), pp. 1-27, quote 17. Similar cultural, economic distinctions in early nineteenth century politics are noted in T. B. Alexander, "The Basis of Alabama's Ante-Bellum Two-Party System," *Alabama Review,* XIX (1966), pp. 243-276.

32. Ibid. Main, "Political Parties," p. 17; J. R. Haeuser, "The Maryland Conventions, 1774-1776; A Study in the Politics of Revolution" (M.A. thesis, Georgetown University, 1968). Haeuser's conclusions, based upon a sample of 21 votes, and mine, using 66 of 68 votes to determine affiliation, agree closely as to the groups into which individual delegates fell. See also R. Hoffman, "Economics, Politics, and the Revolution in

Maryland" (Ph.D. dissertation, University of Wisconsin, 1969), pp. 271–301, for a discussion of the convention. The conclusions of J. C. Rainbolt in "A Note on the Maryland Declaration of Rights and Constitution of 1776," *Maryland Historical Magazine,* LXVI (1971), pp. 420–435, relative to the geographic distribution of voting patterns conflict with mine. This is primarily due to methodological differences coming from his subjective choice of what constituted the "Democratic" side on various votes and an unfortunate combining of the votes of the Baltimore and Anne Arundel County delegations with those from Baltimore Town and Annapolis. I am particularly grateful to Professor Peter H. Smith of the Department of History, University of Wisconsin, and Mr. David R. Olson of the Madison Area Computer Center for their kind assistance to a novice in setting up programs using factor analysis, the BOGUETAB system to create a matrix of voting blocs, and Automatic Interaction Detection to ascertain the optimal combination of variables predicting voting behavior. In most cases, place of residence was the most important variable, with those delegates from the northern (Baltimore, Harford, and Ann Arundel counties) and western (Frederick County) districts allied against the others. The other variables were age, occupation, and legislative experience.

33. Carrollton to C. Carroll, August 20, October 4, October 10, and October 18, 1776, same to same, no date (August-October, 1776), Charles Carroll of Annapolis Papers, Maryland Historical Society.

34. This and all subsequent discussion of the deliberations, and quotations from the Declaration of Rights and Constitution, are taken from *Proceedings of the Convention . . . of August, 1776.* Considered the most conservative whigs were: Barnes, Carroll of Carrollton, J.T. Chase, S. Chase, Horsey, Johnson, Plater, Gustavus Scott, J. Smith, and T. Smyth. On the most liberal democrat list were: Bowie, Deye, Fitzhugh, Hammond, Love, Mackall, Ridgely, Shepherd, Stevenson, and Williams.

35. Douglas, *Rebels,* pp. 21–32; "Charles Carroll's Plan of Government." P.A. Crowl, editor, *American Historical Review,* XLVI (1941), pp. 592–595.

36. Good published analyses of the 1776 constitution are found in P.A. Crowl, *Maryland During and After the Revolution: A Political and Economic Study* (Johns Hopkins University Studies, Series LXI, Baltimore, 1943), pp. 29–40, and Douglas, *Rebels,* pp. 45–54, 266–271.

37. For a convenient reprinting of both documents, see F. N. Thorpe, editor, *The Federal and State Constitutions,* 7 vols. (Washington, D.C.: Government Printing Office, 1909), III, pp. 1686–1701, VII, pp. 3812–3819.

38. Douglas, *Rebels,* pp. 50–54, 266–271, quote 54.

39. D. Jenifer to Carrollton *et al.,* February 2, 1771, in Crowl, *Maryland,* pp. 39–40.

EPILOGUE

Maryland is a little beside itself I think, but presently it will blaze out like a little Fire ship or a Volcano.

John Adams to Cotton Tufts,

June 23, 1776

10

THE QUEST FOR DEMOCRACY

Was colonial Maryland a democracy? If not, did the revolutionary ferment bring about an impulse toward change in the provincial society? These are the questions raised in the introduction to this monograph and they remain important to the understanding of colonial America.

In attempting to answer the first question, we are using the criteria for a democracy defined in the model created by Ranney and Kendall.[1] One must always remember that their ideas remain a "model," not an example of any actual state of the present or the past.

Their first principle was that of *popular sovereignty,* tested by four criteria.

The first of these criteria holds that the ultimate authority for all decisions rests with all members of society. Of course, one could not say that the ultimate decision-making authority rested with all the citizens of colonial Maryland. Instead, it rested with the Lord Proprietor, who held an absolute veto over all political decisions. This, however, was an undemocratic feature imposed from the outside and had little bearing on whether political democracy existed within the province. Where did sovereignty within the colony reside? This is the vital question.

Throughout the colonial period, it becomes apparent that ultimate authority in Maryland resided in the hands not of the masses but rather of the economic and social elite that controlled the political processes. Sovereignty resided with those who had property. Thus, while the voting regulations of the proprietary were far more liberal than those of England, they were patently discriminatory, so much so that they excluded a large segment of the populace from participation in the political processes. In an economy based upon agriculture, political participation required property ownership. Since the agrarian system required few tools and household utensils, landownership became a prerequisite to the franchise. But fewer than a third of the white adult freemen owned land, and probably not more than half—certainly not more than two-thirds—possessed the right to vote.

Moreover, with land as the prime indicator of wealth, an increasing population saw a decreasing percentage of the population becoming landholders. Tenantry became an increasingly common phenomenon of land tenure in colonial Maryland. Since upward social mobility required the acquisition of land, the opportunity for social advancement became increasingly more difficult and discouraged any tendency to move up the social ladder. Thus, internal political sovereignty resided in an increasingly smaller proportion of the population.

Second, popular sovereignty must mean that the formal as well as the legal governing institutions must respond to an orderly and non-violent expression of popular will. The idea that the Lower House or its successor, the convention, responded in anything but a negative fashion to the popular will expressed in many of the county meetings and militia resolutions is difficult to accept. Some elements in provincial society—elements which seemed to grow in strength, so that by the time of the Declaration they were a prominent factor in the decision-making process—concluded that only by violence could they force their opinions upon even the most "democratic" element in their government—the conventions. Substantial portions of the community felt it necessary to use techniques of expression outside those provided in the existing political system. Finding that the system failed to provide a legitimate means of expressing their desire for political change, these groups often resorted to violence or threats of violence to achieve their objectives. The existing institutions, whether proprietary or extra-legal revolutionary ones like the committees, conventions, or Council of Safety, thus responded ineffectively to many demonstrations of the concept of popular sovereignty.

The third criterion concerns the feeling of community within the geographic area—whether the desire to live together was at least as strong as the selfish desires of individual citizens and groups. To a large extent, Maryland met the test of community. One does see examples of a sense of separatism on the Eastern Shore, but on the whole there existed a commonality of interests within the province. Moreover, there was a tendency to include more and more groups within that community, although the traditional concept that elements of a society not homogeneous with the majority ought to be excluded still prevailed in some cases. At the end of the colonial period, the Roman Catholics and the Germans saw themselves accepted not as a divisive force but as another contributing element in a plural society. The Constitution of 1776 eliminated all restrictions on their full participation in political life. The concept of a plural society was more fully appreciated as the colonial period ended, although slaves, servants, and women found their liberties restricted in varying degrees.

The fourth criterion of political sovereignty holds that political power is not vested in any class or classes but in the community as a whole. Although political power may not have been vested in the gentry, it certainly rested there. The top fourth of the freeholders held three-fourths of the public offices, and most of the rest went to persons bound to them by class, kinship, or friendship. These included the vestry, militia, judiciary, civil, ecclesiastical, and legislative offices. Plural officeholding was another common feature of eighteenth-century life This concentration of office in the hands of one socio-economic group was part of a generally accepted principle. That the wealthiest members of society tended to hold public office does not of itself mean that government was undemocratic or unresponsive to the wishes of all elements of the community. In an era when Roosevelts, Kennedys, Javitses, and Harrimans allegedly represent the masses of society, it can hardly be argued that men of wealth are inherently unresponsive to the public weal. In Charles Ridgely, William Fitzhugh, and Rezin Hammond, a similar trend can be seen in revolutionary Maryland.

But this concentration of office in the hands of one socio-economic group was part of a generally accepted concept of the period which held that those with the greatest financial stake in society should govern it. This was coupled with a pervading and prevailing opinion of deference to one's social superiors at the polling place. This intellectual construct of a deferential society constituted an important constraint upon popular sovereignty.[2]

Ranney and Kendall's second principle of democracy, *political equality,* proceeds from the first. This involves not only the concept of one man-one vote (the limitations upon which have already been discussed), but also the belief that in other ways no group or individual should hold more power than other members of the community. If this principle is denied, a privileged class is created which makes democracy impossible. For political equality to operate, the individual must have genuine alternatives, information sufficient to make a choice between the alternatives, and freedom to exercise choice once the decision is made.

It is quite obvious that before the revolutionary ferment reached its climax in the mid-1770s, the voter was presented with few genuine alternatives and lacked sufficient information to make a choice between them. The editors of the *Maryland Gazette* adopted a generally non-partisan policy towards letters published in their journal and thereby allowed diverse opinions to circulate. However, virtually all the attitudes represented late in the colonial period came from the gentry and did not reflect any demand for wider electoral participation. They rather reflected the whiggish concept of political interplay between propertied gentlemen. Until the existence of the various local committees and militia units—from which emerged voices of social and political unrest— the gentry dominated the political scene by determining both the issues and the candidates among themselves. Sometimes they blatantly disregarded the pressing needs of the community in order to continue a petty jurisdictional quarrel with the Lord Proprietor.

Admittedly, the eligible voters had the right to make their choice freely, and many did so. Often their options were meaningless. A choice between two gentlemen whose only differences apparently were concerned with interfamily disputes over patronage plums was not enough to excite the average citizen to leave his warm home for a journey, usually in mid-winter, to a distant polling place.[3]

Popular consultation, the third of the Ranney-Kendall principles of democracy, demands that there be institutional devices by which the popular will may become known. It can be successfully argued that elections were frequent and gave the eligible electorate an adequate opportunity to express their opinions regarding the choices offered. For the freemen without the franchise, for the Roman Catholics, and for the immigrants, the only recourse was to express grievance through petition. This device did not achieve any significant results in those rare instances when it was tried. Still, one can hardly deny that the principle of popular consultation was available in the colony.

Majority rule, the last and most controversial of these principles, holds that the popular will must, eventually, become a matter of public policy. Before 1776, there is almost no evidence that the leading politicians of Maryland, save such renegades as Fitzhugh, Ridgely, and the Hammonds, ever believed in a democratic system in which the popular will determined public action. Response to the fickle will of the unpropertied masses was not a function of good government. Clinton Rossiter correctly perceived the nature of the whiggish revolutionists' concept of government when he wrote that their thoughts were "of liberty and self-government rather than of equality and mass participation." The most glaring confirmation of this disbelief in majority rule came when three Anne Arundel County delegates resigned their convention seats rather than support the principle of universal manhood suffrage demanded by many of their constituents, a principle which they felt to be "incompatible with good government and the public peace and happiness."[4]

It appears, then, that in colonial Maryland severe restrictions hampered the free exercise of democracy. The financial restrictions upon suffrage were not excessively limiting. But other legal, non-legal, social, and ideological limitations were imposed and they dominated the political scene.

Assuming, at least for the sake of argument, that colonial Maryland was not a democracy, one comes to a second question concerned with the political scene. Was there a demand for a more democratic political and social order in the years before the final break with the British crown? One must ascertain whether there were any attempts to change the legal limitations upon the exercise of the franchise and officeholding, and whether the ideological limitations of a deferential society continued.

There can be little doubt that the expansion of the electorate to include Catholics and Germans as full participants constitutes a remarkable change in the colonial order. The relative ease with which this was accomplished makes it apparent that colonial Maryland was probably well on the road to religious and ethnic toleration before revolutionary ferment led Marylanders further down the trail. More important were the assaults upon the "stake-in-society" concept of voting requirements. Here one finds the more democratically oriented elements of society waging a full-fledged attack upon entrenched interests, and winning a concession in the size of the property requirements for voting, but not a concession in the continuance of the principle of "stake-in-society." Moreover, to secure their principle, the whigs instituted property requirements for officeholding for the first time in Maryland history. Such restraints upon popular government indicate that by the time the new constitution went into effect during the winter of 1776-1777, democracy had not yet come to Maryland.

Further democratization of governmental structure came with the creation of two new counties and the admission of delegates from Baltimore Town. This meant that the new General Assembly would have representation more closely approximating population distribution than had the colonial Lower House. The provision that four delegates should represent each county meant that many of the counties with small populations would be over-represented in comparison with the more populous ones. [5]

More important than the structural changes occurring in Maryland political life were the ideological changes wrought by the movement towards independence. Of particular importance was the idea that the populace at large must be consulted on major public issues before action was taken. Writing in May, 1776, from Philadelphia, Continental Congressman Thomas Stone informed James Hollyday: "The vox populi must in great measure influence your determination" whether or not to declare independence from Britain. A month after this request for popular determination of the question of independence, Stone and Congressman John Rogers wrote of seeking to provide "an Opportunity to our constituents to communicate to us the Sense of the Province upon" this issue. On the eve of the constitutional convention, "Watchman" proclaimed: "The voice of the people should be heard with a solemn attention, and duly regarded." Such principles belied the whiggish tradition that elected officials were independent entities.[6]

The concept of consultation embodied a belief that constituents could instruct their delegates on how to vote. In late June, assemblies all over the colony resolved that Convention delegates should support the independence resolutions. Not only could they instruct, but the delegates felt bound by instructions. In mid-August, a convocation of 885 Anne Arundel County freemen urged their representatives to support this constitutional provision: "That all freemen, natives of this State, above twenty-one years of age, and well affected to the present glorious cause in which we are engaged, shall have the right of a free vote in the election of all officers who are to be chosen by the people." Feeling themselves "bound by your instructions although ever so contrary to our opinion," three of the county's four delegates resigned their seats rather than support "measures, in their opinion, incompatible with good government and the public peace and happiness." They asked for a new convocation of citizens at which they explained their positions. At an ensuing by-election, two of those three were again returned to the Convention.[7]

A corollary to this development was the emergence of a policy by which representatives had to justify their voting records before the assembled electorate at the next regular election. Benjamin Rumsey, member of the Council of Safety and of the June Convention, explained his votes to a friend back in Harford County. He felt that the manner in which he voted "was agreeable to the Desires and Wishes of the People." Rumsey's duties on the Council precluded his attending the election for constitutional convention delegates, so he hoped that his friends would rescue his "Character from any injurious Aspersions that may be thrown on it" so that he might preserve the good opinion of his "Countrymen."[8]

At the same time that the electorate were being more assiduously consulted by their representatives, they were being presented with more meaningful choices at the polling place. The best known example of this was the defeat of Thomas Johnson, William Paca, and Charles Carroll, barrister, in the 1776 elections for Anne Arundel County. In fact, a startled Council of Safety reported their defeat despite the fact that "very few people from Elkridge or the lower part of the County," the sections most inclined toward egalitarianism, had come to the polling places. At the same election in Baltimore County, there were at least seven known candidates for four positions. Although John McClure thought only a few candidates were "clever" (for which read "gentlemen"), he acknowledged that there were viable alternatives afforded the electorate.[9]

Probably most significant was the declining deference to gentry leadership, or at least to gentlemen who did not cater to the vocal demands of the populace. The most graphic examples of this occur in the most democratic elections of the revolutionary era— those for militia officers. Concern for gentry domination of civil elections affected a traditional leader like Daniel of St. Thomas Jenifer, who wrote to ex-Governor Sharpe on the eve of Maryland's independence: "I confess that should there be a departure from the old system of laws in the province I shall be totally unfit to have anything to say as to public matters." In order to prevent the feared "departure from the old system," the delegates to the constitutional convention wrote probably the most conservative of the revolutionary constitutions. By requiring a rather large amount of property for officeholders and by making most public offices either indirectly elected or appointive, they hoped to preserve Maryland whiggery.[10]

The tradition-minded gentry were, of course, attempting to hold back a rising flood. As this flood was a long way from its highwater mark, some temporary shoring of the levees would be effective. Still, the rising waters of democratic revolution swept through Maryland during the 1770s, and the restraints placed upon it by the Convention could not long endure.

This meant that when Jacob Funk, leading German-American patriot of Frederick County, spoke of "a Gentleman whose opinions I have generally received with much Deference," he was in reality expressing a philosophy of deferential politics that no longer prevailed in many sections of the new state. In 1767, the Rev. Thomas Cradock preached how the true Christian "shews deference to his superiors, is open, clear and friendly with his equals, [and is] easy of access to Inferiors." Less than nine years later, his son would resign a major's commission received from the Convention because the enlisted men of the Soldier's Delight battalion declared they would "be commanded only by officers recommended by themselves."

Instead of deference, politicians might find themselves confronted with the ridicule heaped upon Robert Alexander and "some of the Great Men of Baltimore-Town" in a broadside apparently printed in 1774. Published by the backers of Charles Ridgely, it was allegedly an appeal by "the principal Merchants" for Ridgely to resign from the Lower House so that Alexander could be elected in his place. Signed "Captain BOB-AD-ILL," the broadside mockingly praised Alexander in doggerel:

> For his eloquent Speech is so pow'rful and strong,
> He'll make *Wrong* appear *Right* and make *Right* appear *Wrong*.

The versifier made the merchants confess:

> And our Int'rest is such, so designing our Ways,
> That each man in the County shall *Vote* as We please.

While admitting they had "the greatest Regard" for his father, these "Great Men" "resolv'd [Ridgely] sha'nt sit in the House." They acknowledged that the usual structure of voting restrictions had broken down during the revolutionary ferment and to overcome Ridgely's popularity with the masses they proposed "to demand and insist on a regular Poll." All this comment and satire was a far cry from the politics of the colonial period.[11]

This same resort to ridicule of the establishment and its ideas appeared in a poem entitled "The Song of the Man in the Moon," published shortly after the adoption of the Constitution of 1776. Commenting upon the fact that legislators under the new government must have property worth £ 1,000 currency before they can serve, the moonman observed:

Alas! we've lost our liberty.
When thousand pounds must bear the sway,
While men of merit's cast away;
Because they thousands can't produce,
They're render'd quite unfit for use,
While naves and fools may strut and flutter,
About their money make a splutter,
Persuading people all they can
It is the money makes the man;
    Tho' man has often money made,
And by it often been betray'd,
To think himself did far excel,
Him that in humble station dwell.

    Let Virtue be the moving cause,
Or *summum bonum* of your laws,
Then may your state continue long,
And be the burden of my song.
    But if old Mammon bear the sway,
He'll drive your virtuous sons away
To other states, and you, when scant,
Will fall a venal mendicant. [12]

As the discussion of militia elections in Chapter 8 illustrated, the masses were often not content to defer to social superiors who made no commitment to support measures endorsed by the populace.

Controversies over the drift toward revolution became so heated that gentlemen were impelled to hurl vindictive charges at one another. Probably the heights of this were reached in Maryland when a whig calling himself "A Citizen" charged, in a handbill issued in January 1775, that a "shameless" person, *"bankrupt . . .* both in fortune and reputation," led "a band of bravoes" from the Elkridge section of northern Anne Arundel County. This "son of distraction" and his followers allegedly threatened by "a dagger or a torch, to destroy the lives and properties of those he hates or *fears."* Under the appellation of "An American," the accused replied in kind. It may have been Rezin Hammond who felt the impact of the charges of "A Citizen" and who hid under the pseudonym of "An American" and, later,

"Watchman." The egalitarian-oriented politicians were not above expressing their desire to communicate directly with the citizenry, regardless of their social position. Col. William Fitzhugh posted a notice in the *Maryland Gazette* expressing pleasure at having received an anonymous piece signed "Freeman." He then indicated he "would be happy in an interview with the author (however humble may be his station) whose sentiments are so favourable, and so timely calculated, to preserve the rights and liberties, and promote the happiness of the people."[13]

Such exchanges helped to undermine the tradition of deference to one's social superiors. The consequences of these quarrels between gentlemen and nondeferential expressions became most apparent in the quest for political equality for all freemen. Time after time, the rioters and demonstrators at the polls during the critical election of July 1776 demanded, as they did in Kent County, that "every associator resident of the county one year, and 21 years of age, might be enabled to vote." Similarly, the freemen of Prince George's County resolved "that every taxable bearing arms, being an inhabitant of the county, had an undoubted right to vote for representatives at this time of public calamity."[14] The concept of deference was closely intertwined with the whiggish ideology of a stake-in-society suffrage concept, so that when one of these was attacked, both were in fact being destroyed as accepted political ideals.

Because of the temporary triumph of whiggery in the Constitution of 1776, one must not reason that revolutionary Maryland was a backwater into which none of the principles of the American political tradition strayed. On the contrary, the dominant whiggish ideology made major contributions to the development of American concepts of political rights during the years of its dominance. One such contribution concerned the right of an individual to believe in and publicly advocate pacificism while the state was engaged in a total war. More particularly, this concerned the activities of Quakers and Methodists on the Eastern Shore during the Revolution. The gentry leadership, at a time when their new state was fighting for its very right to exist, allowed men such as Freeborn Garrettson, a Methodist preacher, to continue their work in behalf of pacificism. To do this, when pacificism combined with loyalism posed a threat to the new nation, the whigs exhibited a spirit of toleration which the more "democratic" faction was not willing to accord.[15]

Another such contribution occurred when the *Maryland Journal's* editor, William Goddard, found himself driven from Baltimore because some of his irresponsible editorial decisions aroused the ire of demagogic political leaders. Twice the gentry leadership of the state secured Goddard's safe return to his press and, thereby, championed the right of a newspaper to support actions considered contrary to the war effort by local superpatriots.[16] In both these instances, the popular majority probably favored a curtailment of the activities of Garrettson and Goddard. The gentry's response did much to further an American civil liberties tradition. Whiggery was not, then, an unmixed blessing. It added significantly to the American political tradition.

In conclusion, the disruptive effects of British imperial politics upon traditional politics in Maryland resulted in major attempts to change not merely the ties to the Mother Country, but also the connections with whiggish thought. Bernard Friedman found similar developments in revolutionary New York, and what he wrote about that colony could, with a few name changes, be written about His Lordship's province:

Provincial politics became less exclusive. Party affiliations seem less secure, political issues are less related to denominational quarrels of the De Lanceys and the Livingstons. The General Assembly appears less at the center of provincial affairs. In short, the powers of the ruling aristocracy in New York are qualified at almost every significant point at the very time that these gentlemen battle so furiously for power.[17]

The demands made by the democratic or egalitarian politicians were part of a conscious attempt to wrest control of the province from the great planters of whiggish persuasion who maintained townhouses in Annapolis and who saw to it that they, their brothers, their cousins, and their in-laws received the most influential and lucrative offices. These demands were not an attempt to secure a leveling of society; instead, they represented a desire for the creation of an environment in which a greater degree of social, political, and economic mobility might exist. When one takes into consideration the provisions of the Constitution of 1776, their efforts appear to have failed.

In this context, a study of the revolutionary movement in Maryland indicates that the most influential segment of society desired the preservation of the existing social, economic, and political order, and it was willing to exert extensive energies and talent to preserve that society from threats directed against it either by the British government or by domestic malcontents. Despite the virulent attacks against their position, the whig leadership of Maryland—Matthew Tilghman, both Charles Carrolls, Samuel Chase, and Thomas Johnson—never lost its nerve. That the whigs won should not disguise the fact that in the years just prior to the Declaration of Independence, other social elements began to demand a more drastic revision of society than the gentry anticipated was necessary to end parliamentary tyranny. Such demands indicate that many colonial Marylanders desired a more democratic social, political, and economic order than existed before 1776.[18]

Although the major trust of this monograph has been to show that economic, social, and political democracy was severely limited in colonial Maryland, and that there were attempts to modify this situation in the decade before the Constitution of 1776, it must be pointed out that what were merely the roots of a democratic impulse in 1776 became the dominant political ideology of Maryland a quarter of a century later. The ideas of the Anne Arundel militia, of "Watchman," of "An American," did not become political reality until 1801; but they were part of the revolutionary heritage of the Free State. Maryland's Revolution did not end until these ideas became embodied in its constitution. When, at the turn of the century, Free Staters modified their fundamental law so as to allow for universal manhood suffrage and to forbid property restrictions on office-holding, they culminated a quest for democracy begun in the 1770s. Merely because it took several years after the fighting ended to achieve the egalitarian goals, one can hardly argue against the idea that many who fought the war of the Revolution in this particular state did so because they desired to change the existing social order, to see the enactment of what Carl Becker has called an "internal revolution."[19]

NOTES

1. A. Ranney & W. Kendall, *Democracy and the American Party System* (New York: Harcourt, Brace, & World, 1956), pp. 1–39, esp. pp. 23–39. For a more detailed definition of what he calls "populistic democracy," see R. A. Dahl, *A Preface to Democratic Theory* (Chicago: University of Chicago Press, 1956), pp. 34–62.

2. C. S. Sydnor, *Gentlemen Freeholders: Political Practices in Washington's Virginia* (Chapel Hill: University of North Carolina Press, 1952), pp. 92–93; R. Buel, "Democracy and the American Revolution: A Frame of Reference," *William and Mary Quarterly,* Series 3, XXI (1964), pp. 165–190.

3. C. Williamson, *American Suffrage from Property to Democracy, 1760–1860* (Princeton: Princeton University Press, 1960), pp. 43–45; D. C. Skaggs, "Editorial Policies of the *Maryland Gazette,* 1765–1783," *Maryland Historical Magazine,* LIX (1964), pp. 341–349

4. C. Rossiter, *The First American Revolution: The American Colonies on the Eve of Independence* (New York, 1956), p. 101; *Maryland Gazette,* August 22, 1776.

5. See particularly *Maryland Journal,* July 3, 1776; *Maryland Gazette,* July 18, August 15, August 22, September 12, 1776; *Proceedings of the Convention Held at the City of Annapolis, on Wednesday, the fourteenth day of August, 1776* (Annapolis: Frederick Green, [1775]); D. Cunz, *The Maryland Germans: A History* (Princeton: Princeton University Press, 1948), pp. 133–135; C. H. Metzger, *Catholics in the American Revolution: A Study in Religious Climate* (Chicago: Loyola University Press, 1962), pp. 177–207.

6. T. Stone to J. Hollyday, May 20, 1776, Stone Papers, Library of Congress; Stone and J. Rogers to Council of Safety, June 15, 1776, *Letters of Members of the Continental Congress,* E. C. Burnett editor, 8 vols., (Washington, D.C. Carnegie Institution, 1921), I, pp. 492–493; *Maryland Gazette,* August 15, 1776.

7. *Maryland Gazette,* June 27, July 4, July 18, August 22, September 12, 1776; *Maryland Journal,* July 10, 1776; (Baltimore) *Dunlap's Maryland Gazette,* July 23, 1776; *To Walter Tolley, Benjamin Nicholson, John Moale, Robert Alexander, and Jeremiah Townley Chase, Esqrs.* [Baltimore: Mary K. Goddard, 1775 or 1776].

8. B. Rumsey to B. E. Hall, July 26, 1776, B. E. Hall Papers, Maryland Historical Society.

9. *Archives of Maryland,* XII, p. 163; J. McClure to M. Gist, August 1776, Gist Papers, Maryland Historical Society.

10. On the democratization of the militia, see Chapter 8; D. Jenifer to H. Sharpe, June 22, 1776, in H. E. Klingelhofer, "The Cautious Revolution: Maryland and the Movement Toward Independence: 1774–1776," *Maryland Historical Magazine,* LX (1965), p. 297; *Proceedings of the Convention . . . of August, 1776.*

11. J. Funk to J. B. Bordley, n.d. (sometime between May 25 and June 21, 1776), Bordley Papers, Maryland Historical Society, box 3, item 272; T. Cradock, Sermon on Patience, Heb. 6:12, Maryland Diocesan Archives; J. Cradock to Council, July 1, 1776, *Archives of Maryland,* XI, pp. 195–196; *Where are ye All now? A very*

curious and modest Address, lately sent to Mr. Charles Ridgely, by some of the Great Men of Baltimore-town, versified (n.p., n.d.). This broadside is cataloged, Evans no. 18884, as being published in Baltimore by William Goddard in 1784; L. C. Wroth, *A History of Printing in Colonial Maryland, 1684–1776* (Baltimore: The Typothetae, 1922), p. 245, correctly has it printed in 1774 by Mary K. Goddard.

    12. *Maryland Gazette,* October 24, 1776.

    13. *To the Citizens of Annapolis, January 11, 1775.* [Signed] *A Citizen* [Annapolis: Frederick Green, 1775]; *To the Citizens of Annapolis, January 13, 1775.* [Signed] *An American* [Annapolis: Frederick Green, 1775], broadsides in MS Div., Library of Congress; *Maryland Gazette,* October 31, 1776

    14. *Proceedings of the Convention . . . of August, 1776,* pp. 2, 6.

    15. T.O. Hanley, "The State and Dissenters in the Revolution," *Maryland Historical Magazine,* LVIII (1963), pp. 325–332. For a more detailed account of the status of religious groups in the Revolution, see T. O. Hanley, "The Impact of the American Revolution on Religion in Maryland: 1776–1800" (Ph.D. dissertation, Georgetown University, 1961).

    16. W.L. Miner, *William Goddard, Newspaperman* (Durham, N. C.: Duke University Press, 1962), pp. 152–162, 167–173.

    17. B. Friedman, "The New York Assembly Elections of 1768 and 1769: The Disruption of Family Politics," *New York History,* XLVI (1965), pp. 3–24; B. Friedman, "The Shaping of the Radical Consciousness in Provincial New York," *Journal of American History,* LVI (1969–1970), pp. 781–801.

    18. In his analysis of the quest for democracy in the Atlantic community during the late eighteenth century, Robert R. Palmer provided an insight into the situation in Maryland when he observed: "The tendency of history to follow the big battalions is well known; but it seems hardly necessary to maintain that, because the democratic movement failed, no such thing existed." "Notes on the Use of the Word 'Democracy,' 1780–1799," *Political Science Quarterly,* LXVIII (1953), p. 226. Conclusions similar to those in this paragraph may be found in C. S. Olton, "Philadelphia's Mechanics in the First Decade of the Revolution, 1765–1775," *Journal of American History,* LIX (1972–1973), pp. 311–326.

    19. For an introduction to political developments in Maryland after 1776, see P. A. Crowl, *Maryland during and after the Revolution: A Political and Economic Study* (Baltimore: Johns Hopkins Press, 1943); J. T. Main, "Political Parties in Revolutionary Maryland, 1780–1787," *Maryland Historical Magazine,* LXII (1967) pp. 1–27; Williamson, *American Suffrage,* pp. 138–151; J. R. Pole, "Suffrage and Representation in Maryland from 1776 to 1810: A Statistical Note and Some Reflections," *Journal of Southern History,* XXIV (1958), pp. 218–225; L. L. Verstandig, "The Emergence of the Two-Party System in Maryland, 1787–1796" (Ph.D. dissertation, Brown University, 1970).

I

CORRELATION OF ASSEMBLY AND VESTRY SERVICE[1]

Assemblymen	Assembly Elections	Parish	Vestry Service
	Baltimore County		
Adair, Robert	1767	St. John's	1755-1758
Buchanan, Lloyd	1754	None[2]	
Deye, Thomas Cockey	1758,1761,1764, 1767,1771,1773	St. Thomas'	1755
Dorsey, John Hammond	1758,1761	St. John's	1762-1765
Govane, William	1754,1758	None[2]	
Hall, Aquila	1773	St. George's	1756-1759,1769-1773
Hall, John, Jr.	1764	St. George's[3]	
Heath, James	1764	St. George's	1762-1765
Lee, Corbin	1761,1764	St. George's	1760-1763
Moale, John	1767,1771	St. Paul's[4]	1730-1733
Owings, Samuel	1758	St. Paul's	1735-1738,1744-1745
Owings, Samuel, Jr.	1771	St. Thomas'	1768-1771,1776
Paca, John	1754,1761	St. John's	1748-1751,1753-1756
Ridgely, Charles	1773	St. Paul's	1750-1753,1767-1768
Ridgely, John	1767	St. Paul's	1752-1754,1758-1761
Risteau, George	1771	St. Thomas'	1763-1766
Tolley, Walter	1754	St. John's	1749-1753,1761-1772,1775
Tolley, Walter, Jr.	1773	St. John's	1767

APPENDIX I - Continued

CORRELATION OF ASSEMBLY AND VESTRY SERVICE[1]

Assemblymen	Assembly Elections	Parish	Vestry Service
Prince George's County			
Addison, John	1754	St. John's	1747-1750-1753-1756,1758-1762, 1766-1769
Beall, Josias, Jr.	1758,1761,1764, 1767,1771,1773	Pr. George's	1760-1763
Contee, Thomas	1771,1773	St. Paul's	1755-1758,1770-1772,1772-1775
Fraser, George	1754,1758	St. John's	
Hawkins, John; Jr.	1754	St. John's	1748-1751
Jacob, Mordecai	1761,1764	Queen Anne's	1748-1751,1755-1758,1758-1761 1770-1771
King, Francis	1758	St. John's	1754-1757,1762-1765
Murdock, William	1754,1758,1761, 1764,1767	Queen Anne's	1753-1755
Sim, Joseph	1771,1773	St. Paul's	1756-1759,1766-1769,1769-1771, 1771-1774
Tyler, Robert	1764,1767,1771 1773	Queen Anne's	1756-1759,1771-1772
Waring, Francis	1761,1767	St. Paul's	1748-1751,1758-1761
Queen Anne's County			
Bracco, John	1754	St. John's	1752-1755,1756-1759
Brown, John	1773	St. Luke's	1765-1768,1769-1772
Casson, Henry	1754	St. John's	1752-1755,1757-1760
Earle, Richard Tilghman	1771,1773	St. Paul's	1756-1759,1764-1766,1769-1772
Harris, Thomas	1758	St. Paul's	1749-1752
Hollyday, James	1761,1764,1767	St. Luke's	1751-1754
Hopper, William	1758	St. Paul's	1748-1751,1758-1761
Lloyd, Robert	1754,1758,1761 1764,1767	St. Paul's	1753-1756
Tilghman, Edward	1754,1758,1761 1764,1767,1771	St. Paul's	1754-1757,1764-1767
Wright, Solomon	1771,1773	St. Luke's	1782
Wright, Thomas	1761,1764,1767 1771	St. Paul's	1752-1755,1761-1764,1768-1771, 1773-1776
Wright, Turbutt	1773	St. Luke's	1770-1773

APPENDIX I (Continued)

CORRELATION OF ASSEMBLY AND VESTRY SERVICE

Assemblymen	Assembly Elections	Parish	Vestry Service
Talbot County			
Bowman, Samuel	1758	(Quaker)	
Chamberline, James Lloyd	1771,1773	St. Michael's	1765-1768
Dickinson, James	1767	St. Peter's	1750-1753,1759-1762,1766-1769
Edge, James	1754	St. Michael's	1756-1757
Edmondson, Pollard	1754,1758,1761 1764	St. Peter's	1750-1753,1753-1756,1760-1763
Gibson, Woolman	1758,1764	St. Michael's	1759-1762,1764-1767
Goldsborough, John	1754,1758,1761 1764	St. Peter's	1747-1750,1761-1764
Hollyday, Henry	1764	St. Michael's	1754-1756,1768-1771,1774-1777
Lloyd, Edward, IV	1767,1771,1773	St. Michael's	1766-1769
Thomas, Nicholas	1767,1771,1773	St. Michael's?	
Thomas, William	1761	St. Peter's	1758-1761
		St. Michael's	1754-1758
Tilghman, James	1761	St. Michael's	
Tilghman, Matthew	1754,1767,1771, 1773	St. Michael's	1762-1765,1767-1770

1. See the Vestry Proceedings of the following parishes in Maryland Hall of Records: Baltimore County— St. George's, St. John's; Prince George's County— Queen Anne's, St. Paul's; Queen Anne's County— St. John's, St. Luke's, St. Paul's; Talbot County— St. Michael's, St. Peter's; Frederick County— Prince George's, Rock Creek (which included part of Prince George's County in its jurisdiction). A nineteenth century copy of the proceedings of the St. Thomas Parish, Baltimore County is in Maryland Hall of Records, and the author is indebted to the late Richard H. Randall for his tracking down a list of vestrymen of St. Paul's Parish. Baltimore Town.

2. "None" indicates that no record of vestry service, 1750–1776, has been found.

3. Of the many John Halls in the county, it is difficult to determine whether this was the one who had vestry service.

4. It is doubtful that John Moale, vestryman, is the same John Moale, delegate.

II

THE ANNE ARUNDEL COUNTY RESOLVES

A. The Militia Resolves*

We are informed, that the following instructions were drawn up by the conferees appointed by the several battalions of militia of Anne-Arundel county, and afterwards signed by a great number of the inhabitants of the county, and in consequence thereof, moved in the late Convention.

To *Charles Carroll,* barrister, *Samuel Chase, Thomas Johnson, William Paca,* and *Charles Carroll,* of Carrollton, Esquires, delegates in Convention for Anne-Arundel county.

Gentlemen:

WE, the freemen of Anne-Arundel county, taking into serious consideration the present alarming situation of this province, have determined to exercise our unquestionable right of instructing our delegates in Convention: no apology is necessary; neither is any, we presume, expected from us: from the very nature of the trust, and the relation sub-

---

*Maryland Gazette, July 18, 1776.

sisting between constituent and representative, the former is entitled to express his sentiments and to instruct the latter upon all points that may come under his consideration as representative.——We therefore instruct you as follows:

1st. That you move for and endeavour to obtain a resolution in Convention, that the instructions given by the Convention in December last, and renewed by the May Convention, to the deputies of this province in Congress be rescinded, and the restrictions therein contained removed.

2dly. That you move for and endeavour to obtain a resolution in Convention, that this province be united with the other twelve colonies represented in Congress and that the deputies of this colony be authorized and directed to concur with the other united colonies, or a majority of them, in Congress, in declaring the United Colonies free and independent states, and in forming such further compact and confederation between them, in making foreign alliances, and in adopting such other measures as shall be adjudged necessary for securing the liberties of America, provided the sole and exclusive right of regulating the internal government and police of this province be reserved to the people thereof.

3dly. That you move for and endeavour to obtain a resolution of the Convention, that the exercise of every kind of authority under the crown of Great-Britain be now totally suppressed, and that a government be formed for this province under the authority of the people only.

4thly. That you move for and endeavour to obtain a resolution of Convention, that a government for this province ought not to be formed and carried into execution by this present Convention.

5thly. That you move for and endeavour to obtain a resolution of Convention, that a full and equal representation of the people be appointed, and a new Convention be immediately elected, with full powers to form and establish a new government; which Convention to continue until the last day of December next, and such government to be subject to such alterations and amendments as the people may judge necessary.

6thly. That you move for and endeavour to obtain a resolution of

Convention, that a Council of Safety be appointed to exist during the intermediate time between the dissolution of the present and the meeting of the next Convention, and also deputies to represent this province in Congress.

7thly. That you move for and endeavour to obtain a resolution of Convention, that all public and private interest of monies cease and determine during this time of general distress, such monies only to be excepted as have been actually lent within the three last months, which shall be proved by the lender to have been lent within the time above-mentioned, to the satisfaction of such persons as shall be appointed to determine the same, and that country produce be a lawful tender for the interest of the same, at the market price, to be regulated by two unexceptionable freeholders upon oath, one to be appointed by each party.

8thly. That you move for and endeavour to obtain a resolution of Convention, that the monies appropriated by act of assembly for opening, clearing, and straitening the roads in this county, be immediately applied to the payment of the public charge of this county.

9thly. That you move for and endeavour to obtain a resolution of Convention, that all rents may be paid and shall be received, in country produce, at the same rates which such commodities bore at the time such contract was made or renewed; and the same to be set by the committees of observation until other persons are appointed.

10thly. That you move for and endeavour to obtain a resolution of Convention, that no person be allowed to bring fire arms, or any other weapons offensive or defensive, to the ensuing election of delegates in Convention.

Anne-Arundel county, June 26, 1776.

At a meeting of the deputies of the several battalions of militia of this county in convention at the house of Mr. John Ball, in the city of Annapolis.

It was proposed, that the following do pass as a resolve of this committee:— That this committee do proceed to draw up a sketch of a form of government for this province to be laid before the people of this county, for their consideration. A question was put on the passage of the same, and determined in the affirmative.

For the affirmative:— Edward Gaither, Thomas Tillard, A. Warfield, James Tootell, Philemon Warfield, Vachel Gaither, Thomas Harwood, Richard Cromwell, Thomas Mayo, Andrew Ellicot, Rezin Hammond, Matthias Hammond.

The following gentlemen declined voting on the above, conceiving that they had no power from their constituents for that purpose:— Thomas Dorsey, John Dorsey, E. Howard, Benj. Galloway, John Dorsey, son of Michael, Samuel Harrison, jun. John Thomas, Joseph Ellicot, Richard Stringer, Michael Pue.

The committee then adjourned until 9 o'clock tomorrow morning.

June 27, 1776.

Committee met according to adjournment.— The committee proceeded to take up the resolve of yesterday, respecting the drawing up of a form of government for this province, to be laid before the people of this county for their consideration. Whereupon the following form of government was approved of by a majority of the committee, ordered to be published, and laid before the people of this county.

A FORM OF GOVERNMENT proposed for the consideration of the people of *Anne-Arundel* county.

The right to legislate is in every member of the community: But, for the sake of convenience the exercise of such right must be delegated to certain persons, to be chosen by the people. When this choice is free, it is the peoples *[sic]* fault if they are not happy.

That the legislative may be so constituted as never to be able to form an interest of its own, separate from the interest of the community at large, it is necessary its branches should be independent of, and balance each other, and all dependent on the people.

1. That there be chosen by the people a lower house; also, that there be chosen by the people an upper house— these two bodies to form the legislative power.

It is essential to liberty, that the legislative, judicial, and executive powers of government be separate from each other; for where they are united in the same person, or number of persons, there would be wanting that mutual check which is the principal security against their making of arbitrary laws, and a wanton exercise of power in the execution of them.

2. That there be a council of seven persons, appointed by the joint ballot of the two houses of legislature, from their bodies to hold the executive power.

3. That these several bodies, legislative and executive, hold their powers for one year; as annual elections are most friendly to liberty, and the oftener power reverts to the people, the greater will be the security for a faithful discharge of it.

4. That the vacancies created in either house of legislature, by the appointment of the council aforesaid, be filled up by the people of such counties where such persons were sent from, that there may be always a full representation of the people in both houses of the legislature.

5. That judges of a provincial court, be annually appointed by joint ballot of the two houses; also a clerk for the provincial office (having no secretary for that office as heretofore) with reasonable fees for their respective services.

6. That commissioner and clerk of loan office, attorney general, treasurer, register for land-office, judge, marshal and clerk for the court of admiralty, be annually appointed by the joint ballot of the two houses of legislature.

7. That the justices of the peace, sheriffs, clerks of counties, and surveyors, be annually chosen by the people of each county.

8. That the chancery business be done by the respective county courts, subject to an appeal to the council, who shall have power finally to determine on such appeal.— The official business to be done by their respective clerks of each court, with reasonable fees for their respective services.

9. That there be annually chosen, by the people of each county, a person to serve as register of wills, granting letters of administration, &c and that the business heretofore done by the commissary of this province, be done by the county courts, with an appeal to the council, with reasonable fees for their respective services.

10. That no fees be allowed to be taken agreeable to the old table, but that a new and equitable table of fees be established.

11. That trial by jury be held and kept sacred; also the habeas corpus preserved.

12. That no person shall be eligible to sit in either house of legis-lature, or council, or congress, who holds any office of profit, or any pension, receives any profit, or any part of the profit thereof either directly or indirectly, or who holds any office in the regular military service, or marine service, either continental or provincial.

13. That all officers of the regular or marine service be appointed by the joint ballot of both houses of legislature.

14. That the present resolves of the conventions of this province, restricting suits at law, stand and remain during this time of public calamity.

15. That no standing armies be kept up only in time of war.

16. That a well regulated militia be established in this province, as being the best security for the preservation of the lives, liberties and properties of the people.

17. That every militia company chuse its own officers, battalions their field-officers, and the district battalions their brigadier-generals.

18. The adjutants, drummers, and fifers, with drums and fifes, and cartouche-boxes, be provided at the public expense, for the different battalions of militia; and guns for such unarmed men who are not able to purchase the same.— And that the colonels of each battalion be empowered to contract for the above, and procure the same, and draw on the treasurer for the amount.

19. That a congress be appointed annually, and composed of mem-bers of each colony, to convene at any place they may agree on, as occasion may require; to have power to adjust disputes between colon-ies, regulate the affairs of trade, war, peace alliances, &c.— reserving to the people of each colony the exclusive right of regulating the inter-nal government and police thereof.— That there be seven deputies appointed by the joint ballot of the two houses of legislature of this province, for congress annually, out of their bodies, and that the va-cancies created in either house, by such appointment, be forthwith filled up, by election by the people of such counties where such mem-bers were sent from.— That there may be always a full representation of the people in assembly as well as in congress.—The continuance of such persons in assembly when public business requires their con-tinual attendance in congress, would be nugatory, and serve only as a mark of respect, which could not compensate for the injury done the public, by their absence from either station.

20. That all the votes and proceedings of the assembly be published, except such parts as relate to military operations, and measures taken to procure arms and ammunition, and that they sit open, except when particular business requires their being private.— And that the votes and proceedings of congress be published, except as aforesaid.

21. That an oath be taken by every person who shall hold an office of profit or trust, to stand true, be faithful, maintain and support the constitution, and to the utmost of his power promote the interest of the people.— Such constitution, however, to be subject to be changed, or altered, or amended, from time to time by the people, as they may judge necessary.

22. That all monies to be raised on the people be by a fair and equal assessment, in proportion to every person's estate— and that the unjust mode of taxation by the poll, heretofore used, be abolished; and that assessors be chosen by the people of each district in each county annually.

Signed per order of the Committee.
BRICE T. B. WORTHINGTON, Chairman.

B. Instructions to Convention Delegates**

Instructions

To Charles Carroll, barrister, *Brice Thomas Beal Worthington, Samuel Chase,* and *Rezin Hammond,* Esqrs. representative for Anne-Arundel county.

Gentlemen,

WE the subscribers, freemen of Anne Arundel county, taking into our most serious consideration the important business you are to meet upon the 12th of this instant, think it our indispensable duty to give you the following instructions.— It is with much concern and displeasure we find, that the last convention excluded all such of our countrymen who did not possess fifty acres of land, or a visible estate of forty

---

**Maryland Gazette, August 22, 1776.

pounds sterling, in the election of representatives, thereby unjustly depriving near half of the free inhabitants of this state, of the inestimable right of free suffrage: nevertheless subjecting them to all the pains and burthens of government. This glaring injustice, hateful distinction and apparent impolicy, we are determined to use our utmost efforts to get redressed; and that our free, honest, well affected brethren, as they proportionably bear with us every burthen and brave every danger, shall equally share every privilege: WE therefore direct and instruct you to move for, and use your utmost endeavours to establish, in the *New Government,*— That all freemen, natives of this *State,* above twenty-one years of age, and well affected to the present glorious cause in which we are engaged, shall have the right of a free vote in the election of all officers who are to be chosen by the people, provided such person shall have resided one year next preceding the election in the county, district, city or town, where he shall offer to vote.— Also that every foreigner, above twenty-one years of age, well affected to the present glorious cause, having a visible estate of thirty pounds currency, or a freehold of fifty acres of land, and who has resided as a freeman two years next preceding the election in the county, district, city, or town, where he shall offer to vote, shall have the right of free suffrage in the election of all officers who are to be chosen by the people.— Also that all elections be free and made *viva voce* in the manner heretofore used in this state.— Also that Annapolis be represented, but that the inhabitants thereof be not allowed to vote for the representatives for this county. That there be chosen by the people a lower and an upper house annually: these two houses to be distinct and independent of each other, and to form the legislative power.— And also that the persons appointed to hold the executive power, have no share or negative in the legislature.— Also that no persons shall be eligible to fit in either house of legislature or congress, who holds any office of profit, or any pension, or receives any profit, or any part of the profit thereof, either directly or indirectly, or who holds any office in the regular military service, or marine service, either continental or provincial.— That the trial by jury be held and kept sacred and the *habeas corpus* preserved.— Also that justices of the peace, sheriffs, clerks of counties, and surveyors, be chosen by the people annually, of each county.— That a well regulated militia be established in this state, as being the best security for the preservation of the lives, liberties, and properties of the people.— That every militia company chuse its own officers, and battalions their field officers.— That adjutants, drummers, and fifers, with drums, fifes, colours, and cartouche-boxes, be provided at the public expence, for the different battalions of militia, and guns for such unarmed men who are not able to purchase the same, and that the colonels of each battalion be empowered to contract for the above, procure the same, and draw on the treasurer for the amount.— That all monies to be raised on the people be by a fair and equal assessment, in proportion to every person's estate: and that the unjust mode of taxation heretofore used, be abolished; and that assessors be chosen by the people of each district, in each county annually.—Also that the votes and proceedings of the assembly be published, except such parts as relate to military operations, and measures taken to procure arms and ammunition; and that they be open, except when particular business requires their being private: also that the votes and proceedings of congress be published, except as aforesaid.

Signed by eight hundred and eighty-five freemen.

To the ELECTORS of Anne-Arundel county.

Gentlemen,

WE were honoured on Saturday afternoon with instructions from a considerable number of the inhabitants of this county, on points of very great importance, relative to the formation of a new government for this state. As your delegates, we esteem ourselves bound by your instructions, though ever so contrary to our opinion. We conceive several of your last instructions, if carried into execution, destructive of free government. We are reduced to this alternative, we must either endeavour to establish a government, without a proper security for liberty or property, or surrender the trust we have received from you. We submit to you the propriety of reconsidering your instructions. We would with pleasure wait on you at the most convenient places in the county to explain our reasons against the restrictions you are pleased to impose on us, but are prevented by our necessary attendance on the public business. If you could make it convenient to meet at the city of Annapolis on Monday the 26th instant, we will attend you. We are now ready (as we ever have been) to serve our country at every hazard, but we cannot submit to be instruments for its destruction.

We are, gentlemen, with sincere respect and esteem,

Your obedient servants,

Annapolis,
Aug, 19, 1776.

CHARLES CARROLL,
BRICE T. B. WORTHINGTON,
SAMUEL CHASE.

Appendix

III

PERSONAL DATA ON CONSTITUTIONAL CONVENTION DELEGATES

Name	County	Dates	Occupation
Archer, Dr. John*	Harford	1741–1810	Physician
Barnes, Richard of Tudor Hall	St. Mary's	–1804	Planter
Bayly [Bayley], William, Jr.	Montgomery	1741–1824	Planter?
Beall, Samuel Jr.	Washington	–1778	Manufacturer
Bishop, Dr. Smith	Worcester	–1783	Physician
Bond, Jacob	Harford		Farmer?
Bowie, Walter	Prince George's	1748–1811	Merchant?
Brevard, Benjamin	Cecil	–1793	Farmer?
Bruff, William	Queen Anne's		Merchant
Carroll, Charles, barrister	Anne Arundel	1723–1783	Manufacturer, Planter

*For the data on these delegates the author is indebted to various files and indices at the Maryland Historical Society, to the wills and other court records pertaining to them in the Maryland Hall of Records, to landholding records in the quitrent Debt Books at the Maryland Hall of Records, and to a large number of citizens from across the country who responded to his "Query" relative to the delegates, which appeared in *Maryland Historical Magazine*, LXII (1967), pp. 212–215.

PERSONAL DATA ON CONSTITUTIONAL CONVENTION DELEGATES

Name	County	Dates	Occupation
Carroll, Charles of Carrollton	Annapolis	1737–1832	Planter, Manufacturer
Chaille, Peter	Worcester	1725–1802	Planter?
Chamberlaine, James Lloyd	Talbot	1732–1783	Planter
Chase, Jeremiah Townley	Baltimore Town	1748–1828	Lawyer
Chase, Samuel	Anne Arundel	1741–1811	Lawyer
Dent, Gen. John	Charles	1733–1809	Planter
Deye, Thomas Cockey	Baltimore	–1808	Planter
Dickinson, Henry	Caroline	172?–1789	Planter
Earle, Joseph	Kent	1739 1799	Lawyer
Edelen, Christopher	Frederick	1723–1786	Merchant
Edmondson, Pollard	Talbot	–1794	Planter
Ennalls, Lt.Col. John	Dorchester	c.1735–c.1778	Planter
Ennalls, Lt.Col. Joseph	Dorchester	1735–1782	Planter
Ewing, Patrick	Cecil	1737–1819	Farmer, Miller
Fenwick, Col. Ignatius, Jr.	St. Mary's		Planter
Fischer, Dr. Adam	Frederick	1736–1787	Physician
Fitzhugh, Col. William	Calvert	1721–1798	Planter, Merchant
Gibson, John of Tuckahoe	Talbot	1729–1790	Farmer
Gilpin, Joseph	Cecil	1727–1790	Farmer
Goldsborough, Robert III	Dorchester	1733–1788	Lawyer, Planter
Grahame, Charles of Lower Marlboro	Calvert	–c.1790	Lawyer
Hall, Benjamin or Francis?	Prince George's	1710?– ? / 1709–1803	Planter? / Planter?
Hall, John of the Vineyard	Anne Arundel	1729- 1797	Lawyer, Planter
Hammond, Rezin	Anne Arundel	1745–1809	Lawyer. Planter

231

Name	County	Dates	Occupation
Handy, Samuel	Worcester	1752- ?	Planter
Hooe, Robert Townshend	Charles	1743–1809	Merchant, Planter
Horsey, William	Somerset	–1786	Miller, Planter
Hughs [Hughes], Samuel	Washington	–1782	Manufacturer
Johnson, Thomas, Jr.	Caroline	1732–1819	Lawyer, Planter
Jordan, Jeremiah	St. Mary's		Merchant Farmer?
Kent, James	Queen Anne's		Farmer?
Lee, Thomas Sim	Prince George's	1745–1819	Planter
Love, Dr. John	Harford	1749–1831	Physician
Lowes, Henry	Somerset		Merchant?
Mackall, Benjamin of Hollowing Point?	Calvert		Lawyer
Mackall, John of St. Leonards?	Calvert	1740–1799?	Planter?
Marbury, Luke	Prince George's	c.1745–1809	Planter? Merchant
Mason, Richard of Tuckahoe Neck?	Caroline	–1785	Farmer?
Mitchell, Josiah	Worcester		Farmer?
Murray, James of Hunting Creek	Dorchester	1739–1819	Miller, Planter
Paca, William	Annapolis	1740–1799	Lawyer, Planter
Parnham, Dr. John	Charles	1740–1800	Physician
Plater, Col. George III	St. Mary's	1735–1792	Planter
Potter, Nathaniel	Caroline	–1783	Merchant, Planter
Richardson, Col. William	Caroline	1735–1825	Planter
Ridgeley Capt. Charles of Hampton "The Mariner"	Baltimore	1733–1790	Merchant, Planter, Manufacturer

232

Name	County	Dates	Occupation
Ringgold, Thomas, Jr. of Chestertown	Kent	–1776	Merchant
Ringgold, William, Jr. of Eastern Neck	Kent	1723–1808	Planter
Robins, John Purnell	Worcester	1742–1781	Planter
Schnebely, Dr. Henry	Washington		Physician, Planter
Scott, George [Day?]	Somerset		Farmer?
Scott, Gustavus	Somerset	1753–1801	Lawyer,
Semmes, Thomas	Charles	c.1750–1832? or 1754–1824?	Planter
Shepherd, Peter	Baltimore	–1787	Farmer?
Sheredine, Upton of Midhill	Frederick	1740–1800	Manufacturer?, Planter
Shriver[Schriver], David	Frederick	1735–1826	Miller, Farmer
Smith, David	Cecil	1739–1813	Clerk
Smith, John	Baltimore Town	–1794	Merchant
Smyth, Thomas	Kent	1730–1819	Merchant? Planter
Sprigg, Osborn	Prince George's	c.1740–1815	Planter?
Stevenson, John of Edward? of Popular Hill?	Baltimore		Planter?
Stull, Col. John [Jr.?] of Hagerstown	Washington	–1791	Planter
Tilghman, Matthew	Talbot	1718–1790	Planter
Williams, Elisha	Montgomery		Farmer
Wilson, Henry, Jr.	Harford	1744–1800?	Farmer?
Wilson, Jonathan	Montgomery		Planter
Wootton, Dr. Thomas Sprigg	Montgomery		Dentist
Worthington, B.T.B.	Anne Arundel	1727–1794	Planter
Wright, Solomon	Queen Anne's	1727–1792	Lawyer, Planter
Wright, Turbutt	Queen Anne's	1741–1789	Lawyer, Planter

BIBLIOGRAPHICAL ESSAY

General bibliographic introductions to the study of colonial and revolutionary Maryland can be found in Charles A. Barker, *The Background of the Revolution in Maryland* (New Haven: Yale University Press, 1940) and Donnell M. Owings, *His Lordship's Patronage: Offices of Profit in Colonial Maryland* (Baltimore: Maryland Historical Society, 1953). Additional listings may be found in Jack P. Greene, *The American Colonies in the Eighteenth Century, 1689-1763* ("Goldentree Bibliographies in American History") (New York: Appleton-Century Crofts, 1969). These works, plus the policy utilized in the notes of this work to provide a full citation to each printed source the first time cited in each chapter, obviate the necessity for a complete formal listing here. Additional citations within each chapter are short titled.

Manuscript Sources. Of considerable importance in the compilation of data for this study have been the quitrent debt books kept in each county to assess the amount of funds owed the proprietor in these feudal dues. They list not only the amount owed, but also the names and acreages of the individual tracts by the owners' names. Formerly housed in the Maryland Land Office, they have recently been transferred to the Hall of Records in Annapolis. This same archival agency also has the existing court records through 1788 and has the originals, photocopies, or typescript copies of most of the Anglican parish vestry proceedings. Duplicate copies of the vestry records are often found at either the Maryland Historical Society, Baltimore, or the Library of Congress. Many pertinent official government letters are also found in the "Rainbow Series" of books at the Hall of Records. To understand these collections one should begin by consulting the *Publications of the Hall of Records Commission* (Annapolis: The Commission, 1943-present) and A.J.M. Pedley, *The Manuscript Collections of the Maryland Historical Society* (Baltimore: The Society, 1968).

The manuscript sources utilized in this study are found in the following depositories:

Duke University Library, Durham N.C.
  Joseph Chaplin Papers, 1741-1793
  William Henry Hall Papers, 1758—1862
  Maryland Colony and Revolutionary Papers, 1703-1783
  Purviance-Courtenay Papers, 1757-1789

Johns Hopkins University Library, Evergreen House, Baltimore, Md.
   Alexander Hamilton, History of the Tuesday Club
Library of Congress, Washington, D. C.
   John Leeds Bozman Papers
   Carroll Papers
   Galloway, Maxcy, Markoe Papers, 1750–1776
   John Glassford & Co. and Successors Records, 1753–1776
   Thomas Sim Lee Papers
   Public Record Office Transcripts
   Stone Papers
   "Time, Oar, Coal, Iron Book"
   William Tong, Autobiography, 1756–1834
Maryland Diocesan Archives, Baltimore (In Maryland Historical Society)
   Ethan Allen Collection
   Cradock Sermons
   William Duke Journal, 1774–1776
   William Duke Papers
Maryland Hall of Records, Annapolis
   Annapolis City Records, 1753–1767, 3 vols
   Commission Records, 1726–1786
   Court Records and Papers
      Baltimore County
      Charles County
      Frederick County
      Prince George's County
      Queen Anne's County
      Talbot County
   Debit Books
      Baltimore County, 1753–1773
      Prince George's County, 1755–1773
      Queen Anne's County, 1753–1769
      Talbot County, 1755–1773
   Executive Papers
   Prerogative Court Records
      Accounts
      Balance Books
      Inventories
      Wills
   Rainbow Series
      Blue Books
      Brown Books
      Red Books
   Vestry Proceedings
      Prince George's Parish, Rock Creek, Frederick County
      Queen Anne's Parish, Prince George's County

BIBLIOGRAPHICAL ESSAY

St. George's Parish, Old Spesutia, Baltimore County
St. James Parish, Anne Arundel County
St. John's Parish, Copley, Baltimore County
St. John's Parish, Piscataway, Prince George's County
St. John's Parish, Tuckahoe, Queen Anne's County
St. Luke's Parish, Queen Anne's County
St. Michael's Parish, Talbot County
St. Paul's Parish, Prince George's County
St. Paul's, King George Parish, Queen Anne's County
St. Peter's Parish, Talbot County
St. Thomas' Parish, Baltimore County
Maryland Historical Society, Baltimore
Bordley-Calvert Papers
Bordley Letterbooks, 1727-1759
Bordley Papers
Calvert Papers
Cradock Papers
Dulany Papers
Fisher Transcripts
Gilmor Papers
Gist Papers
Aquila Hall Papers
Benedict Edward Hall Papers
Henry Hollyday Papers
Lloyd Papers
Purviance Papers
Ridgely Account Books
St. Paul's Church (Baltimore) Records
Stone Family Papers
William L. Clements Library, University of Michigan, Ann Arbor
Gage Papers
Shelburne Papers

Newspapers. The newspapers used were the Green family's *Maryland Gazette* (Annapolis), 1750-1776 (with occasional earlier and subsequent citations where necessity demanded it), the Goddards' *Maryland Journal* (Baltimore), 1773-1776, and *Dunlap's Maryland Gazette* (Baltimore), 1775-1776.

Printed Primary Sources. While most sources are adequately cited in the notes, particular emphasis must be given to the *Archives of Maryland,* William H. Browne *et al..* eds. (Baltimore: Maryland Historical Society, 1883-1971), to date there are 71 volumes in the series which constitutes the single most important printed source for colonial Maryland history. Particularly significant for this study were the volumes dealing with "The Correspondence of Governor Horatio Sharpe, 1753-1771," "Proceedings and Acts of the General Assembly, 1637- 1774," "Proceedings of the Council, 1637-1770," and "Journal and Correspondence of the Council of Safety, 1775-1777."

237

The "Maryland Imprints" bibliography in Lawrence C. Wroth, *A History of Printing in Colonial Maryland, 1686–1776* (Baltimore: The Typothetae, 1922) is indispensable. Coupled with the "Early American Imprints" series published in microprint, the researcher has easily available all the material printed in colonial America.

Unpublished Secondary Sources. Full citations of the various typescript studies concerned with this study are made in the chapter notes. A virtually complete listing of such works is in Dorothy M. Brown and Richard H. Duncan (compl.), *Master's Theses and Doctoral Dissertations in Maryland History* (Baltimore: Maryland Historical Society, 1970).

INDEX